Words of
The Be

Frances Hogan is a Catholic scripture teacher who is working as a lay missionary in the Church. She has taught Science and Scripture in West Africa and Ireland for ten years. Since 1975 she has worked full-time as a lay missionary, giving scripture courses, retreats, and working in parishes opening up the scriptures to the people.

Frances Hogan has committed her life to making the Word of God known to lay people in the Church in order to deepen their prayer life and commitment to Christ. She has made a series of Scripture Tapes on books of the Bible and on various spiritual themes.

Frances Hogan

Words of Life
from Luke
The Beloved Physician

Collins
FOUNT PAPERBACKS

First published in Great Britain by
Fount Paperbacks, London in 1990

Copyright © Frances Hogan 1990

Made and printed in Great Britain by
William Collins Sons & Co. Ltd, Glasgow

Unless otherwise stated, biblical quotations are taken
from *The Jerusalem Bible*, © 1966, 1967 and 1968
by Darton, Longman & Todd Ltd of London
and Doubleday & Company, Inc. of New York
and are used by kind permission of the copyright holders

Contents

Introduction

The gospel of Saint Luke is the best known gospel among the people of God. It has been the textbook of every child studying the Christian faith. As such it was learned by heart and exams passed or failed on it. They had "done" Luke. They had the stories off by heart, but had they "received" the Gospel? I doubt it. There is much more to this wonderful document than just learning the stories it tells. There is an inner depth one must penetrate as Luke strives to introduce us to the Christ he knew and loved.

Luke has been the favourite gospel among painters and artists also, because of his famed gift of painting word-pictures. He has given us the Madonna, the crib, the shepherds and that wonderful rogues' gallery littered throughout this gospel, because he loved to use "baddies" as examples to put across a point. As a master storyteller he has given the Church the priceless gems of the Prodigal Son, the Good Samaritan and the Walk to Emmaus, which so fire the imagination. He has provided the Church with her daily hymns, the Magnificat, the Benedictus and the Nunc Dimittis which never lose their appeal. As such he is the "dear doctor", the beloved physician of the soul who has comforted and strengthened us all on our journey through life.

Luke portrays Jesus as a man of prayer throughout his gospel, putting Him before the early Christians as their model. He shows that prayer was the power behind the mighty works, and the source of His inner strength. He shows Him also as a man filled with the Spirit, and obedient to His Father in all things. In fact, the Holy Spirit is seen to be the very source of His life. Luke portrays Jesus as a very gentle Master, one who loved sinners and had great compassion on the weak, a man who showed real tenderness to the poor and the suffering, especially to those on the margins of society. As such he has made the Saviour very attractive to anyone who is willing to change their ways in order to let God into their lives. The story of the Good Thief is his masterpiece, where a good-for-nothing criminal gains the first place in Paradise.

Luke also has a strong feeling for women in this gospel. He goes out of his way to show Jesus treating them with the same respect and acceptance as men, for he treated them as persons in their own right. He shows that Jesus understood the particular sufferings of women and tried to alleviate them. He called them to be His disciples just as He called the men, but allowed them to do very personal service for Him (Luke 8:1–3). Throughout the gospel Luke balances any story or parable that has a man at its centre with one dealing with a woman. For example the man with the hundred sheep in chapter 15 is followed by the woman with the ten drachmas. Jesus raises the widow's son at Nain and later he goes on to raise the daughter of Jairus. The women are represented as the faithful disciples, those who do not deny Jesus. They remain with Him right up to Calvary and become the important witnesses to the fact that Christ died, was buried, and rose again. It was to them that the message of resurrection was given.

This gospel also deals with the social needs of Christians in the Graeco-Roman world, where Luke demands radical commitment to Christ and the Gospel. Like Jesus, Christians must be poor servants of God, fully at the service of their neighbour. They are warned of the dangers of riches and of false religion.

He wants them to see the life of the Church as a continuation of the mission of Jesus, who is its source. Christians are to see themselves as pilgrims on a spiritual journey from Pentecost to the Parousia, and they are to remain watchful in prayer and faithful to the mission given to them. They are to be good stewards of the Lord's gifts.

There is a gospel within a gospel in the infancy narratives, where the author of this two-part work Luke-Acts wants us to grasp the sound Old Testament background to the gospel story. Following the instruction of Jesus in Luke 24:27 he searched the Old Testament documents to find the explanation of the Messiah-Saviour. There he found words to put on the Christ-Event, and a way to illustrate the changeover from the Old Covenant to the New.

As the text of the gospel is not included in this book, it will be necessary to have it to hand as you read, otherwise the commentary may be difficult, as it follows the text exactly. The argument in any particular section will be clear only if the text is read first.

Chapter One
The Rising Sun Has Come to Visit Us

Luke dedicated his two-part work (Luke-Acts) to a person in high office named Theophilus. Because this name means "beloved of God", he could have written "dear Christian" since his message was aimed far beyond this one individual who needed to have his ideas clarified on *the events that have taken place among us*. Luke is anxious that everyone will realize how well founded their faith is, so he has researched the matter for us. Others had already written accounts of the Christ-event and these documents were available to him. There was also the oral tradition passed on by the first eye-witnesses and preached by the ministers of the word. So, armed with this material, and also with an extraordinary gift for communication through writing he set about giving us the third gospel which has so inspired artists, poets and saints alike.

Luke says that he wrote *an ordered account* so it is important for us to grasp what that order was. Examination of the gospel shows that that order was logical rather than chronological, based on God's order of promise and fulfilment in the Bible. This becomes clear as soon as we approach the infancy narratives.

The infancy narratives form the prologue to Luke's work, and like a great musical overture we hear the theme songs throughout. Luke's concern is to set out Jesus' personal identity and heavenly origins clearly, and at the same time clear up any misunderstanding regarding the relative greatness and mission of John the Baptist.

11

Looking at His origins we can see that Jesus was human, born of woman (Galatians 4:4), a person related to His biblical past and identified with His people and their history, a man who enjoyed human relationships and was socially concerned. But this in no way explains Jesus, for he was also born of God. Both His identity and His origins transcend the merely human. The Son of God and son of Mary, was destined to return whence He came, so Christians must come to grips with His physical absence from their midst, and discover His risen presence among them (2:41–52, 9:31).

The infancy narratives comprise chapters one and two of the gospel and form a distinct unit. This material is so complete that even if Luke had concluded his book here we would have a finished work, a gospel of the infancy. There are several levels on which the work has to be read, because Luke is not just recounting events that happened, he is also interpreting them in the light of the Old Testament, so that we, his readers, begin to understand that there is no break in the salvific work of God. What God began in the Era of Promise was now being fulfilled before their own eyes (24:27, 44–48).

At the second level, Luke addresses the Christians of his own day, asking them to look at themselves in the light of these events, and judge if they were real disciples of Jesus. Since the Church had, by then, moved its centre from Jerusalem to Rome, its present context was the Roman Empire, so we will look at gospel characters in that light. For example "Pharisees" will refer to characteristics of Christians, rather than the Jews of Jesus' day. They become character "types" from whom Christians must learn, just as they are to learn from Peter and Judas.

The Conception of John the Baptist (1:5–25)

From the fluent Greek style of the introduction which indicated the second half of the first century, where the Church was identified with the Roman Empire and the Gentile mission, Luke suddenly plunges us back into the Jewish biblical world at the time of Herod the Great, who ruled over Palestine from 37 to 4 BC. The shock effect is great. To add to the drama we are taken into the interior of the Temple of God in Jerusalem and allowed to see and hear what went on in its sacred precincts, a thing unheard of for Gentiles! If you need a moment to recover wait for the Angel, for Luke casts us into the very Presence of God. If we are to proceed we must get used to the divine and the extraordinary, yet told in a context of such amazing simplicity and love. It's a new world where human beings allow God to have His way with them, with the result that hope and joy are given to a weary world of violence and corruption.

One of the themes in the gospel is that the Lord seeks you out wherever you are. Here He finds a priest in the Temple doing his duty. In the next scene, God seeks out a young girl at home, also doing her duty. Later He will look for the fishermen at the Lake of Galilee (chapter 5), the tax-collector at his desk (5:27–28), the farmers in the fields and the children playing in the market squares (7:32). With the coming of Jesus God has entered our world, and is calling us to new life. It is up to us how we respond. In the infancy narratives Luke is showing us how Zechariah, Elizabeth, Mary, the Bethlehemites, shepherds, prophets and Doctors of the Law received and responded to Jesus. And it is all given to us for our learning (2 Timothy 3:14–17).

Zechariah belonged to the Abijah section of the priesthood, an interesting detail, as there were 18,000 priests

13

serving the Temple at that time who were chosen by lot for each task (see 1 Chronicles 24; also J. Jeremias, *Jerusalem at the time of Jesus*; London 1969, pp. 198–204). Following Moses' instructions in Exodus 30:6–8 the priest was to offer fragrant incense in the Holy Place morning and evening. The privilege of being chosen for this task came once in a lifetime, since that person was considered ineligible in all future lots until his entire section had served (see A. Edersheim: *The Temple, its Ministry and Services as they were at the Time of Jesus Christ*; London 1959).

Both Zechariah and Elizabeth were from priestly families. Both were "worthy" in the sight of God, and kept the commandments, yet they were childless, which was normally considered a punishment from God (see Leviticus 20:20). Luke insists that, in this case, it is merely the prelude to a divine intervention, not only in their personal lives but also in human history. He describes this couple as the best of the Old Testament. They were all that God expected them to be, but they had two problems: Elizabeth was barren, and now they were too old to have a child. It was way past the time even if it were possible to give birth (1:5–10).

Luke presents us here with the new Abraham and Sarah, through whom God will begin a new way of salvation, just as He did with the original pair (Genesis 18:11–12). Zechariah's name means "God remembers", and as God has remembered that the time has come for the Messiah to be given, Zechariah needs to remember how God overcame the problems of barrenness for Sarah, Rebecca (Genesis 25:21), Rachel (Genesis 29:31), the mother of Samson (Judges 13:2), and Hannah (1 Samuel: 1–2). The gift being offered to him and Elizabeth had precedent in God's way. None of these women was barren because of sin, but to show forth the glory of God (John 9:3). John the Baptist, therefore, is to be born into the long line of specially chosen friends of God and prophets.

The angel Gabriel, whose duty is to stand in God's Presence, and await His pleasure (1:19) is despatched to announce the birth of the Forerunner of the Messiah. This approach of God through the angel strikes fear and awe into Zechariah (1:12), yet God's messenger brings good news: a child is to be born through whom the promises of God are to be fulfilled – just as had happened to Abraham (Genesis 17:16). Not only has Zechariah's personal prayer for a child been heard, but so has the prayer of all God's people been heard for a child who will be their Messiah. As the angel spoke to the priest, the congregation were at prayer outside the sanctuary. Luke has introduced another theme of his gospel, namely that prayer is the context for the intervention of God on our behalf. The people do not realize that their prayer is being heard even as they speak to God.

The good news was that Elizabeth, the barren one, was to bear a son, and the child was to be named John, which means "God is gracious" or "the grace of God", the name signifying the future mission of the child, who was to herald the coming of the Grace of God in Jesus. The child's mission is now explained to the stunned father, who is expected to remember that Daniel's prophecy of the seventy weeks of years before the coming of Messiah are now up (Daniel 9:24–27), and that it was indeed a great privilege to participate in its fulfilment, and play a major role in the salvation of the people, but it seemed he could not comprehend it all.

His son was to be a great prophet, coming to Israel at this crucial moment in the spirit and power of Elijah (1:17). The prophet Malachi had predicted that God would prepare Israel for her Messiah by a prophet in Elijah's style, hence he would have great zeal for God and power to bring the nation back to God (see 1 Kings 17). The healing of the nation is described as the reconciliation of fathers to their children and vice versa (see Malachi 4:6). Just as family breakdown is seen as national breakdown, so the healing of the family unit begins the renewal of the nation and the restoration of its strength. John the Baptist was to have the great privilege of preparing Israel to meet her God spiritually and temporally (see Sirach 48:1–12; Matthew 17:9–13).

The coming of John the Baptist will be a cause of joy because it will herald first the spiritual resurrection of Israel and later that of the rest of the world. To prepare him for this task he is given a unique privilege among the prophets in that he will be anointed with the Spirit from his mother's womb, a unique visitation of grace for the Old Testament (1:16).

Zechariah echoes Abraham's inability to comprehend such a miracle (even though Abraham's questioning was not read as a lack of faith on his part), as it is clearly seen here (1:18 see Genesis 15:8, 17:16–21). It seems that Zechariah did not accept the power of God to resurrect what was dead. This would be essential in the preparation for all that Jesus was to do, namely to bring to life what has been destroyed either in this case by barrenness and old age, or by the destruction of sin in the case of forgiveness (spiritual resurrection) and then the resurrection of the body as a result of illness, and finally death itself, for the last enemy to be overcome is death (see 1 Corinthians 15:26). Unfortunately Zechariah does not remember that with God all things are possible (1:38). Not even Gabriel's reminder that he stood in the Presence of God shifted him from a position he thought impossible. He is the first example in the gospel of a mind-set that will not allow God's creativity to work (1:19).

Because of this Zechariah is given a sign with a double effect. First the priest is not permitted to proclaim the good news until he has experienced God's power to re-create and make all things new (1:20; see Daniel 10:15 and Acts 9:9, where the prophet was made speechless, and Paul blind for a time). When Zechariah asked *"How can I be sure of this?"* it seems he expressed the Jewish failing of asking for a second sign to confirm the first one (11:29; Judges 6:36–40; 2 Kings 20:8).

Second, the waiting crowds became anxious at Zechariah's delay. His reappearance and dumbness made them assume that he had seen a vision in the sanctuary (1:22)! He cannot give the expected blessing of Aaron now and can only make signs to them (Numbers 6:24–26). The blessing of the new High Priest will be given at the end of the gospel from the Mount of Olives as Jesus ascends into Heaven, having accomplished all that humans could not comprehend in their combined unbelief (24:50–52).

Although Zechariah represents the best that was in the Old Testament, he showed its limitation too, its inability to open up fully to God or believe in a practical way in His mighty power to save. But God is not blocked by this, because Zechariah's dumbness had the effect of making the people remember the messianic prophecies, which awakened in them an expectation that alerted them to the working of God in their midst. God had communicated with the people in spite of Zechariah, a timely warning for all who are meant to speak in God's name.

Another theme message of Luke appears now as Zechariah went home to share his good news with his wife (1:23). The messenger to Zechariah was an angel of the winged type, but the messenger to Elizabeth was an angel of the unwinged type! It does not matter who is sent to us even if, as in this case, the messenger only half believes the message. If Elizabeth can hear the word of the Lord through her husband she will conceive and bring forth against all the odds – and she does. Her faith is presented as greater than that of Zechariah. She represents all those who believe without seeing (John 20:29). Unfortunately priestly office is no guarantee of holiness or of openness to God. She went into seclusion for five months to rejoice in what the Lord had done for her (1:23–25). At the end of the gospel Luke will return to the two types of angels in the resurrection narratives and here again the emphasis will be on the unwinged types who are sent out to all the world on mission.

The Conception of Jesus (1:26–38)

The scene that follows parallels the previous one. Luke obviously intends us to compare the faith of Zechariah and Mary, as well as the missions of Jesus and John and their relative greatness. It is like the second scene of a well planned play. The first scene gave us a priest at prayer in the Temple. Here we have a young girl in prayer in her home. For Luke, prayer is the context where God intervenes in our lives to answer the cry of the human heart. Whereas for Zechariah God had answered too late, here for Mary it is too early, for she had not yet come to live with her husband Joseph. God's timing of events and ours often do not coincide.

It was in the sixth month of Elizabeth's pregnancy that Gabriel was sent to a virgin many miles north of Jerusalem in the little town of Nazareth (1:26–27). Its name means "branch town", an allusion to the prophecy that God would raise up a righteous branch to the House of David (Zechariah 6:12). The virgin's name was Mary, which means both "exalted one" and "bitterness", and this woman was to experience both. Mary had as yet only gone through the first stage of her marriage to Joseph of Nazareth, where the vows are taken, but they had not begun to live

18

together. This first stage was legally binding and the couple pronounced man and wife. The bond could only be broken by a legal divorce (Matthew 1:19–20; Deuteronomy 22:20). Mary, then, is still a virgin (1:28). Even though Joseph is of the House of David, and it is through his legal adoption of Jesus that the Child will become a Davidid (3:23), yet Luke focuses completely on the mother. Thus he alerts us to the fact that Joseph was not Jesus' father (1:32).

The contrasts between the origins of Jesus and John are already apparent. John was born of human parents by the ordinary method of human intercourse, whereas Jesus was born of God by a divine intervention of an altogether higher order, for God intervened as Creator. Mary's son would not be conceived by the human agency of Mary and Joseph but by the power of the Most High (1:35). John was born of a barren woman, whereas Jesus was born of a fruitful virgin. John was quickened by the Holy Spirit in his mother's womb but Jesus was conceived by the Holy Spirit. Since the Holy Spirit is the true source of Jesus' life there was never a moment when He was not filled with the Holy Spirit.

Gabriel's greeting to Mary indicates that she is chosen to be the mother of the Messiah (see Zechariah 9:9–10; Genesis 6:9; Zephaniah 3:14–17). She was reassured that God was with her in a special way so there was nothing to fear (see Judges 6:12). She had God's protection, presence and grace for He wanted to fulfil His promises to Israel through her. Out of all the women in Israel Mary is the chosen one for the exalted privilege of mothering the Messiah. Sitting at the feet of the angel, much like a disciple before her master, Mary receives the good news about Jesus. At the dawn of the New Age God's Word comes to her through the agency of the angel, but it will not always be this way, as we will see.

Mary was to bear a son and call him Jesus, a name which means "God saves" (1:32). He will be the great prophet (Deuteronomy 18:15–18), but also the Son of God. He will be the Davidic Messiah who was so long expected (2 Samuel 7:8–16; Psalm 2:7) and the king whose rule would be everlasting (Daniel 2:44). This Davidic branch was to be holy, as foreseen by Isaiah 4:2–3, 11:1–9. Mary is now "evangelized", for the Word of God had been declared to her. She is free to accept or reject it like every other disciple who follows her, and to whom she is presented here as the model. Instead of going into raptures about this extraordinary grace, Mary presents her virginity as an obstacle that would have to be overcome. She is as yet unaware that God has already overcome many obstacles for Elizabeth, and none of them, not even Zechariah's unbelief, proved too difficult for God. God is a Creator, who works from nothing. He is about to create a child in Mary's womb, a child who will come into being as a result of His own creative love for Israel and for the world. He initiated and carried the process through against all the odds (see Genesis 18:14, 31:38).

God's answer to Mary was that she would experience an absolutely unique visitation of grace in that the power of the Creator would come to her, and she would be overshadowed by the Holy Spirit, just as the Spirit of God had hovered over the void at the dawn of creation (1:35; see Genesis 1:2). The void in her virginal womb would be filled by the same Creative Hand that had brought all things into being from nothing. The ineffable Presence of God was to come upon Mary now as It had upon the the Tabernacle in the wilderness, and the Temple in Jerusalem in bygone days (see Exodus 40:34–35; 1

Kings 8:10–12), and she was to become the first Christ-bearer to the world.

Mary leads the way for all disciples in her perfect and enthusiastic surrender to the Will of God. Having heard the Word, she allows it to transform her life according to God's salvific plans. As both a hearer and doer of the Word (see James 1:22) she shows us the way to spiritual fulfillment, namely to let God's word be our guide in life. "*Let what you have said be done to me*" (1:38) is the motto of all disciples to come.

Like her father Abraham, she put her faith completely in God. Since God had promised it, she refused either to deny it or even to doubt it, but drew strength from faith and gave glory to God, convinced that God had the power to do what He had promised (Romans 4:21). Later Jesus will ask disciples to model themselves on her: "*My mother and my brothers are those who hear the word of God and put it into practice*" (8:21). This is what constitutes "family" for him (see Acts 1:14). At that moment all the promises of God to Israel came alive in Mary's womb. Her "yes" was a costly one if the Law of Moses were to be imposed when it became known later that she was pregnant before coming to live with Joseph (Deuteronomy 22:21–22).

She was given a sign, one which had no negative aspect like that of Zechariah. Elizabeth's pregnancy is made known to her (1:36–37). We have already been told that Elizabeth had hidden herself for five months once her own miracle manifested itself (1:25), so it was not possible for Mary to have known it. But now she knows that two unknown women carry the future of Israel and the redemption of the world in their wombs! Two women who accepted the circumstances of God's Will for their lives, who received God's message in whatever way He sent it, by an angel in Mary's case, by an unbelieving husband in the other, between them carry the hope of the world.

It is not difficult to understand why the Fathers of the Church in the first six centuries, those who were closest to the sources, compared Mary with the first woman of the Bible. At the time of Eve's fall she too was a virgin espoused to a husband (Genesis 2:21–25). Like Mary she had been created in innocence and holiness, but she listened to the wrong messenger and took the wrong message, thus bringing disaster upon the human race. The contrast with Mary here is obvious. We can understand why the early Church Fathers said that both the fall and the redemption came through the agency of a woman. Mary and Eve are truly the mothers of all who live, Eve our natural mother and Mary the mother of all believers. As life-givers women carry great responsibility for the spiritual well-being of the human race. (see chapter 1 pp. 35–59 of *"The Blessed Virgin in the Fathers of the First Six Centuries"* by Thomas Livius, London 1893 where he quotes Justin, Irenaeus, Tertullian, Origen and many others).

As soon as the miracle of the Incarnation occurs Mary becomes another Ark of God, the precious container of Him who is both Word of God, Bread of Life, and Priest. The Ark of the Covenant was the precious container placed in the Temple in the olden days. At different stages in its history it had three objects inside it. Moses placed the two tablets of stone there, and a jar of manna. These together symbolize the word and bread of God. After the rebellion against Aaron, the high priest, was settled he put Aaron's rod which budded into the Ark as the symbol of priest (Hebrews 9:4–5). The cloud of God's presence was seen over the Ark between the golden cherubs, so the Ark was overshadowed by the presence of God. Just as the Ark carried the mystery of God's presence, so Mary now carries the mystery of God's presence in the Incarnation (Exodus 25:20–22).

Jesus Comes to John (1:39–56)

Luke gives a supplementary scene here which confirms the greatness of Mary and of her son, who meets John for the first time. This meeting of mothers and sons gives further opportunity to the Lord to reveal His wonderful works. He has already revealed Elizabeth's pregnancy to Mary. Now He is about to reveal Mary's pregnancy to Elizabeth, so both women can confirm the gift of grace in the other. Likewise John will prophetically recognize Jesus, thus confirming that Mary is the mother of the Lord. The unborn prophet recognizes the greatness of the unborn Lord.

After the revelation of Elizabeth's pregnancy Mary went quickly to visit her, even though it was a long and arduous journey into the hill country of Judah, to a place called Ain Karim in Christian times, about eight kilometres west of Jerusalem. From the time of Nehemiah it was known that many of the priests did not live in Jerusalem, as their service was not required in the Temple frequently (Nehemiah 11:3). Mary's greeting to Elizabeth was the occasion for great grace to be outpoured upon the House of Zechariah, as both Elizabeth and her son were filled with the Holy Spirit simultaneously, and both responded with exuberant joy (1:39–42). Thus, through Mary's loving visit, God's promise to Zechariah was fulfilled (1:15). The unborn prophet recognized his Lord and jumped for joy in anticipation of the redemption to come. This sign confirmed Elizabeth's prophecy regarding Mary's wonderful secret, that she carried the Lord in her womb, not just in her heart as a holy person would do, but incarnate in her womb by an extraordinary act of God's mercy to the human race.

Inspired by the Holy Spirit Elizabeth declared Mary the most blessed of all women. Women were considered to be blessed in their children, so she who bore the *Kyrios* (the Lord) is the most blessed (see Judith 13:18). Other women will recognize this later (11:27). Elizabeth considers herself unworthy of Mary's presence because Mary brings THE LORD wherever she goes. This is the first time in the gospel that Jesus is recognized as the Lord. Elizabeth congratulates Mary on her faith which stands in contrast to Zechariah's unbelief. Mary is blessed, first in God's choice of her as mother of the Lord (1:43), then in the fruit of her womb (1:42), and lastly she is blessed in her great faith that gave God the freedom to work (1:45). Mary is thus presented as the first disciple to believe without seeing a sign, and Jesus Himself pronounced this a blessing and made it the standard for real faith (John 20:29). Again, Mary is the model disciple.

Another way of viewing this scene is to see it in the light of the Ark of the Covenant coming to Jerusalem. In 2 Samuel 6 David took the Ark to Jerusalem with great joy and celebration. In 2 Samuel 6:9–11 David exclaimed in fear: *"However can the Ark of the Lord come to me?"*. And he took the Ark to the house of Obed-edom of Gath where it stayed for three months and the Lord blessed the house of Obed-edom because of the Ark. At the end of this period the Ark was taken to Jerusalem. It would seem that Luke is thinking of Mary in these terms as she went to Zechariah's house a few miles from Jerusalem, and the Lord blessed the family on account of her presence. Afterwards Mary will go to the Temple in Jerusalem and it will be her great privilege to be the first to offer the Son of God to God in the Temple. At long last a gift worthy of God will be offered to Him in the Temple (2:22–28).

The Rising Sun Has Come to Visit Us

The Magnificat (1:46–55)

Mary's response was to sing God's praises in words that came almost exclusively from the Old Testament Scriptures that had been her food since childhood. Matthew 12:34 says that our words flow from the abundance in our hearts and reflect what is there. This song of Mary echoes that of Hannah in 1 Samuel 2:1–10 where Hannah had asked God for a child and her prayer was answered in the same way as for Elizabeth. She too brought forth a great prophet and she blessed God for this grace. Mary's song also echoes the themes of Luke's gospel and anticipate the ministry of her son, so there is a backward and forward movement in it.

Mary glorifies God for His great works. He who is the Saviour of the human race does not despise the poor (Psalm 22:24). Because of what God had done Mary knows that all generations will acknowledge her blessing, but it is God's work that is being blessed, He who takes care of the little ones of the earth through all generations. God's ways are as different to ours as the heavens are from the earth (Isaiah 55:8–9). He resists the proud (12:45; Job 12:19) and raises the lowly of every rank and race. Only those who relate to Him correctly with reverence and awe will experience His wonderful mercy, but it is offered to all. Those hungry for God will have their needs met but the "rich", whose lives are already filled with other gods, materialism, worldliness and selfishness, these will not be filled with the Lord's good things since there is no room in their lives for God. This anticipates the Beatitudes (6:21). Through the infant in Mary's womb God has answered the promise He made to Abraham and the prophets of old, so we are to experience Him in the gospel as the One who keeps His promises.

Mary's song is definitely good news for the little people

25

on the earth, but bad news for the rich and the great who don't need God in their lives, (1 Samuel 2:7). She indicates the social revolution that would occur if God's will were to be done, for this would mean that all those in need would be taken care of, and God would reign (Psalm 111:9) not some earthly potentate (Isaiah 2:12; Job 22:9).

The Birth of John (1:57–80)

The birth of John the Baptist and his manifestation to Israel are given here and then followed by the birth and manifestation of Jesus, and Luke compares and contrasts them just as he did for the annunciation scenes. Elizabeth's time came, and she gave birth to a son in accordance with God's word (1:13). Since she had hidden herself during her pregnancy it is only now that her neighbours and relatives hear of God's gift, and they share her joy. The setting for John's birth is that of family and friends and the special rejoicing at the intervention of God to Elizabeth. For John the earth rejoices in the advent of one of its greatest sons, but for Jesus the heavens rejoice in the advent of the Saviour of all the world.

According to custom the child was circumcised and named on the eighth day (Genesis 17:12). This was John's incorporation into the Community of Israel, when he is marked with the sign of the Covenant of Moses (Joshua 5:2–9). When Elizabeth rejected the family name in favour of the angelic one, the neighbours objected and turned to Zechariah who had been silent and in the background since his return home. Luke seems to imply that Zechariah was deaf as well as mute, for they had to make signs to him (1:62). This means that he would not have heard the name pronounced by his wife (1:22, 62). Elizabeth, the believer, had taken front stage up to now, but the time for Zechariah's restoration has come with his obedience to the word of God when he wrote that the name was John (1:20). Instantly cured, Zechariah praised and thanked God for His goodness in the fulfilment of His word, something he should have done before, in faith. The people are amazed at all these wonderful happenings. The mother's womb had been cured, the father's speech and hearing had been cured, the child is given a special name indicating a special mission: yes, surely the Hand of God is present (1 Chronicles 28:19).

Again (see 1:22) Zechariah has the effect of making the people wonder concerning the fulfilment of the Messianic prophecies. They ask who will this child become since God has been so manifestly present in his generation. Luke thus prepares his readers to ask the same question of Jesus since his birth is of an altogether higher order than John's. The news spread quickly and the people treasured it in their hearts as their expectations of the Messiah were aroused. This too was a cause of great joy and prepared the people for John's retirement to the wilderness before his manifestation to Israel in adult life (1:65).

The Benedictus (1:67–79)

But who is John? This question is answered by Zechariah in his canticle, which is a prophetic interpretation of the events taking place among them. One of the tragedies of human existence is that we can have an experience and miss its meaning. The biblical authors were very concerned to ensure their readers grasped the meaning of the events they proclaimed. Mary has already done this in the Magnificat, and Simeon will do so later in the Nunc Dimittis (2:29–32). Only when we grasp the meaning can we enter into the reality presented to us. Zechariah will try to explain the special role John has in Israel's destiny and his relationship to Jesus. He can only do this after he, too, was filled with the Holy Spirit (1:67).

This hymn falls into two distinct parts, the first relating to Jesus (1:68–75), and the second to John (1:76–79). It was when Elizabeth was filled with the Holy Spirit that she was able to discern the true blessedness of Mary. Now Zechariah can discern the true blessedness of Jesus and John. Like Mary he calls upon the Old Testament to give expression to his thoughts. He begins by blessing God for intervening in history to bring about salvation by raising up a saviour from the House of David (Psalms 41:13, 72:18, 111:9, 132:16–17; Ezekiel 29:21; 1 Kings 1:48). Thus He would vindicate every prophetic promise ever truly made in His Name (Isaiah 49:6; Psalms 105:8–9, 106:10, 45; Micah 7:20). It will mean redemption (1:68), salvation (1:69), deliverance from servitude, freedom to serve God in holiness and to walk in His presence (1:74–75), forgiveness of sins which brings freedom from the fear of death, and finally, peace (1:77–79). The great horn of salvation who will bring all these gifts is the saviour from the House of David, not John (Numbers 24:17).

Zechariah looks down at his infant son convinced that these great events will be prepared by him, for he is the gifted forerunner. The people must be prepared by the confession of sin and this is John's task, to preach repentance to Israel. Jesus is the Rising Sun whose light will fill the world, now shrouded in the darkness of sin and unbelief (Isaiah 9:1, 42:6–7). Jesus alone can show us the Way of Peace, but John will point people to Jesus, thus setting them on the path of salvation. The people will now be made aware that the Sun is Rising for them. In the meantime John disappears into the wilderness, like Moses and Elijah before him, to mature in spirit and await the time for the Word of God to come to him (3:2).

The Birth of Jesus (2:1–20)

As we move into the scene of Jesus' birth Luke shifts us from the homely private circumstances of John's birth to the universal context of the coming of the Son of God. The events that lead up to this moment compare with the final hours before dawn. Wonderful as they are, they cannot compare with the rising of the Sun of Justice. As Isaiah said: the people that walked in darkness will see a great light. A wondrous joy is about to break upon us in the birth of the child who is the Davidic ruler, and at the same time Mighty God and Prince of Peace, yet the child of a humble virgin of Nazareth (Isaiah 9:1–7).

If the son of an emperor was born, his date of birth went down in the annals of history to indicate his importance. On the balcony of the palace the proud father presented the child to the people with great fanfare. His birth was announced like this: "We have a great joy, one to be shared with all the people. We have a son"! Since the emperors were worshipped as gods, the son was presented as the "son of god". At the time of Jesus' birth it was Caesar Augustus who reigned over most of the known world from 42 BC to AD 14. Since he had achieved peace in his far-flung empire he was hailed as the saviour of the world, and prince of peace. His edicts were proclaimed as "good news" to the world and he was worshipped as a god.

Luke has a powerful message for us. The emperor is merely a tool in the hands of God, like King Cyrus before him (Isaiah 45:1) to issue a decree that sends Mary and Joseph to Bethlehem in time for the birth of the true Son of God, the heir to the throne of David, who must be born in Bethlehem, David's city (23:3; Micah 5:1–4; John 7:42). Caesar's edict opens the way for the real good news, the Gospel, to be proclaimed throughout the Roman

Empire, *urbi et orbi*. The census ordered by him was for tax purposes, but the one about to replace him as King of kings and Lord of lords will enrol his people as citizens of heaven for their salvation (10:17–20). This child born in utter poverty pales the "divine" Caesar into nothing by His importance as the Saviour of the world and Prince of Peace. Luke makes sure that we see the universal significance of Jesus' birth, by placing Him in reference to imperial Rome and world events. The most earth-shaking event of that era was not the *pax romana* but the humble entrance of the Son of God into history.

The Roman Empire took periodical censuses for the double purpose of discovering who was liable for military service, and for assessing taxation. The Jews were exempt from military service and therefore the census in Palestine was for taxation purposes only. It was taken every fourteen years, and the one Luke referred to under Quirinius took place about 7–8 BC, the time of Jesus' birth. There is considerable controversy over the dates for this census, although it is known from inscriptions in Antioch of Psidia that Quirinius was Legate of Syria at that time. The rule for the census demanded that a married woman present herself with her husband.

Joseph and Mary set out for Bethlehem in obedience to the civil law even though it was very costly in terms of personal suffering since Mary's time for delivery had come. Luke presents them as obeying both civil and religious authority (2:4, 22–52). Obviously since the Church in Luke's day had its centre in Rome, he wanted to show the Christians their obligations to both church and state (Romans 13:1–7). Bethlehem means "house of bread", and as such carries a reminder that Jesus will become the bread of life for us. He will be our nourishing food, and the Church itself can be called the house of bread since it is where we are provided with the heavenly food. When the child was born Mary swaddled her son. The swaddling cloths were baby-wraps to keep the infant warm and snug. Even King Solomon was wrapped like this (Wisdom 7:4–6). She then placed Jesus in a manger, which is an animal's food box, again emphasizing the Eucharistic element, since Christians now meet Jesus, in this mystery.

Jesus is called Mary's first-born not only because He was the first to open the womb, but to highlight His privileges according to the Mosaic Law (2:22–24; Exodus 13:2; Numbers 3:12, 18:15–16). Mary's "other children" will be all those who hear the Word of God and put it into practice (8:21; John 19:26). The place of the birth is not stated by Luke except to say that Jesus was not born in a house, but presumably in a stable because of the manger. It is noteworthy that neither Joseph nor Mary demur at the awful circumstances of the birth of God's Son. They accept reality as it presents itself to them. Their surrender to God's Will is complete, and so with simplicity, humility and freedom they get on with it, without fuss. I wonder if Luke intends us to see the "no room in the inn" problem as the first sign of the rejection of Jesus, that He came unto His own but they received Him not? (John 1:11). If so, then the Bethlehemites have already rejected their Davidic king in the child born to them that night (Isaiah 1:3; Jeremiah 14:8).

God Reveals the Birth of His Son (2:8–20)

Who will ever know that the Messiah has come? Who will proclaim him to Israel? Who will tell the world that *"When peaceful silence lay over all, and night had run the half of her swift course, down from the heavens, from the royal throne leapt your all-powerful Word"* (Wisdom 18:14–15a)? The answer lies with the *anawim*, those little people whom the world considers contemptible. As Scripture says: the humble will hear and rejoice (Psalm 34:2). The shepherd's way of life came to represent those with enough time to listen to God, and Israel had famous shepherd leaders in the past, Moses and David to name but a few (1 Samuel 16; Exodus 3; Psalm 23). These unlettered, simple folk who were on the fringe of society, and, in Jesus' day, despised because their work left them unfree to observe all the requirements of the ceremonial law, are just the right people to hear and proclaim the wonderful works of God. They also represent the type of people that Jesus will be interested in later in life.

Just as the angel of the Lord looked for the priest in the Temple and Mary at home, so here he looks for shepherds in the fields doing their duty watching their flocks by night, obviously taking it in turns to sleep and keep the watch. As in many Old Testament texts the angel merely alerts the shepherds to the awesome Presence of God Himself. Luke says that *"the glory of the Lord shone round them"* (2:9; Genesis 16:7; Exodus 3:2, 24:16). The announcement of the birth is made by the Father of the child through His chosen messenger, and these simple shepherds receive a direct revelation from God.

An official proclamation is made just like an imperial announcement: *"Today in the town of David a saviour has been born to you; he is Christ the Lord"*, both Christ (Messiah) and Lord (God). The emphasis "to you" means that Jesus is God's gift to humanity. Mary's child belongs to everyone, and is given by God as the solution to the needs of the world. Isaiah 9:6–7 is fulfilled here: *"For there is a child born for us, a son given to us and dominion is laid on his shoulders; and this is the name they give him: Wonder Counsellor, Mighty God, Eternal Father, Prince of Peace. Wide is his dominion in a peace that has no end, for the throne of David and for his* royal power, which he establishes and makes secure in justice and integrity. From this time onwards and forever, the jealous love of the the Lord of Hosts will do this". The titles given to the Roman emperors truly belong to Jesus, the Son of God and Saviour.

The fulfilment far exceeds the promise even though the angel's words fulfil Isaiah 52:7:I *"How beautiful on the mountains are the feet of one who brings good news, who heralds peace, brings happiness, proclaims salvation, and tells Zion, 'Your God is King!' "*.

Yet the prophets did not ever consider that God would become incarnate among them. They understood these texts in a spiritual way. Now that they discover that it is the Lord they were seeking, where would they go and what would they find? They were given a sign just as Zechariah and Mary were. They were to look for a baby, not in a palace, but in a manger. Since any baby born in Bethlehem would be wrapped in swaddling bands it is the place where he lay that constitutes the sign. They would know to look for him where the animals were kept. Does this mean that Luke is saying that Isaiah 1:3 is about to reversed? *"The ox knows its owner and the ass its master's crib, Israel knows nothing, my people understands nothing"*. These shepherds represent the remnant believers who will recognize their Master's crib among the animals and will give praise to God for His wonderful works (2:20).

As they try to absorb what has been said, the heavens open and the shepherds see the choirs of angels, a great throng, praising and glorifying God (Isaiah 6:3). The birth is celebrated in Jesus' true Home. They are also shown the correct response to the birth of the Son of God. Human beings should give glory and praise to God for His wondrous mercy and for the fact that Jesus is our peace through the gift of forgiveness He brings to all

(2:14). If we reject the Prince of peace we seek peace in vain, because it comes through God's good will, in Jesus, towards us (19:41–42). As the disciples proclaim Jesus later they know that this peace comes from heaven (19:38).

Just as Mary had responded to the angel's message by visiting Elizabeth in haste, so here the shepherds go to Bethlehem in haste to seek out the Saviour newly born. They, too are hearers and doers of the word, and they illustrate for all disciples to come that those who seek will find, and if they knock the door will be opened unto them (11:9–10). The shepherds found the holy family and the baby *was* lying in a manger. As they recognized the sign given them *they* proclaimed the good news of the birth of Christ the Lord to Mary and Joseph (2:17). The family were not alone as Luke says that "everyone" who heard this message was astonished at the news.

The shepherds are the first unwinged messengers of the birth of Christ. Throughout the infancy narratives Luke intersperses the two types of messenger that God uses to proclaim His wonderful works, and we are shown that it does not matter whether the messenger sent to us is winged or not. What matters is that we hear the Word of God and put it into practice. Both Zechariah and Mary received the winged messenger type, but Elizabeth was given her husband first, then Mary to confirm her grace. Now Mary and Joseph receive very humble messengers to confirm the grace given to them. As usual they consent to God's ways whether extraordinary, as in the birth itself, or ordinary, in the shepherds. God seems to want to spread the privilege around, for it was the shepherds who received the winged messengers this time round! This was a forecast of the future for it will be the little people who will spread the message of Jesus Christ around the world, and the nations of the earth will hear the word of God from these unwinged messengers sent to them. As they do they find like Elizabeth that they experience everything God has for them. We must grasp that it is not the messenger but the message that is all important, as John the Baptist will declare later (3:5).

Luke gives three reactions to the announcement of the shepherds: the people are astonished, Mary treasured all these things pondering them in her heart, and the shepherds went away glorifying and praising God for all that they had heard and seen. First of all the people hear but go no further than amazement that such stories should be told of a new-born infant. This is an incorrect response to the good news as the devil may remove it from their hearts if they do not accept and respond to it (8:5-6). Mary is the ideal disciple again, listening to the word taking it into her heart, and holding it there for God to give her full enlightenment, and fulfilment (8:15; Acts 1:14; see Sirach 39:1-3; Proverbs 3:1-2). And the shepherds are models for future disciples, who, when they have heard the whole of the good news about Jesus, will glorify and praise God continually (24:52-53), and proclaim this good news to all nations (24:47). For Luke, the Church, like the shepherds and Mary, is the humble recipient and proclaimer of the Gospel.

Eight days later Jesus was circumcised and named in obedience to the Word of God through the angel and the Law of Moses. The manifestation of Jesus will come in the next two scenes so this one is merely mentioned as a family event whereas it represented the manifestation for John.

Jesus Comes to Jerusalem (2:22-40)

Just as Luke had one extra scene to show the greatness

of Mary, so here he gives two scenes to show the greatness of Jesus and His destiny. It is a solemn moment for Israel, even if she is not aware of it, when the Son of God comes to the Temple for the first time. If we follow the imagery of the Ark, as in the Annunciation and Visitation, then the Ark arrives in Jerusalem bringing the presence of the Lord with it. The Ark was very precious to Israel because it was overshadowed by the glory of God. At the time of Christ the Ark was long since lost (Jeremiah 3:16) and the Holy of Holies was empty, save for the invisible Presence of God. The shock of the gospel is that, in Jesus, the presence of God has left His prison in the Holy of Holies and made His dwelling among His people. He is no longer inaccessible (John 1:14).

As we move into this scene we see that the Law and the prophets are fulfilled in Jesus. Malachi 3:1–5 said that one day the Lord would send a messenger before Him and then suddenly He would come to the Temple. But many would not endure the day of His coming because He would discriminate between them causing some to fall and others to rise (2:34). In Daniel 9:24–27 the prophet speaks of the seventy weeks of years that must lapse before the anointing of the Holy of Holies and the coming of the Anointed Prince, who after a short while will be cut off in death resulting in the destruction of the city and the sanctuary. Now, Mary's child is the Holy One (1:35), who is brought to the Temple because as the first-born, he is consecrated or "holy unto the Lord" (2:23). There are echoes in this scene of the offering of the boy Samuel to the Lord in 1 Samuel 1–2 by Hannah and Elkanah.

Just as the Roman civil law brought Mary and Joseph to Bethlehem, so now God's law brings them to the Temple in Jerusalem. Exodus 13:1, 14–16 demanded the consecration of the first-born to the Lord. The original idea was that the person would be in the Lord's service, as Samuel was, for the whole of his life. But as the tribe of Levi eventually took over the service of the Lord, Numbers 18:15–16 laid it down that the first-born could be redeemed or bought back from the Lord by the payment of five shekels to the Temple. Leviticus 12:1–8 said that a woman was to be purified after child-birth, for in the case of a boy, she was considered unclean for forty days. After this period she went to the Temple bringing a lamb for sacrifice. If she was poor she could substitute the lamb for a pair of turtledoves or two young pigeons.

Luke connects both of these customs in this incident, and does not mention the five shekels because, like Samuel, Jesus stayed consecrated to the Lord for the whole of His life. He is the true Lamb of God who will be sacrificed for the sins of the world. Out of His poverty He will enrich everyone (2 Corinthians 8:9; Hebrews 10:1–10). It was Mary's special privilege to offer the Son of God to God in the Temple for the first time, anticipating the priestly privilege in the Church.

Jesus is offered and received in the Temple by the priests, but not recognized by them! He was just another infant. It was two lay people who recognized and proclaimed who He was. Both Simeon and Anna are Spirit-filled people who listen to God in prayer, so they are able to penetrate the mystery of the person of Jesus. This is not just any infant. He is the long awaited Messiah, and they rejoice in the fulfilment of God's promises to Israel. Just as the prophetic spirit became alive in Elizabeth at Mary's arrival in the Visitation so here it comes alive in Simeon and Anna at the arrival of Jesus, Mary and Joseph in the Temple (see Joel 3:1–2). A son and a daughter of Israel who represent the remnant of believers, the *anawim* or the Lord's poor, who live in hope of Israel's comforting,

realize that with this infant the last days have *now* arrived
(2:29). Israel could only be comforted by the coming of
her redeemer (Isaiah 40:1–11; 52:7–10). The words that
Jesus spoke to his disciples in 10:23–24 apply to them:
"*Happy the eyes that see what you see, for I tell you that
many prophets and kings wanted to see what you see, and
never saw it; to hear what you hear, and never heard it*".

Simeon had received a specific revelation from God
that before he died his eyes would behold the Christ of
the Lord. His personal expectation of the Messiah was
different from that of the nation where it was vague.
Moreover, he was open to the leading of the Holy Spirit
on a given day to go to the Temple and see what was
hidden to all others there, including the priests (2:25–27).
How often the Lord works in this manner revealing His
secrets to His friends and hiding them from the high
and mighty (10:21–22). Mary and Joseph were astonished
that this complete stranger was telling *them* who Jesus
was and why He came. They had said nothing to anyone.
It was the Lord who was making the secret known to
others. All they had to do was fulfil the Will of God
in all details of their lives (2:33).

Zechariah, the priest, was unable to bless the people
in the Temple because of his unbelief (1:22), but this
layman filled with the Spirit, blessed God and the parents
of the Messiah because of his lively faith and hope in
God. Luke is telling the Church that Jesus is only
recognized *today* by all those who love and serve God
faithfully, those who live a true spiritual life, guided by
the Holy Spirit.

Simeon's canticle is the shortest and loveliest in the
infancy narratives explaining the relationship of Christianity
to Israel. Through Simeon, Israel, the servant of God
under the Mosaic law, can sleep in peace now that the
Messiah has come. He will enlighten all the nations and

be Israel's greatest glory, for, through Him God's promises will be fulfilled. Jesus is the Prince of Peace (Isaiah 9:5–6; Psalm 72:7) bringing peace to people like Simeon, Anna, the shepherds, Mary and Joseph, Elizabeth and Zechariah, all of whom enjoy God's favour (2:14).

Both Micah and Isaiah had predicted that God would include the Gentiles in His salvific plans, and this Simeon is shown now (Micah 4:1–4; Isaiah 2:2–5, 49:6, 52:9–10). The "glory of Israel" was the Lord's own presence in the sanctuary which marked them out as God's special people (1 Kings 8:10–12; Ezekiel 44:4; Isaiah 49:6). Jesus is pointed out by Simeon as the glory of Israel, the new tabernacle of God's presence. Here Zechariah 2:14–15 is fulfilled: "*Sing, rejoice, daughter of Zion; for I am coming to dwell in the middle of you – Yahweh it is who speaks. Many nations will join Yahweh on that day; and they will become his people.*" Israel who has been the Lord's watchman in the Old Testament is now off duty and happily hands over to Jesus. It is not that she is irrelevant but that all her hopes will be fulfilled and surpassed in Jesus her Saviour (Matthew 5:17–19).

Having blessed God for the fulfilment of the promises, Simeon speaks an oracle to Mary concerning the destiny of her son. There is bitterness ahead for this exalted woman (both meanings of her name). She is told of the suffering awaiting all those associated with Jesus since He will be a sign that will be rejected. Though Prince of Peace He is also the sword of division for families and nations as people choose for or against the Light of the world. No one will feel this more keenly than the mother who bore Him as the sword will be felt even in their own family (see John 7:5; Mark 3:21). Now the full message is revealed which includes both suffering and glory. The joy of His coming is followed by the suffering of His rejection and the glory of His victory. Christians must accept the whole package if they are to be true followers of the Prince of Peace, and the peacemakers of the earth.

Mary is told *"a sword will pierce your own soul too so that the secret thoughts of many may be laid bare"*. Malachi 3:1–5, 16–18, 3:19–4:1 states that the day of the Lord will also be a day of judgement. Jesus will be, like the Lord, in Isaiah 8:14 "a stone of offence" uncovering the secret thoughts of the people. Isaiah chapters 6–8 put the facts clearly before the people: either they listen to the Word of God and obey it, or reject it and take the consequences . . . which is judgement. Jesus is God's sign to Israel now, but one that will be opposed and rejected with drastic consequences for Israel. The sword, a symbol of the decisive Word of revelation coming from the Son of Man demands decision from everyone (Isaiah 49:2; Ephesians 6:17; Hebrews 4:12; Revelation 1:16, 2:12, 16, 19:11, 13, 15, 21). The ministry of Jesus would go through Israel like a two-edged sword leaving no one neutral. It would bring strife into families (12:51–53; Matthew 10:34) and provoke a crisis for the nation, which would, in the end, reject Him for the status quo. Mary as the mother would suffer in the heart of it all, suffer for Jesus her son, for Israel, and for God. Later she would understand with the rest of the disciples that this sword was then destined to go through all nations. She was to be mother of sorrows, and like her son, acquainted with grief.

Jesus' Final Destiny (2:41–52)

The Presentation of Jesus in the Temple closes the infancy narratives proper. Luke adds one more scene in which Jesus Himself declares who He is and why He came. Luke is the only evangelist to give us a scene from the hidden life of Jesus and it gives insight into the religious life of the holy family revealing the harmony and peace in the home. The event occurs in the Temple during the feast of Passover, one of the three pilgrimage feasts. The journey of about eighty miles normally took three days. For safety from robbers and unknown dangers people travelled in large convoys, where the women and men were separate in their own groups until nightfall when each family came together. The children were free to roam during the day, rejoining their parents at night.

The Law commanded every male Jew to go to Jerusalem for the three pilgrimage feasts of Passover, Pentecost and Tabernacles (Exodus 23:14–19, 34:23; Deuteronomy 16:16). Women were not obliged to go but frequently did, like Samuel's parents in 1 Samuel 1:3–28: Boys at the age of twelve were considered to be at the age of discretion. Modern Jewish boys have their Bar Mitzvah at that age, after which they take their place as an adult and must fulfil all the prescriptions of the Mosaic law. We do not know if there was a comparable ceremony in Jesus' day. All we know is that Jesus took his place among the Doctors, listening to them expounding the Law and asking them questions. He astounded them by his clear intelligence and insight. How could someone so young have such deep insight into the Law? It would immediately evoke the question among them as to *who his father was*, and therefore sets the scene for Jesus' revelation that His origins transcend his human family.

In sheer relief at finding Jesus after a fruitless search for three days, Mary reprimands Him as a child. *"See how worried your father and I have been, looking for you"* she said. Just as the doctors of the Law look at Joseph and wonder that he had brought forth such a child, Jesus intervened, reprimanding His human parents and reminding them of His true origins and His true Father.

Since Jesus is now an adult why would they look for Him? His commitment is to his *Father* and He will always be found in the Father's presence and doing his Father's will. He has a mission to fulfil, and no human attachments will prevent His carrying it through (2:49, 4:43, 9:22, 13:32, 17:25).

What a shock for all present, the doctors of the Law no less than the parents. Here is a boy claiming what no man on earth had ever claimed before, not even Moses himself who had seen God face to face and built the original Tabernacle; nor Solomon who first built God a temple. No one had called God's House his Father's house, thus claiming specific sonship. Jesus was conscious of a relationship with God that no one could conceive of, let alone express, and with it went the great passion of His life: "My Father's business". Jesus' origins and His destiny transcend created humanity and the limitations of human history.

It would be a great shock for ordinary country folk like Mary and Joseph to have their son speak up in front of the Doctors of the Law, quite apart from the claim He so publicly made. Luke says that they did not understand what He meant (2:50), which is a difficulty if we remember what the angel Gabriel told Mary about Him, and what the shepherds and Simeon added to that. Was it that they did not understand that being His family would not give them privileged tickets into the Kingdom of God? Was it that ordinary family ties which were very strong in Jewish families were to be put aside, and that Joseph and Mary would have to step down from parental control to a position of disciples which would be very difficult in a home? Their puzzlement is understandable if He had given no sign to them, and then suddenly there is this very public declaration.

Immediately afterwards He went home to Nazareth and

resumed His hidden life under their authority (2:51). So it was a long-distance warning they were given. Mary had time, not only to store up these things in her heart, but to pray for enlightenment about them, and for the strength to cooperate when the time came for their fulfilment. Luke has prepared his readers too for the fact that Jesus will begin a new family, and it will have nothing to do with earthly ties, but will consist of all those who hear the Word of God and put it into practice. Even though Jesus grew in wisdom and stature and favour with both God and men He still managed to hide who He was from the unseeing eyes of those who lived at Nazareth.

This final scene of the infancy narratives links with the final scenes of the gospel as a whole. Luke has a strong emphasis on journeys throughout his gospel. Mary and Joseph travelled to Bethlehem for the fulfilment of the Messianic prophecies concerning the birth of the Messiah. Mary journeyed to Elizabeth, then the family travelled to Jerusalem for the presentation and purification, and here they come for the Passover feast. This particular journey has parallels with the final journey to Jerusalem which begins in 9:51 in which Jesus travels up for Passover with His disciples, His new family, (8:21, 11:28, 2:41, 22:1). On both occasions Jesus got "lost" for three days (2:43–45, 22:47–23:56), causing consternation to his "family" (2:48, 24:19–24). When He is found on the third day (2:46, 24:1–49), it is discovered that His absence had to do with the will of God and the mission given to Him (2:49, 24:25–27), and that they should have known that he was about his father's affairs (2:49, 24:50–53). Perhaps the puzzlement of Mary and Joseph has more to do with this "losing" than the original one, for here the sword will have pierced Mary's heart.

In this final scene Luke completes his overture to the

gospel and leaves us with the picture of the victorious Jesus having returned to the Father's side when He completed the work He was given to do. His physical absence from the Church today has to do with the same divine necessity and there should be no confusion or consternation among His "family" today as we cooperate with all that He has asked of us in this same mission.

Chapter Two

The Hours of Day: Preparation Day

The main topic of the infancy narratives was the arrival of the Son of God into our world. Eighteen years have passed in silence since those events. Now, at thirty, Jesus is ready to be launched into His official Ministry. Luke makes it clear that even though Jesus' coming was spectacular, yet His birth and childhood passed unnoticed by most. The shepherds of Bethlehem disappeared off the scene almost as soon as they entered it. Besides, their sphere of influence was not very great. Indeed many of those involved in the infancy may have been dead by now, because Zechariah, Elizabeth, Simeon and Anna were old at the time of Jesus' birth, and Joseph is no longer mentioned. The political scene is very different too as Herod the Great had died in 4 BC and Caesar Augustus in AD 14 (1:5, 2:1). This section of the gospel which deals with His transition from private life to public activity falls into four parts: the ministry of John the Baptist (3:1–20), the Baptism of Jesus (3:21–22), the Genealogy of Jesus (3:23–38) and the Temptation of Jesus in the wilderness 4:1–13.

The Ministry of John the Baptist (3:1–20)

Luke opens this section as if he were beginning the gospel again, confirming the thesis of scholars that the infancy narratives were inserted after the gospel as a whole was completed. It concerns the mission of the prophet John who was called by God to prepare Israel for the coming of the Messiah. *"The Word of God came to John, son of Zechariah, in the wilderness"* (3:2). Because this led to the earth-shaking events of salvation through Jesus, Luke places it in the context of world history, highlighting the political, religious and geographical ambience of John's mission.

The fifteenth year of Tiberius Caesar was approximately AD 27 or 28. After the death of Herod the Great, the kingdom was divided between his four sons. Herod Antipas was given the regions of Galilee and Perea, and was popularly known as "king" even though his title was that of tetrarch. He reigned from 4 BC to AD 39. His brother Philip had the regions east of the Jordan and to the north bordering on Syria, and he ruled from 4 BC to AD 34 (Mark 6:17–18). Little is known about Lysanias and the tetrarchy of Abilene which centred around the city of Abila about twenty miles northwest of Damascus. The southern tetrarchy was given to Archelaus and consisted of Judaea, Samaria and Idumea (Matthew 2:22). He was deposed and exiled in AD 6 and replaced by Roman Procurators. Pilate was Governor of Judaea from AD 26 to 36.

For the religious context of this new move of God Luke mentions the high priesthood of Annas and Caiaphas, a curious fact because Jewish high priests were normally elected for life. However, Rome had interfered and deposed Annas in AD 15, but since his successors were his five sons and then his son-in-law Caiaphas from AD 18 to 36 AD, perhaps the old man did not resign in reality, but merely let the title go (John 18:13–24). Alternatively, the Sanhedrin or even the people may not have accepted secular intereference in their religious affairs, and so may have considered Annas the true high priest (Acts 4:6).

It was during this time that the Word of God came to

John. Unlike the political and religious rulers, John was in the wilderness waiting for God's Word and God's moment to begin a new move of the Spirit to Israel. He came forth from his solitude where his soul had been tried and tested, to preach repentance and forgiveness of sins to a people that had become hardened by political intrigue and religious cynicism. Many believe that John must have lived in the monastery at Qumran in order to survive the wilderness. These monks used a baptismal rite as purification but only for their own members. It would never have occurred to them that God would want this repentance for everyone. So it was not to any of these separatists that the Word of God came, but to Zechariah's son, who obviously had a more universal vision of salvation. John came to the Jordan valley where there was a plentiful supply of water, to preach to anyone who would listen (3:3).

Each one of the four gospels identifies John as the desert voice prophesied by Isaiah 40:3–5: Isaiah said that God would send a voice from the desert to prepare a way for the Lord. Isaiah used an image from antiquity where if a sovereign were visiting a city, the people were instructed beforehand to prepare a roadway for the king's chariots. For this they would level the low hillocks and use this material to fill in depressions, so that a highway was prepared for the solemn entry of the king. John had come to make a spiritual highway for the Messiah's entry into the hearts of His people. The high places of pride and arrogance had to be levelled and the valleys of their depressions and unbelief filled in so that the Lord would find His people ready at His arrival. Only a turning away from evil and a commitment to God's Will could prepare the heart of Israel for the message of universal salvation. Repentance was the key to salvation, for only then could the for-giveness of sin be offered (3:4–5).

As adults, both Jesus and John begin in the desert (3:2, 4:1). Both seek explanation for their mission from Isaiah (3:5, 4:18). Both preach God's Word which demands a change of life in the listener (3:7–18, 4:43–44). Both preached the Good News except that for John it was still in the future; for Jesus it was in the present (3:6, 18, 4:18, 43). Both are questioned regarding their identity (3:15, 4:34), and ultimately rejected (3:19–20, 4:28–30). But the contrasts remain. The Word of God "came to John" whereas Jesus *is* the Word of God. He *is* salvation. John can only baptize with water, but Jesus baptizes with the Holy Spirit and fire (3:3, 16). John is introduced simply as the "son of Zechariah", while Luke gives an elaborate genealogy to Jesus to make sure *we* know who He is.

John directed his preaching to the crowds who came for baptism. It was strong medicine for a people who considered themselves special because of their physical descent from Abraham. Many Jews thought this was an automatic ticket into the Kingdom of God. They were in for a rude awakening. God, for whom nothing is impossible (1:37) can raise up children to Abraham from the stones (3:8). In fact God was about to raise up children to Abraham from the Gentiles, a fact many of them would reject. A true son of Abraham is one who lives *like* Abraham and thus bears fruit in his life (3:8; Romans 4:13). Physical descent is not the issue for anyone (13:28–30, 19:9). As we have seen in the case of Jesus' conception (1:26–38), of John's word (3:1–2) and the mission to the Gentiles (10:1–11:18) human origins are of no consequence. What matters is that we respond positively to the call of God and the salvation He offers us through Jesus.

Using desert language John asked them if a brood of vipers could escape a fire (3:7)? This strong language evoked the image of the devil in Genesis 3 (John 8:44). If their lives are governed by evil, then they *are* a brood of vipers and there would be no escape from the judgement to come except by repentance, which entails a real turning from sin and commitment to God's ways (John 8:33–44). Baptism was not an escape route, but a sign that the penitent had begun a new life of holiness. This change was urgent because for John the judgement was imminent (3:9). For John the axe was already laid to the root of the tree, a beautiful image taken from the forest of the Jordan, which John must have observed many times.

While the leaders reject John's teaching (7:30), the response from the people was an urgent *"What must we do then?"* (3:10). This gives John (and Luke) an opportunity to explain that repentance is not a feeling of sorrow or regret, but a decision to change one's way of life. It has social consequences that involve sharing with those in need (3:11), being just in one's dealings with others (3:12), and refusing to manipulate or dominate others, or to use one's position of authority to get things by underhand means (3:14). It was a very practical spirituality that was demanded of them, something they had heard many times from the prophets. Take for example Micah 6:8: *"This is what the Lord asks of you: only this, to act justly, to love tenderly and to walk humbly with your God"*. They are only asked to do what should have been their true way of life anyway. John did not demand that they join him in the rigours of the desert life at all. Just plain upright living, for God is not demanding the impossible.

John's preaching had the effect of raising the expectation of the Messiah among the people again (1:66). Could anyone be holier than John, or greater than he? Maybe John was the Christ (3:15–16)? John declared

49

that there was Someone greater coming to them, who was close at hand. So great was He that John was not worthy to be His slave. Both John and his baptism are inferior to the One who is to come and His baptism, because John is of the earth, earthly, just as his baptism is (John 3:29–36), but Jesus will baptize with the Holy Spirit and fire (3:16, 11:20–22). To be baptized means "to be immersed". In John's case the immersion was into repentance and newness of life, but Jesus' baptism would immerse us in the Holy Spirit, and it brought its own fire of judgement. Anyone submitting to Jesus' baptism would be immersed in the Love of God, but they would have to undergo the fire of purification in order to be a fit dwelling for the Holy Spirit. Jesus was the One to bring judgement not only to Israel, but to everyone who hears the good news, for the Word will discriminate between the wheat and the chaff. The latter will be burnt in a fire which will never go out, an image of hell or final destruction (3:17–18). There are serious consequences to hearing the good news from John and even more so from Jesus.

History records two reactions to the prophets: the people either repent or kill them. The latter was John's fate for pointing the finger at sins in high places. The immorality of the Herods was proverbial, and John, following the teaching of Leviticus 18:16, criticized the immoral relationship of the petty king with his brother's wife. Luke also alludes to political crimes and says that he added a further crime to the list by shutting John up in prison. The historian Josephus wrote that John was imprisoned in the fortress of Machaerus on the east side of the Dead Sea. Thus Luke removes John from the scene before introducing Jesus, even though Jesus has not yet been baptized (3:19–20).

The Baptism of Jesus (3:21–22)

The One who was to come was in the crowd unknown to the people (John 1:26). He stepped forward for baptism like the rest, identifying himself with the sinful people of Israel. He who bore no sin did not worry that others might consider Him a sinner (John 8:46; 2 Corinthians 5:21; Hebrews 4:15, 7:26, 9:14). Why would Jesus submit to baptism since it was for repentance? Why does Luke omit the mention of John as the baptizer? He made sure to have John already in prison in the last scene as we pointed out. Is this deliberate? Mark 1:9 and Matthew 3:13 emphasize the baptism part of this event. Luke takes up the story *after* the baptism as does John 1:31: Since the repentance involved a turning towards a new life, we can say that this baptism is Jesus' beginning His new life as a public prophet, leaving His hidden life behind. It represents the beginning of a New Exodus of God's people, and, like Moses before Him, He goes ahead of His people in baptism, as He will not ask anything of His disciples that He will not do Himself.

Luke wants us to see that it was not John's baptism that inaugurated Jesus' ministry. The source of Jesus' life and ministry is the Holy Spirit Himself (1:35). Jesus was at prayer after his baptism when the heavens opened *and the Holy Spirit descended upon him in bodily shape like a dove*. The descent of the Spirit upon Jesus is the source of His anointing and power. It is Jesus' baptism in the Spirit which John said He would give to all disciples afterwards (24:49; Acts 2: 1–4). And it was His prayer that had opened the heavens to produce this extraordinary effect. As Luke shows throughout his gospel prayer is the key that opens the heavens releasing the glory of God upon us.

The Spirit is described as *like a dove*, perhaps an

allusion to the hovering of the Spirit over the waters at
the dawn of Creation (Genesis 1:2)? This would mean
that here at the dawn of the New Creation, the Spirit of
God is even more in evidence since He descends upon
Him who can hold the fullness of the Spirit (John 3:34).
Perhaps it is an allusion to Noah's dove pointing to Jesus
as *the* messenger from God to humankind, the mediator
(Genesis 8:8), the one who would bring the peace of God
to our troubled world. If the dove alludes to the Song
of Songs 2:14, then it points to Jesus as the Lord's
Beloved, the Father's delight.

The opening of the heavens was the final answer to
the fervent prayer of Isaiah in 63:19: *"Oh, that you
would tear the heavens open and come down"* asking
God to come at last for the definitive act of redemption
that would solve the problems of the human race. Jesus
is also the Servant of God who will bring justice to the
nations thus fulfilling Isaiah 42:1: All in all, this event
points Jesus out as the Servant of the Lord, Beloved by
God, filled with the Spirit, a man of prayer and commitment to God's Will, and a fitting instrument in God's
hands for the redemption of the world. The voice of the
Father was heard affirming Jesus' sonship and choice.
The One who said "My Father" in 2:49 now hears the
response "My Son" after His baptism, paving the way
for the Son's special prayer later (chapter 11).

The Genealogy of Jesus (3:23–38)

Although the modern reader finds biblical genealogies
boring, they were vitally important to the Jewish people.
Even today aristocrats need them to prove their "noble
blood", or to make claims to a throne. The general chaos
which followed the return from Exile made genealogies
important to establish membership of a particular tribe,

and to make claims for property. They were vital to establish the priestly families for the restoration of public worship (Ezra 2:59–63; Nehemiah 7:61–65). The Old Testament gives genealogies for famous leaders, sometimes before telling their story, like Noah in Genesis 5, or Abraham in Genesis 11: Matthew follows this pattern in his gospel. Luke follows the pattern for Moses where the genealogy is given as he is about to begin His public ministry in Exodus 6:14–27:

The purpose of Luke's genealogy is to point to Jesus as the climax of human history, hence he traces His ancestry back through Joseph, David, Abraham, to Adam and ultimately to God Himself. No matter how great His lineage in human terms, it does not explain the person of Jesus nor the source of his Ministry, as these come from God Himself (1:32–33, 3:21–22). Although identified with the greatest in Israel, Jesus transcends the boundaries of history. He belongs to the whole human race, as Adam does. As Adam caused us to lose Paradise, so Jesus restores it (23:43).

This is the only genealogy in the Bible that traces a person back to "son of God". It is Luke's unique contribution to make sure that *we* know who Jesus is before we move into the public ministry and the rejection of the Beloved Son. We need to see Jesus' ministry in the context of universal history, not as a consequence of the baptism by John or limited by any human lineage, not even a biblical one. Jesus both fulfils and surpasses the expectations of his biblical background, as the hand of God is creatively present in His conception, birth, anointing and the final action that crowns His life, namely His resurrection.

Luke both affirms and denies the parentage of Joseph. *Jesus was about thirty years old, being the son, as it was thought, of Joseph* (3:23). Jesus was thought to be the son of Joseph because Joseph was the head of that particular household, and men were known as "the son of . . ." whoever was the leader of the family (4:23). At thirty, men were considered ready for public office, and mature enough to teach. It was at this age that Joseph was given high office in Egypt (Genesis 41:46), that David began to reign (2 Samuel 5:4), and that men could bear arms or become priests (Numbers 4:47, 8:23; John 8:57).

The Temptations in the Wilderness (4:1–13)

The genealogy showed that this son of Adam was also Son of God. This fact will be challenged in the desert by the Tempter where we see Jesus' humanity in His prayerful vigil, and also the divine sonship in His response to the Tempter. We can judge Him by His own standard: *"You will be able to tell them by their fruits"* (Matthew 7:16, 6:43–45). Jesus proved He was a Son of God by His actions and behaviour. The testing of Jesus is the last preparatory text before the public ministry.

We understand that an aircraft needs to be tested minutely in order to be passed as airworthy, since the lives of so many people depend on it. The same holds for public office. An untried person is unfit to hold the reins of government. We must not consider it unusual that a servant of the Lord would be tested and proved before taking on a great mission (see 1 Timothy 3:6). Abraham's faith had long years of testing before being rewarded. Moses was tested in the wilderness before being given leadership of the people of God on their Exodus journey. The people themselves were tested for forty years in the wilderness before taking possession of the Promised Land. Adam, too, had been tested to see if he would keep the Word of God, but he failed the test.

The experience of Jesus fits this testing of the Servant

of the Lord, to see if He really is a Son of God. When Adam and Eve encountered the Evil One in the garden they were seduced away from full commitment to God's Will and Word into error, sin and death. Jesus clings to God's Will and Word, and becomes the source of Life and light and redemption to all. As God had explained to Cain in Genesis 4:8 temptation must be overcome to conquer the Evil One. Every person who decides to be a friend of God must struggle with and overcome evil in their own lives and in the world. They must cling to God Himself, and to His Will and Word as Ben Sirach explained so well to his disciples in Sirach 2: He says that *"chosen men are tested in the furnace of humiliation"* as Jesus is here, and will be in the Passion particularly.

After the experience of the Exodus, God led His people into the vast and terrible wilderness for forty years. There He tested them with hunger, thirst, and privations of all kinds, as this would reveal what was in their innermost hearts and show if they would remain faithful to God or not (Deuteronomy 8:2–6). As they marched triumphantly out of Egypt no one but God knew that their hearts were not fully committed to Him, but the testing of the wilderness showed it up. When He allowed them to feel hunger, they rebelled and demanded food. God responded by giving them the miracle of the manna (Exodus 16). Shortage of water made them rebel too, and He gave them water from the rock (Exodus 17). Instead of trusting God, they demanded the extraordinary all the time. They tested God and His goodness, instead of allowing God to mature them through this testing (Deuteronomy 6:13, 16). They had refused the lesson that would have made them the first nation to truly worship God with lives of holiness. The servants of God allow God to test them, while they cling to His goodness and remain humbly committed to His Will (Acts 7:36–43, 13:18).

Luke presents Jesus re-living the experiences of Israel's past history, but whereas Israel failed God's testing, Jesus is seen to be a true Son of God in everything. Throughout this passage Luke also addresses the Christians of his own day, lifting up Jesus as their model when they are tested by life's experiences (22:31–32). The Church is to live by God's Word, clinging to the will of God in everything. Adoring and serving God alone, they were not to seek power or domination in the political, religious or social spheres. They were to be true servants of God, and the greatest in the Kingdom of God are the servants and the least (22:24–27).

It was not a person in inner conflict who approached the wilderness to have solitude with the Alone for forty days. No, it was the spirit-filled and Beloved Son, whose relationship with the Father has just been affirmed after His baptism, who is *led* by the Holy Spirit into this school of suffering just as every servant of God is brought into it at some point in their lives (see Romans 8:14, 18–19). Luke makes it very clear that the testing came from *outside* of Jesus, not from inner conflict, just as it had for Adam and Eve. The wilderness was seen as the place where wild beasts and demons lived (Isaiah 13:20, 30:6). No one would go there if not led by God Himself, for they would encounter the struggle with evil, while facing the weakness of their own humanity. Only the strong, like Moses and Elijah and, of course, John the Baptist, would risk it, and each one had a deep experience of God there too (Exodus 34:28; 1 Kings 19:8).

The first suggestion is not what it seems on the surface. *"If you are the Son of God, tell this stone to turn into a loaf"* (4:3). The "if" is important. The Tempter is not sure, yet knows that a son of God would have power. The suggestion is that he use that power for his own benefit rather than for the redemption of others. Use it for self-love, rather than *agape*-love. What a hypocrite Jesus would be if instead of fasting and praying in the wilderness, He was working miracles to take care of Himself! Should we not put the spirit before the body, and the eternal before the temporal (9:23–24)? Jesus responded from Deuteronomy chapters 6–8, from that passage which deals with the great commandment to love God, and reminds Israel of the lessons of its own wilderness experience. *"Man does not live on bread alone"* Luke quotes, and the rest of the sentence is that man lives on everything that comes from the mouth of the Lord. If we are to live a spiritual life, then we must be fed on the Will of God, and the Word of God. We must rely on God, not on materialism. Material food is for the material body only. The Church must always remember that the Kingdom of God is not of this world, and that the power given to it must be used only for the glory of God (John 18:37). Jesus' choice was to remain hungry, poor, lonely and dependent on God (6:20–23), and He became the Bread of Life for all those who hunger for God (see John 6).

The second suggestion was equally subtle. The devil showed Jesus the kingdoms of the world, obviously in vision, offering Him political power and world domination, an attractive suggestion if one lusted for power. The Devil claimed that the world empires belonged to him (4:7), and he would give them to anyone who would worship him (John 12:31, 14:30). The temptation was to use wrong means to achieve good ends. Could Jesus use political power to establish the Kingdom of God? Would He become a political Messiah as the people expected? The people of Israel had run after political power, and alien gods, to their own ruin in the past. Jesus rejects all this to cling to the Father. He will bring the Kingdom of God on earth by doing the Will of God (Exodus 23:20–33; Deuteronomy

12:30–31). The Devil may have usurped God's right to be called King of the Universe, because the perversity of human nature gave him that loophole, but Jesus will re-establish God's Kingship over the universe (Psalms 24:1, 33:8; 47:2, 7). Later Jesus himself will be proclaimed King of kings and Lord of lords (Revelation 19:16), the one who will reign over all the earth (Revelation 20).

In the final temptation Jesus was brought to the Temple in Jerusalem and made to stand at its highest point. Then He was challenged to throw Himself down (4:9). Jesus had twice foiled the Tempter by quoting Scripture, so here the Devil takes Him on and suggests that Jesus attempt suicide on the grounds of a misquotation of Psalm 91:11–12: This psalm promises God's protection to one who does His will, the one who trusts God to save him from deadly perils. The psalm does not guarantee us protection from the results of our own actions. This temptation also gives rise to the question of signs and wonders which the Jews were prone to demand, but Jesus refuses to do anything spectacular, unnatural or unnecessary, for God does not work like that. He works through quiet ordinary, humdrum "natural" ways, so much so that we are hardly aware of His Presence and action on our behalf.

Jesus refuses to be a Messiah who will force acceptance of Himself through extraordinary means. As the divine Son He refuses to accept any special protection that would save Him from the pain of being human. He will not ask to come down from the cross. Israel had tested God in the wilderness many times by demanding miracles as proof of God's love. This was particularly so at Massah and Meribah (the names mean trial and contention) where they distrusted God's providence on their behalf (Exodus 17:1–7; Numbers 20:2–13). In reply, Jesus reiterates the command of Moses in Deuteronomy 6:16 that no creature has the right to test God.

In conclusion Luke says that the Devil left Jesus but he would return *"at the appointed time"* (4:13). The appointed time is the Passion and the place Gethsemane, when the Hour of Darkness will come upon Jesus (22:3, 53; 23:44). Here He had His first struggle and victory over Satan. There the final struggle and victory will take place. The results of His struggle here will be seen in the exorcisms when the demons will flee before Him.

Chapter Three
The Ministry in Galilee

God ... has visited his people, he has come to their rescue and he has raised up for us a power for salvation in the House of his servant David (1:68–69). In a series of incidents Luke sets out the programme for the mission which evokes the entire course and meaning of Jesus' life. Jesus left the wilderness *with the power of the Spirit on him.* This *dynamis* is the power behind the ministry, and the source of His teaching with authority. The wilderness experience both strengthened and empowered Him for mission. He emerged as a man of prayer, filled with the Spirit, ready to go about doing good (Acts 10:37–38; Luke 24:19). He began in Galilee, His homeland, in the synagogues where the people gathered every Saturday to hear the Word of God read and explained to them. The initial response was good: *"everyone praised him"* (4:15).

The Inaugural Sermon at Nazareth (4:16–30)

Jesus chose His home town to lay out the programme for His mission. He chose the Sabbath when the people gathered in the synagogue, so His audience consisted of relatives, friends and neighbours as well as the other townspeople. He chose a passage from Isaiah to reveal that, in Him, the prophets were to be fulfilled. Unknown to them their town had been highly honoured by God, but they were to refuse the honour of giving Israel its Messiah. Jesus declared that the Spirit of the Lord had been given to Him, as we saw in His baptism. Like the prophets of old He was anointed for mission, for the Spirit was never given for personal reasons (Isaiah 42:1–9).

Jesus said that His mission was to preach the good news to the poor, but what type of poverty? Later He gives examples of two Old Testament people who were helped by the Lord through His prophets. One was a poor widow (4:26), the other was a rich man impoverished by his illness (4:27). The poverty consists of our need for God. Some may be rich, like the tax collector in 5:27, but be poor morally and spiritually. Our need for healing and redemption puts us all into the category of the poor, as well as all those who are marginalized by their social position. The good news for the poor was that Jesus came to set the captives free. The release of captives (*aphesis*), not only means the release of prisoners of war, but Luke uses it with the special meaning of "forgiveness", meaning the release from the slavery of sin (7:36–50), and the crushing power of Satan (8:26–39). Jesus will be anxious to free anyone from any bondage in order to release them to become sons and daughters of God.

Next Jesus offers new sight to the blind. Again this covers both the spiritual and material aspects of blindness (Acts 26:17–18). Unless our eyes are opened we will not penetrate the mystery of the person of Jesus, nor will we be able to benefit from the redemption that He brings. But for all those who do accept Him Jesus declares that this is the beginning of *the Lord's year of favour*, the beginning of the Era of God's Mercy to all. In a dramatic move Jesus stopped in mid-sentence omitting the words about " a day of vengeance for our God" in Isaiah 61:2, because that would not come in His lifetime. He was to inaugurate the Era of Mercy and let history take its course from there. He rolled up the scroll and everyone's eyes were riveted on Him as He said: *"This text is being fulfilled today even as you listen"* (4:21). Here before the people who knew Him best Jesus claimed to be the Messiah. They all expected the "day of the Lord" to be a day of wrath. Even John the Baptist had prepared them for judgement (3:9, 16–17). There will be discrimination between those who accept and those who reject as will be shown even in this scene, for Jesus is the sign that will be ultimately rejected, even if the initial response is favourable, as it is here (4:22, 2:34).

After the initial response of astonishment at His gracious words, a negative reaction set in with the people's refusal to accept that anything good could come out of Nazareth (John 1:46). Jesus was only Joseph's son, and they knew His relatives (4:23). They could not believe that behind the simplicity and humility could be the answer to all their hopes and desires. After all their experience of the prophets they still would not accept the divine coming to them through the human. Anyway He had done nothing significant here, at home. All they had were rumours from abroad. As far as they were concerned He had not supplied any evidence that He was the Messiah. They had seen no miracles, and would not believe unless they did (Mark 6:5; John 4:48; Deuteronomy 13:2). They were not prepared to trust Him and His message without the signs (see John 20:28). Jesus knew that prophets were not accepted in their own country (4:24), and that He would ultimately be rejected by the Jewish nation. His acceptance would come from the outsiders as the prophets had experienced of old, for "familiarity breeds contempt" (11:49–51, 13:33).

Jesus then gave them two case histories from the prophets to ponder which might explain His ultimate rejection by the Jews and acceptance by the Gentiles. The first was that of a widow whom Elijah challenged to give her last cake to him even though it meant death for herself and her son (4:25–26; 1 Kings 17:8–16). The request was outrageous at first glance. Sure he promised that miracles would follow, but how was she to know that she was not being duped? Why did she trust him? Basically, she had nothing to lose. She and her son were going to die anyway. If this man were right there was hope of life, otherwise death stared her in the face. It wasn't credulity that made her risk trusting him, but the hope of life to follow. She acted on no other evidence than Elijah's promise in God's name. This is precisely the risk that the Nazareans refuse to take with Jesus, because they will not admit their poverty before God. They were good-living respectable people who worshipped God. Insulated by this respectability they would not admit that they needed release from the slavery to sin, or that they needed their eyes opened to the wonder of what God was doing in their midst. They were not poor.

This is where the second case becomes relevant. The next story is of a very rich man, Naaman, who became impoverished through leprosy, an illness that neither the privileges of his high office nor money could cure. (Notice that Luke likes to balance stories of women and men). His desperation made him listen to the words of a young Jewish slavegirl to seek out the prophet Elisha. He had nothing to lose but everything to gain from this encounter. Death stared him in the face if this prophet had no power, but if the words of the prophet were right then life was possible, and hope. He risked the humiliation of having to dip in the Jordan in order to be healed. The Jordan is a symbol of death, so this man learned that he had to die to himself, listen to the Word of God through the prophet and then he would be healed and live, not a pagan life, but a true life as God ordained. The gift to Naaman was a spiritual resurrection (4:27; 2 Kings 5:9–14). But the Nazareans would not acknowledge the leprosy of sin, so there was no urgency to repent or listen to the

Word through Jesus. They refused to die to their own ideas of Messiah or to themselves, so they tried to kill the prophet.

In this brilliant text Luke has managed to summarize the gospel, giving us Jesus' programme of redemption and why it was ultimately rejected by the Jews and accepted by the poor, the sick, the blind and the needy. *"We had to proclaim the word of God to you first, but since you have rejected it, since you do not think yourselves worthy of eternal life, we must turn to the pagans. For this is what the Lord commanded us to do"* (Acts 13:46–47; see also Acts 18:6, 19:9). Now he shows us the frustrated efforts to destroy Jesus, whom they did not know as they thought that He was only Joseph's son. The first "Calvary" is here on the hilltop overlooking Nazareth where His own townspeople tried to kill Him. But He slipped through the crowd and walked away. They demanded a miracle and they got one. They did not have the power to destroy Him because He is full of the power of the Holy Spirit (3:22; 4:14, 18). He went on his way here to continue His mission. After Calvary He would go on His triumphant way to conquer the world for God.

Jesus at Capernaum (4:31–44)

In His visit to Capernaum Jesus begins His work of setting people free from oppression so that the Kingdom of God can be established in their midst. First He preaches the good news (4:31–32), then he releases a man from satanic oppression (4:33–37), and a woman from illness (again note the balance of male and female) and many people from all kinds of problems (4:40–41). Thus the Kingdom of God comes in peace, forgiveness and joy for those in need of God. The hungry are fed (1:53). Unlike Nazareth, Capernaum wants Jesus to stay. In fact the people try to prevent Him from leaving them (4:43), but Jesus must continue on His way to give the good news to all Israel (4:44). His departure from them is a divine necessity. Luke uses the name Judaea for all Israel which was the Graeco-Roman designation for the country. Judaea for them meant "the land of the Jews". For Jewish people Judaea meant the southern province where the tribe of Judah resided.

Jesus preached in the synagogue at Capernaum but we are not given the contents of the sermon because Luke wants us to look at something else, namely His divine authority, which did not rest on human learning, or dependence on great teachers of the past. No, the authority was within Himself, and His word carried the power to heal and to exorcize. His word was Spirit-filled and life-giving, and the people had never seen anything like this before (4:32,36). The victory that Jesus gained over Satan in the wilderness produces fruit here as the demons are afraid of Jesus. They reveal who He is, but He refuses to accept testimony from His enemy (4:34). He will, Himself, open the eyes of the blind and make it possible for humans to recognize Him by their own experience of Him. He refuses help from the devil as he did in the wilderness. Their title *"Holy One of God"* echoes the words of the angel to Mary in 1:32, 35, but it is not enough for angels and demons to recognize Jesus. He must be recognized and proclaimed by humans also, but first they must recognize their sinfulness and need of redemption (5:9). The Kingdom will come in God's way, in God's time, and by God's grace. It will bring about the ultimate defeat of the Devil which is foreshadowed in this deliverance (4:34).

Throughout the ministry there is a close connection between teaching the Word of God and delivering the people from their bondage to Satan, sin, sickness. The

Word of God ploughs up the soil of the soul so that spiritual warfare can take place there and God's Kingdom be established. Jesus sharply commanded the demon to leave (4:35) and rebuked the fever in Simon's mother-in-law (4:39) and the evils of sin and sickness melted away before that divine word so that astonishment was the result. The people were filled with admiration at Jesus' authority that had such redeeming effects. They lead to the recognition of Jesus' true identity as the Son of God (4:34). If the Nazareans had travelled to Capernaum they would have seen the evidence they demanded. Simon's mother-in-law is introduced without explanation because everyone in Luke's church knew who Simon was (4:38). The move from the synagogue to Simon's house was reflected in the growth of the church which held its meetings in private homes which became the *ecclesia domestica*. This woman is the first of many women disciples to serve Jesus. Others are mentioned in Luke 8:1–3, and all of them had opened to Jesus' healing ministry. Anyone in Capernaum that day who was open to God's action through Jesus was healed or delivered according to their need (4:40–41). His departure from them was a divine necessity, part of God's plan, and His own choice, just as it will be in the Passion (23:46) and Ascension (24:51) later (2:49–50).

Jesus and his First Disciples (5:1–6:11)

Up to this point Jesus has been alone on the mission, but now He associates disciples to Himself, and begins to train them to continue the work He has begun. In 4:14–44 Luke showed that Jesus' mission programme and identity were rooted in the Holy Spirit. That of the disciples is rooted in the call of Jesus, which established them in a new way of life patterned on that of Jesus

Himself. There are five main sections here which begins
with Simon Peter's call (5:1–11), followed by the healing
of a leper in which Jesus demonstrates His respect for
the Mosaic law (5:12–16). Next begins a series of con-
frontations with the religious authorities, first on the
question of the forgiveness of sin (5:17–26), then on
Jesus' acceptance of sinners as disciples (5:27–39), and
the final two in the cornfields and in the synagogue on
Jesus' more liberal interpretation of the Scriptures (6:1–11).

The section begins by the Lake of Galilee, called here
Gennesaret, "the garden lake", so called because of the
fertile land west of the lake, south of Capernaum. Again
we see Jesus teaching the people, for they can only be
opened up to the work of God in their lives by having
their eyes opened by His word. Jesus asked His friend
Simon (Peter) to allow Him to teach from His boat, a
foreshadowing of the mission to come (5:3). In this
incident Luke gives prominence to Simon even though
there are other boats and fishermen there, who are mentioned only at the end (5:10). Luke puts Peter in a leading
position vis-à-vis Jesus and the mission right from the
time of his call.

After hearing the Word of God, Peter is challenged by
Jesus to *"put out into deep water and pay out your nets
for a catch"* (5:4), for disciples must learn not just to
hear the Word of God, but also carry out His will in
working for the Kingdom of God in the world – signified
by the "deep water". Although there are others about
(Mark 1:16) the command is given specifically to Peter
who will be the leader in the post-resurrection era. Jesus
had requested to go into Simon's boat, not one of the
others (5:3). Simon objects that there appears to be no
fish about, for they had worked fruitlessly all night. Then
the moment of grace came when he decided to trust Jesus
in this seemingly ridiculous request. They netted such a

huge catch that they signalled to their companions in the other boat to come and help them (5:6–7). Simon immediately took his attention from the catch to the miracle worker, which is the correct response to a miracle. He recognized the Hand of God here, and this stirred his conscience. He threw himself on his knees confessing his sinfulness and unworthiness to be in Jesus' company. His fear (5:10) is normal for one receiving divine revelation (Peter in 5:5 addresses Jesus as "Master", but in 5:9 as "Lord"). Isaiah, too, confessed sinfulness and fear before the revelation of God (Isaiah 6:5) and was immediately asked to go on mission, as Peter is here (5:11; Isaiah 6:8–13). The story finishes with all of these men leaving everything to follow Jesus.

This episode foreshadows the future mission to all the world. The lake itself symbolizes the world, or the abyss, from which the disciples are asked to save people (8:31). The mission begins from Peter's boat in response to the Word of God, and the specific command of Jesus (24:47–49; Acts 1:8). The mission is so difficult that no haul is possible without Jesus' presence and power. They cannot go it alone, as it would be fruitless. Peter was to engage the help of companions who were to be his partners (5:10) in the mission, for each one had a role to play. Cooperation between the boats would be needed if many of the fish were not to be lost (5:7). Neither Peter nor the others were called because of worthiness. They, like every other disciple had to repent and have their sins forgiven (5:8), and must feed on the word of God (5:2). Their call was part of the mystery of God's purpose for universal redemption. The hesitation of the Apostles to embark on the Gentile mission is seen in Acts where the Lord specifically commands Peter to go and bring in the Gentiles who were ready (Acts 10:17–23).

The Healing of the Leper (5:12–16)

At this point Luke relates a story told in greater detail in Mark 1:40–45. It concerns touching the untouchables, or the healing of a leper. The ancient world called a group of skin diseases "leprosy". Leviticus 13 and 14 give the background to the disease and its treatment. Since these diseases were contagious the lepers were isolated from their families, their village community and from public worship. They were obliged to stay away from the healthy community, and if they had to emerge for some reason they had to shout "Unclean! Unclean!" (Leviticus 13:45–46) to warn people to stay away from them. Since they had to stay away from the towns Jesus must have just left a town when this leper ran up to Him to implore healing (5:12). Obviously he had heard that Jesus was different to others so he took the risk of breaking the Law to get to Him. Addressing Jesus as "Kyrie", which means either "sir" or "Lord" depending on the context, he told Jesus that he understood that the only possibility of life for him lay in Jesus' healing power. Like Naaman the leper, his illness opened him up to the working of God in his life, and his faith would now occasion a work of God.

Jesus touched him and said "*Of course I want to! Be cured!*" (5:14). This is a very dramatic moment, for lepers were never touched for fear of contracting the disease. Not to be touched for long years of one's life is a great deprivation, as love is communicated by touch in so many ways. This wholesome touch of Jesus told the man that in Jesus' eyes he was not a loathsome person with an ugly illness, but that he was a son of God, and would be treated as such. That acceptance must have healed the psychological scars of having been unclean for so long. Luke said that the man was "covered in leprosy" (5:12), so that instant healing amounted to a virtual resurrection because leprosy in an advanced state meant the loss of fingers and toes and the destruction of the skin. He was a new man. The emotional shock of this must have been enormous.

The Mosaic regulations for the cleansing of lepers included an examination by the priests, and making a sin offering to the Temple. Since Israelite tradition regarded sin and sickness as closely connected, the priests were the public health officers who declared people clean. Jesus honoured that tradition (Leviticus 13:49; 14:4–7). Did He want to give them evidence (5:14) of the healing? or of His power to heal? or that He kept the Law? As we are about to move into scenes of confrontation in which Jesus will be accused of breaking the Law the evidence supplied beforehand is important. Would Jesus want to reveal that he came not only to keep the law but to surpass it? The priests had no power to remove the cause of the person's trouble, they could only declare the person healed after the event. But Jesus removed the disease and became the cause of this man's joy and liberation. While the old rituals were the best that Israel had, God had come in Jesus to give them something much more efficacious... he had set this captive free (4:18). Leprosy would no longer be the horror it had been. The life-sentence was removed by the touch of the Master's hand.

For the Israelites, leprosy was like a parable. As they viewed the ravages of the disease they thought of the ravages of sin to the inner person. They considered the isolation effects of serious sin which breaks relationships with family, community and church, leaving a person in a wretched state, desperately in need of the gentle touch of the Lord's forgiving love to release them to re-form their lives. And the priests are charged with the responsibility of examining us and declaring us clean before returning us to society and normality. Some people today do not like this type of reflection, thinking it says something about disease sufferers today. Ancient peoples were more fortunate than us, for they were willing to learn from all eventualities of life, where moderns appear to be less willing, yet this is put down to greater knowledge. If we were willing to learn from our history, geography, flora, fauna, life, death, sickness, our lives would be richer and more fruitful. Alas, we are so scientific that we forget to be philosophers, poets and prophets also.

Placed after the call of Peter this passage is also a powerful statement regarding the non-exclusiveness of disciples. Jesus was ready to help Peter with his sinfulness, and here He shows that He can deal with any level of uncleanness whether of body or soul. Without this loving ministry of forgiveness none of us can be disciples.

The Paralytic (5:17–26)

In the five scenes that follow Luke shows the progress of the religious leaders' opposition to Jesus. In the story of the paralytic it is hidden in their hearts (5:21), but at the sinners' banquet they challenge the disciples (5:30). On the question of fasting Jesus Himself is challenged (5:33). As they walk through the cornfields Jesus is challenged about the disciples breaking the Law (6:2), and finally they set a trap to catch Jesus out on the Sabbath in 6:7. The series ends with a decision to kill Jesus (6:11).

The Pharisees and Doctors of the Law came from all over the country to a meeting Jesus held in a private house (5:17). In the last episode we met the priests who were in charge of the rituals in the Temple. Here we meet Israel's Scripture scholars and theologians, those who were experts in the Law. Such an audience would trouble many teachers, but Luke says that *"the Power of the Lord was with Jesus"* (5:17). The Lord was manifesting Himself powerfully through Jesus that day . . . especially for these people. Then some men arrived and let a paralytic down through the tiles in front of Jesus. Mark 2:4 says that they stripped the roof. Mark appears to refer to the roofing in Palestinian houses whereas Luke mentions the type his Greek audiences would be accustomed to.

Jesus responded to the faith of the sick man's friends, and to the love that had gone so far to help him. Then to the consternation of all present He forgave the man's sins (5:20)! It was a physical healing that was sought, so why bring sins into it? Surely there is no connection between paralysis and sin? These thoughts would trouble the sick man and his friends. Meanwhile the scholarly audience picked up the implications of the statement and accused Jesus in their hearts of blasphemy, that is, of appropriating God's right to Himself, since everyone knew that God alone could forgive sin. Forgiveness was a future blessing to be brought by the Messiah, but here is a man claiming that Godly Messianic gift to himself. Jesus makes God's forgiveness a present reality in the here-and-now of time. This means that Jesus claims authority from God, on a day when the power of the Lord was especially present in the healings (5:17, 22).

In taking this action Jesus demonstrated that He was a redeemer, interested in the whole person, not just in the body. Real, lasting healing begins with inner healing. The paralysis of sin is more deadly than the paralysis of the body because one could be physically paralysed and go to heaven, and have full physical health and go to hell if the soul is neglected. The priority, therefore, is forgiveness which sets the captive free. But if Jesus does not also heal the man everyone will be disappointed, for that is what they want. Humans think the body more important than the soul, but wisdom values the spiritual over the temporal.

Jesus responded to their need, for now it is the need of the whole group, disturbed by Jesus' forgiveness, by working a miracle. A good teacher, He decided to use the physical healing as a demonstration so that the audience would understand what had just happened before their unseeing eyes. Was it any more difficult to say "you are forgiven" or "get up and walk"? Of course not, but if the second command produced results, then the first did also. When Jesus commanded the man to get up and go home, they all observed that the man was given the power to do so, yet Jesus did not touch him. They were listening to the Spirit-filled and life-giving Word of God. Jesus' word held the power to bring about the effects He wanted, just as the creative Word of God had at the dawn of creation (Genesis 1; 5:23–25). The man went home praising God, and as he did, the audience also sang God's praise, filled as they were with awe and wonder (5:26). It would appear from the following scenes that the praise came from the ordinary people as the opposition from the Pharisees is about to escalate.

A Sinner's Call to Discipleship (5:27–32)

The healed paralytic walked away forgiven and healed. Now Luke tells us that the forgiven sinner is called into a whole new life. Forgiveness and healing are not ends in themselves. They open one up to walk in the way of salvation. As we saw in the infancy narratives, the Lord goes looking for us wherever we are. Here Jesus goes to the tax office to call Levi from his old way of life, and Levi generously responds by leaving everything to follow Him (5:27–28), which of course includes acknowledgement of sinfulness, repentance and forgiveness before experiencing table fellowship with Jesus. Because Levi and other tax collectors collaborated with Rome in an unjust system of taxation they were seen as public sinners and shunned. As a class of people they were fraudulent and extortionate, looked upon as robbers by the rabbis, and their constant contact with Gentiles kept them ritually unclean, so they were socially ostracized. In the expression "tax collectors and sinners" the two were practically interchangeable in the minds of religious leaders. John the Baptist in 3:12 had told the tax collectors to only exact what they had to, no more. Here all the uncleanness and isolation of the tax collector, as well as his love of money, are overcome by the strength of Jesus' love and forgiveness. The condemnation of the religious leaders would leave this man in his sin, but Jesus harvests this life for the Kingdom of God.

Levi understood that his acceptance by Jesus opened the way for others. He invited Jesus to a sinners' banquet, only for the sinners to discover that they were in turn invited to Jesus' Messianic banquet (13:29, 14:15–24, 22:30). This is the marvellous exchange that redemption brings. By accepting their invitation Jesus shows solidarity with the needy. By joining Him they show solidarity with Him and with the redemption that He brings. There is mutual commitment in this meal which we now see as a healing and reconciling event. Luke's own community and the Church as a whole are made up of reconciled sinners in table fellowship with each other and with the Lord. It is thus a prophetic forecast of the future "breaking of bread" which will be the central feature of Christian worship (24:34). Luke reminds us then, that the Eucharistic meal is a call to intimacy and solidarity with Jesus from disciples who have broken with sin and become a loving community serving those in need.

Most of the banquet scenes in the gospels have the

Pharisees as hosts and the poor standing about looking at more of what they can't have, and listening to the learned conversations of the rich religious leaders (7:36–50). This is the one occasion where the tables are turned, and the Pharisees are looking on not because they are not invited, but because their segregationist tendencies will not permit them to join sinners for fear of defilement. They are scandalized that Jesus does not appear to care about this (5:30). His reply is devastating in its unanswerable logic: *"it is not those who are well who need a doctor, but the sick"* (5:31). It is absurd to think that a doctor would stay away from the sick for fear of contracting illness. There is no justification for a doctor's existence if he does not take care of the sick. The Pharisees are challenged to see Jesus, not as someone joining the problem but offering the only solution there is to that problem. His mission is to set these spiritual captives free (4:18), and this cannot be achieved by avoiding them. He must associate with them, which is the exact opposite mentality to that of the Pharisees.

Jesus, the divine physician, made another statement regarding His mission: *"I have not come to call the virtuous, but sinners to repentance"*. Only the hungry can be filled, the rich are sent empty away (1:53). The "virtuous" are those who deem themselves OK spiritually, who have no need of a saviour. The term does not mean people filled with grace and the love of God, but those filled with religion, who have no room for God; the ultimate tragedy. Sin is still associated with sickness here, because to allow this destructive power to operate in our lives is a sick way to live. People who live so far from God's plan for us as humans, and as His family, are seen as "sick" in His eyes, needing the ultimate healing of redemption (Isaiah 1:2–9, 17–20).

The Pharisees did not bargain for all this. They merely complained that Jesus' disciples could not be compared to their disciples or those of John the Baptist, for these were good religious people who *"are always fasting and saying prayers"* (5:33, 18:12). Among the Jews fasting was practised for the expiation of sins on the day of Atonement (Leviticus 16:29–31), for occasions of personal repentance (1 Kings 21:27; Joel 1:14, 2:15–17; Isaiah 58:1–9), or as a sign of mourning (Esther 4:3). Thus there is a time and a place for fasting, if it is to be an appropriate sign, and not empty religion which puffs up pride (18:12). The radical newness of the life to which these sinners are called is shown now. Jesus replied that when a wedding is in progress, and for the time when the couple are still referred to as bride and groom, it is absurd to speak of fasting when one is celebrating new life and love. Jesus is the New Bridegroom, come to bring about the new marriage between God and His people (John 2:1–12, 3:29). This event is a cause for joy, but a time would come when the bridegroom will be forcefully removed from them. That will be the time for mourning and lamenting, and fasting (5:35; Mark 16:10). Luke is also telling his community that Jesus did approve of fasting at the right time (Acts 13:2–3).

Jesus used two lovely parables to illustrate the radical newness of Christianity by comparison with Pharisaical Judaism. Christianity was not a patch on Judaism. It is a completely new garment. God never patches anything. He is a creator, who always does a new thing (see Isaiah 48:6–11; Revelation 21:5). The old garment is worn out and to sew a new patch would only destroy both the patch and the garment. Christianity was also new wine, which could not be put into old wineskins unable to stretch. The grace of the gospel could not be squeezed into the legalism of the old system. The outmoded rituals, forms and traditions of Judaism were too rigid to hold the joy, exuberance and energy of the new Dispensation (5:37). (Notice again the female sewing and the male drinking images: Luke insists on reaching his whole audience with images that suit.)

Finally, Jesus acknowledges how difficult the change-over really is for sincere believers of Judaism: *"And nobody who has been drinking the old wine wants new. 'The old is good' he says"* (5:39). This is an acknowledgement that Israel had good wine. In fact, she had the best wine available in the ancient world. Her reluctance to try the new is understandable if she found the old satisfactory, as so many thousands of them have in every generation. Human beings are always reluctant to give up something that has worked for them in order to take on the untried and untested. This explains why Jesus had most success among those who were considered by themselves and others to be life's failures. Like the widow of Zarephath and Naaman, they had nothing to lose but everything to gain by joining Jesus. The Pharisees had a whole way of life, a long tradition, positions of authority in the old system, and a good life to lose, in order to gain what? the company of sinners? poverty? suffering? Their resistance is understandable.

The New Life and Sabbath Observance (6:1–11)

Will the new converts be bound by the Pharisaic interpretation of the Sabbath observance? They learn here that they must follow Jesus' interpretation of the law. There are two incidents which take place on the Sabbath to illustrate this, one out in the cornfields (6:1–59), and the other in the synagogue (6:6–11). The first deals with the issue of working for one's living on the Sabbath. Harvesting was clearly forbidden in Exodus 34:21, but plucking the ears of corn as one walked through the fields, was allowed in Deuteronomy 23:25. The legalistic Pharisees who are obviously following the group accuse the disciples of breaking the Law. The disciples learn here that their freedom to act responsibly and lovingly, out of concern for one's neighbour's need, is grounded in Jesus as Lord of the Sabbath and the Son of Man.

In 5:24 Jesus called himself "Son of Man", a title which originates in Daniel 7:13–14, and refers to a person of mysterious origin, who comes from God, and is given everlasting universal kingship. The Son of Man has authority on earth, to forgive sins (5:24), and in 6:5 he is Lord of the Sabbath. God himself was the author of the Sabbath observance (Genesis 2:2; Exodus 20:8–11), so His was the ultimate authority which Jesus claims to share, on the principle that whoever has the authority to put double yellow lines on the roadway also has the authority to remove them. Here the Law must give way before real human need as Jesus explains in His rabbinical appeal to Scripture as the highest authority. He cited of King David eating the showbread which was reserved only for priests (Leviticus 24:5–9; 1 Samuel 21:1–6). Surely they would not accuse the great King David of breaking the Law? And a greater King than David was surely here (20:41–44)? The Sabbath was meant by God to remind the people of their redemption in the past and its future fulfilment in the Messianic rest (Hebrews 3:7–4:10) which is being inaugurated by Jesus here.

Another Sabbath day found Jesus teaching in the synagogue. He discovered that the Pharisees had laid a trap for him in bringing along a man who had a withered hand (6:7). They permitted a person to be helped on the Sabbath only *in extremis*, and this case did not measure up to that. If Jesus heals the man they can accuse Him of breaking the Sabbath Law, which was deemed a very serious sin. reading their thoughts, Jesus decided to deal with the real issues for which the sick man was merely a cover, for He never avoided a challenge given to Him. He could so easily have pretended not to see what was afoot, and carry on with His sermon – the temptation of lesser mortals. Instead, he brought the issue out into the open by asking the man to stand out into the middle of the group (6:8).

The sermon was changed to fit the needs of the audience, and the challenge thrown out: *"is it against the law on the sabbath to do good, or to do evil: to save life, or to destroy it?"* (6:10) Since one is forbidden to do evil at any time, the only choice is to do good and to save life, both of which Jesus wants to do for this man. Jesus considers it evil to refuse to do good. He does not accept the middle ground of non-evil, non-good (18:18–23). Here we are at the centre of the controversy because God is the Person who gives life (Genesis 1 and 2) and who works on the Sabbath. The rabbis knew that, in any real sense if God ceased to work on the Sabbath, creation would cease to exist. They also observed that people are born and die on the Sabbath, that neither life nor death respect the days of the week, hence God both gave life and judged on the Sabbath. Here Jesus, the Lord of the Sabbath, is doing what God does on the Sabbath.

When Jesus commanded the man to stretch out his hand he experienced the powerful creative life-giving Word of God in Jesus which restored him to full humanity. The Pharisees, however, had no eyes for this wonderful restoration, but only for the fact that Jesus healed on the Sabbath before their own eyes and succeeded in gaining scriptural authority for doing so. They were bad losers and went out to plot how to deal with Jesus (6:11). Matthew 12:14 says that they decided to kill Jesus at this point, which would strengthen the whole argument that they had evil and death in their hearts while Jesus had life and healing. Jesus, the Sign and the Sword, was exposing the secret thoughts of many hearts, as predicted (3:34–35).

Jesus and the New Israel (6:12–7.50)

Jesus walked out of the synagogue having been rejected by the leaders of the old Israel, so He concentrates on building the new Israel from new foundations (6:12–16, 5:36–39). In the arena of daily life Jesus proclaims the New Word of God for the new Israel made up of people whom He has forgiven and healed (6:17–49). The humble will hear and rejoice, whether Gentile (7:1–10) or Jew (7:11–17). In all this He surpasses expectations so much that even John the Baptist needs reminders from Isaiah (7:18–30), but the perversity of His contemporaries drew anger from Jesus (7:31–35) who explains in a most delicate story how easy it is to join Him (7:36–50).

Luke portrays Jesus as a man of prayer. In 4:42 and 5:16 he told us of Jesus' desire to spend time with His Father. Here He spends a whole night in prayer seeking guidance before selecting His twelve Apostles, who were chosen at dawn the following day, which means that they were somewhere nearby. This significant new moment in Christian history comes from communion with God (see 1:10, 28, 2:15, 27, 37 for other examples so far), and shows that their selection was an important part of God's plan of salvation. The Twelve represent more than a list of names, for they are the New Testament equivalent of the twelve sons of Jacob (Genesis 35:22–26) from whom sprang the twelve tribes of Israel (Genesis 49:28). Later in 22:30 Jesus promises them that they will sit on thrones to judge the twelve tribes of Israel. God's promises to Abraham were transmitted through these twelve sons of Jacob. They are now fulfilled in Jesus (1:55, 72–73) and the resulting salvation will be transmitted through the Apostles (24:47–48, 51: Acts 3:25–26).

At the head of the group stands Simon Peter, whose call was more prominent than the others in 5:1–11. He was the only one given a new name by Jesus, thus indicating his leadership role in the new community. He was to be the rock of strength for the others in the future (22:32), and he is given a special experience of the risen Jesus (24:35; 1 Corinthians 15:5). He is both one of them and set apart (Acts 2:14) like Joseph among the sons of Jacob. He had to overcome evil and rest on the Rock of Israel for his strength (see Genesis 49:24, 22:31–32). The choice of this group is the first stage in the development of Church leadership which is seen to be in direct continuity with Jesus and His mission.

The term *apostolos* means "one who is sent" as the official spokesperson of another. Just as Jesus had been sent by the Father so He is sending them out in His name (6:14). They are different from other disciples now, though they remain part of them. Disciple means "pupil" and He now selected some who would become the masters after He had departed. If one examines the characters He chose we are left in wonder at the wisdom of God which is so contrary to human thinking (see Isaiah 55:8–9). None of them were famous for religion, leadership or learning, and none had access to the corridors of power. They were men who would have to struggle in their personal lives to live up to the standards of Jesus. They would have to struggle with each other for brotherhood and unity, and struggle in prayer for the discernment of God's will for the fast growing body of believers. They were the poor who would succeed only if they lived a life of dependence on God. They were taken from the rank-and-file of the world to show the miracle of the

divine working through the human. And against all the
odds, both inside and outside of them, the leaders of
Israel claimed that they succeeded in turning Jerusalem
and the rest of the world upside down (Acts 5:28, 17:6)!

The Sermon on the Plain

The Word of God for the New Age (6:17–45)

The Apostles were chosen on the mountain, which was
associated with closeness to God, but the word is proclaimed in the plain where all the people are gathered.
This too is a forecast of the future mission where they
would maintain their intimacy with God in prayer, and
there gain the strength and wisdom for the mission when
they "returned to the world" as it were (see Acts 15:28–29).
Luke, in 6:17, says that the crowd came from all over
Israel, but it is a different crowd for it consists of ordinary
people seeking help from Jesus in their troubles. The
leaders are missing when Jesus feeds this hungry people
with the good things of God's Word. Jesus receives
sinners, but expects them to open up to new life and
transformation of character. Though they walk in as sinners,
they must walk out saints. They have a grave responsibility
to hear the Word of God and put it into practice.

Chapter 6:20–45 is a great insight into Jesus Himself,
and what motivated His actions and words. Since disciples
must become photocopies of Himself, it is a revelation
for them as to how a Son of God lives. They, like Himself,
will be recognized by their fruits (6:44). Like a new
Moses Jesus descended the mountain, the place of prayer
and special communion with God (9:28–36; Exodus 34:28),
where He had chosen His Twelve to meet the people in
a level place (6:17) where He proclaims the Word of God
to them (Exodus 32:15). As He descended He was flanked
by the leaders of the New Israel (6:17; Exodus 19:24).
Standing at His side they heard this Christian magna

charta that they were to proclaim from the housetops to the ends of the earth. Luke's sermon is somewhat different to Matthew's Sermon on the Mount, both as to length and content, but we will stay with Luke.

When Jesus proclaimed in his mission statement that He had come to release the captives and downtrodden, and to preach to the poor (4:18), He had in mind not only to release them *from* whatever enslaved them, but to release them *for* a whole new way of life in the New Israel. If the crowd surrounding Jesus (6:17–19) want to live like Him and know happiness and peace, then here is His formula, which is not offered to the strong but to the weak. He contrasts three states of life *now* and prophesies what they will *become* (6:21):

Happy are the poor   ... Alas for the rich
Happy are the hungry ... Alas for the well-fed
Happy you who weep   ... Alas you who laugh

Jesus does not say that poverty, destitution, and mourning are the way to live, rather He does not permit those with excess money, which supplies all of life's necessities, to live in luxury while the slums of the world continue. He demands social responsibility from His followers. It is important to remember that Jesus here addresses *disciples* and how they are to behave. He is not speaking to "those out there" who have no faith in God, no Messiah, and no experience of salvation. The disciples are poor in a special way, because of their relationship to the Son of Man. They have given up everything to follow Him (5:11, 6:28). They have made sacrifices that the worldly-minded think ridiculous. They live austerely, sacrificially, soberly, but enduringly, and their life of dependence on God will be rewarded, unlike the rich, whose money can buy them pleasures, amusement, and present satisfactions. Many of them consider they have no need of God: their kingdom is of this world, and their "heaven" can be measured in monetary terms (12:13–21, 16:19–31, 18:18–23).

The paradox of the Beatitudes is that they leave us uneasy with our acceptance of worldly standards of greatness (Psalm 49:18). The world then, and now, presumes that a person born to prosperity, privilege and power is also "happy". Jesus gives the cause of happiness to a choice of life that is love-orientated towards God and neighbour. In other words you will recognize a disciple of Jesus by the fact that *others* praise God for their existence, because they have received life through that person. Like Jesus they impoverish themselves to make others rich (see 2 Corinthians 8:9). Those who choose to follow Jesus in this dedicated life are the people who attack the desperate poverty and destitution of the have-nots of this world, for they are our neighbour (10:29–37).

Luke's final Beatitude (6:22–23) is addressed to mature disciples who undergo suffering and persecution for the sake of the Kingdom of God. Externally it appears that they have been reduced to the dregs of society, but in fact they are in the long line of prophets who suffered persecution on account of the Lord, and they receive a great reward in heaven (12:32; see Acts 4:23–35, 5:40–42, 7:55–60, 8:3). On the principle that the world loves its own (John 15:19) Jesus ends with a woe to His disciples: *"Alas for you when the world speaks well of you! This is the way their ancestors treated the false prophets"* (6:26). Israel found that so-called prophets who were ready to play the world's game were deceivers who betrayed their calling (see Isaiah 30:10–11; Jeremiah 5:1, 23:16–17; 2 Timothy 3:1–9).

An essential characteristic which marks the disciple as a follower of Jesus of Nazareth, as distinct from any other master, is now enunciated: *"Love your enemies, do good to those who hate you, bless those who curse you, pray for those who treat you badly"* (6:27–28). If the Beatitudes illustrated the different way of life of a disciple, this command of Jesus shows *how far* he wants us to show the world the heavenly life we enjoy. 6:23 had four outrages perpetrated on the disciples which are answered here by their opposites: the enemy hates us, drives us out, abuses and denounces us. We respond by loving the enemy, doing good to those who hate, blessing those who curse, and praying for them. This *agape*-love is a warm, outgoing, disinterested concern for the other person regardless of whether they are on our side or not.

It is obvious that this Christian love demanded by Jesus surpasses all known loves in the world. *Agape* surpasses *eros* which is passionate love, *storge* which is the love of parents for children and vice versa, and finally *philia* the warm love of friendship. It is a gift of God marking one out as a daughter or son of God, because God is kind to the ungrateful and the wicked (6:35). *Agape* shows itself generous in forgiveness (6:29) and in material things (6:30). The standard or golden rule is to treat another person as you would wish to be treated yourself (6:31). But if we love by the world's standards, namely giving love only to those who love us, we are still on the level of sinners (6:32–33), and no reward is offered, for we are operating on a purely natural level. The great reward is reserved for those who love when there is no hope of a return of love in kind or otherwise, when the gift of love is *pure gift*. This is the way Jesus loves, and this is perfection (6:34–35).

To love one's enemies was an unheard of concept in the ancient world. As Psalm 58:6–11 shows taking vengeance on one's enemies was considered normal, even permitted by Moses in the *lex talionis* which stated "an eye for an eye ...". Romans 12:14–21 shows Paul passing on this teaching of Jesus and telling the Christians to leave vengeance to the Lord. Our job is to resist evil and conquer it with good.

Exodus 34:6–7 describes the Lord as "a God of tenderness and compassion, slow to anger, rich in kindness and faithfulness". This is the model placed before anyone who desires to be part of Jesus' new family. Moses commanded in Leviticus 19:2: *"You must be holy, for I, the Lord your God, am Holy"*, but it is the specific attributes of compassion, mercy, forgiveness, and generosity in one's relationships with others that are selected by Jesus, rather than some absolute standard of perfection. He enunciates the principle that such an attitude opens the way for reciprocal generosity both from God Himself and from others, in other words our actions react upon us in the sense that we reap what we sow (see Galatians 6:7; 2 Corinthians 8:6–15).

It was one of the noticable Pharisaical faults to criticize and judge others, and to be legalistic in serving God (7:39, 11:37–54, 15:25–30, 18:9–12). Jesus does not want this for His disciples. Using several parables to illustrate His teaching Jesus demands personal integrity, especially in the leaders, on the grounds that the blind cannot lead the blind (6:39). Teachers and leaders must live what they teach, namely remove the plank from their own eyes before removing the splinter from others. Self-criticism rather than judging others is called for (6:40–42). If they merely pretend to live what they preach they must remember that their disciples will become like them and the problem is perpetuated (6:40).

The pretender or hypocrite will not get away with it because Jesus tells us to judge a tree by its fruit (6:43–45). *"People do not pick figs from thorns, nor gather grapes from brambles"* (6:44). Disciples of Jesus are therefore called to continuous conversion, so that they can call upon "the store of goodness" in their hearts, for *"a man's words flow out of what fills his heart"* (6:45). Jesus is teaching His disciples to become like Him – true sons of God. They must bring their disciples to the same image if the Kingdom is to come.

The sermon finishes with a definition of a true disciple. Jesus does not accept verbal commitment with no behavioural content (6:46). No, everyone who comes to him for salvation, and receives instruction *must act upon it* (6:47). The only sure foundation is a life lived in obedience to the teaching of Jesus. Using the parable of building, Jesus says that the disciple who lives His teaching builds His life on the rock (of salvation). No matter how much testing life brings, it will survive *because* it is on the rock. But the person who lives on words which have no corresponding deeds, is a house built on shifting sands, a definition of disaster, for it will not survive even the incoming tide (see Romans 2:13; James 1:21–25; Luke 8:21).

The Faith of the Gentiles (7:1–10)

In Acts 10:35 Luke tells us that *"God shows no partiality, but anyone who fears him and does what is right in every nation is acceptable to him"*. The salvation that Jesus came to bring will encompass the Gentile nations too, where faith will be present in unexpected abundance. Neither the Gentiles (7:2–10) nor the Jews (7: 11–17) realized that Jesus had come to save them from death, not physical death but what it represented, namely *real death* or the loss of one's soul, one symbolized in the dying Gentile boy and Jewish girl. Whether Jesus finds us dying or already dead, as in the case of the girl, He has come to heal and to give life, and this physical life

symbolizes the *real life* which is salvation and the life
of grace.

*the
Centurion*

Having delivered His magna charta Jesus went again
to Capernaum where a centurion lived who was friendly
and generous to the Jews there. In fact he had built
their synagogue (7:2–5). Ironically it was the Jewish
elders who introduced this man to Jesus telling him
that he was *worthy* of help because of his generosity.
Was he now to experience the Lord's generosity to
Him (6:38)? He was asking nothing for himself but for
a servant who was very precious to him (7:3). The
centurion, who knew the Jewish customs well, realized
that entering his house would incur ritual defilement
for Jesus, something he would never expect (Acts 10:28,
11:12). On hearing that Jesus was actually coming, he
sent some friends to tell him that he *was unworthy* of
such a visit, so unworthy that he did not even dare to
come personally! Like Peter in 5:8, this Gentile knew
that he was on holy ground. The Jews considered him
worthy on the grounds of good works, but Jesus found
him ready for salvation on the grounds of his attitude
of self criticism, humility and openness to the action
of God in his life (6:41).

Jesus marvelled at the centurion's grasp of His authority over sickness and death (4:36), and his respect
for it, saying that He had found nothing to compare
with it in Israel (7:10). The centurion seemed to grasp
that Jesus' word carried power whether He was personally
present or not, a lesson Luke wished to remind his
Church about, now that that word was being transmitted
by the disciples. It still has the same power to heal
and give life at all times. The Church also needed to
hold on to this special gift God had given to the
Gentiles to allow Jesus to be their saviour. This incident
also explains why it was the Jews whom God used to

introduce the Gentiles to salvation historically, even though the nation as a whole rejected Jesus.

The Widow's Son (7:11–17)

Jesus wanted this new life for His own people too, for, in Him, God had visited His people (1:68, 7:17). For the Jews, salvation through Jesus implied a veritable resurrection, one which Jesus was most willing to perform. This is illustrated dramatically in His raising a son of "old Israel" from the dead. Old Israel was a widow in mourning, but Jesus could give her back her son, the cause of her joy. In this incident Luke for the first time gives Jesus the title THE LORD (7:13), a title hitherto reserved for God alone. The Son of Man not only has the power to forgive sins. He is Lord of the Sabbath and Lord of life and death. He can reconstruct Israel again from dry bones (Ezekiel 37:1–14). The Lord had promised through Ezekiel that He would raise them from their graves and put His Spirit into them, and then they would know the Lord (Ezekiel 37:11–14). Jesus worked this miracle without being asked, for salvation is given on God's initiative.

There are Old Testament antecedents for this miracle, namely the raising of the widow's son by Elijah in 1 Kings 17:17–24, where the miracle was a prelude to Elijah's return home to raise Israel, God's first-born (Exodus 4:22–23), to life spiritually (1 Kings 18:20–40). The physical raising was the preparation for the greater miracle of the spiritual resurrection of the nation, which was God's plan through the work of His prophet. So with this boy. Jesus has come to save Israel, to bring the nation to life spiritually, and a greater than Elijah is here, because Jesus only has to command the miracle whereas Elijah had to intercede and lie across the body of the boy and wait for God's action. Jesus merely touched the bier to stop the funeral procession, for this boy, like his nation, has been sitting in the shadow of death, and the Daystar has come in mercy to shine its light upon him (Isaiah 9:1–2).

Noting again that these two miracles concern a man's servant and a woman's son, (Luke's balancing act), there are connections with John the Baptist preparing us for the next incident. The boy is raised by the power of Jesus' word alone, coming from a heart filled with compassion for the poor widow (7:13). That Spirit-filled and life-giving Word put new life into this son of Israel, and he sat up and spoke (7:16). Just as the healing of Zechariah caused awe, so here, and in both cases was followed by praising God, while the people concluded in both cases that God had visited His people through a great prophet who had risen among them (7:16). In both cases the word spread widely, but it was a new word, the realization of the fulfilment of prophecy recently received (7:17, 1:64–75).

Jesus and John the Baptist (7:18–35)

In three incidents Luke concludes what he wants to say regarding the connection between John the Baptist and His relation to Jesus and his ministry. The first episode concerns John's question sent to Jesus from prison (7:18–23), followed by Jesus' testimony regarding John and his ministry (7:24–30), and finally, Jesus' judgement of His contemporaries reaction to both John and Himself (7:31–35).

John had proclaimed Jesus in 3:16–18 as "*Someone who is coming*", that is the One whose coming the prophets spoke about (9:26; Hebrews 10:37–38; Mark 8:38; Matthew 16:27, 25:31–46). According to John, Jesus would have a two-fold ministry. All who repented sincerely would be baptized with the Holy Spirit and fire, but the unrepentant would discover in Him the eschatological judge who would burn the chaff *in a fire that will never go out* (3:17), one who would cut down the trees that failed to produce good fruit (3:9). For John, God's judgement of the wicked was imminent. Now he languishes in prison, facing certain death at the hands of a cruel king, and what he hears from his disciples concerning Jesus disturbs him (3:19–20). Jesus has been working great miracles (7:18), healing the sick, raising the dead, and casting out demons – also preaching the gospel to the poor as He proclaimed in His Mission Programme (4:18).

As far as John could hear, the judgement side of the ministry was being neglected. With all his obvious power, Jesus had made no move to release John from prison, where He was held captive, nor had he done anything to pull the mighty Herod from his throne where he reigned in immorality and injustice (1:52, 4:18). Why was He concentrating on individuals when there were great issues out there waiting to be solved? How was the healing a soldier's servant (7:1–10) or a widow's boy (7:11–17) going to achieve anything against the oppression of Rome? Surely the Messiah should set Israel free? How could Jesus claim convincingly to be the Messiah if He did not put oppressive governments right? John's perplexity has continued down the centuries among people who feel that it is better to deal with political, economic and social evils in the world rather than concentrate on the individuals who make up that system. John sent two of his disciples to ask Jesus: *"Are you the one who is to come, or must we wait for someone else?"* (7:19–20). The question is repeated twice, first as John's question and then as that of his disciples. John did not have the last word on who the Messiah was. He had to send them to Jesus for enlightenment. At the time of writing the gospel John was long since dead, but his disciples lived on and continued his work. They must go to Jesus the Lord (7:19) for the full message of eternal life (Acts 19:1–7).

The Lord's reply to John did not deny that judgement would eventually come to evil individuals, governments and political systems, but right here and now He worked a number of miracles to remind these disciples that He was the fulfilment of the Isaian prophecies concerning God's compassion for the poor and afflicted (see Isaiah 35:1–10, 26:19, 61:1–3). In the passage from Isaiah 35 the prophet says that God is coming in a day of vengeance, and this will occasion the opening of the eyes of the blind etc. as the Lord makes a new way for the redeemed to walk upon. There were priorities in the mission that must be seen to and right now Jesus concentrated on that (7:22). The day of vengeance will surely come, but in God's time (see 2 Peter 3:3–10). This shepherd, as we shall see, is well able to take care of the one sheep without neglecting the ninety-nine others (15:4–7).

Jesus finishes with a challenge to John, and to everyone: *"happy is the man who does not lose faith in me"* (7:23). Jesus asks us to come to Him with no preconceived ideas, so that we can experience Him as He presents Himself, hence He sends back the two disciples as witnesses to John to relate only what they had seen and heard. If they did that in the light of the Scriptures they would understand Him, but if He turns out to be different from what they expected would they still trust Him? Would they put their faith in Him? That is the challenge, and it comes to all of us at some point in our lives. Human beings find it hard to wait for God's timing especially if, like John here, we are experiencing injustice and oppression. We baulk at delay, especially delays in putting the world to rights, forgetting that this involves changing the hearts of thousands of people. It is this change of heart that Jesus works on.

As soon as John's disciples left, Jesus turned and challenged the people about John's mission (7:24). They had flocked to the desert to hear him, but why did they go? And what were they looking for? Did they travel great distances to listen to a desert prophet to be left with an easy life? Surely not! The courtiers living in luxury and ease were those who persecuted him (7:25–26). Jesus asserts clearly that John was not only a prophet, meaning a person who was God's spokesman, but he was the greatest of the prophets, for he had the privilege of ushering in the Messianic Era, of preparing the way of the Lord (Malachi 3:1).

Taking a human estimation of greatness John was the greatest born of woman, yet, paradoxically, *"the least in the kingdom of God is greater than he"* (7:29). This statement has puzzled many for it appears to put John outside the Kingdom of God which he ushered in! Surely not! The Lord would not be so cruel. Although John had been quickened by the Holy Spirit in his mother's womb (1:41, 44) yet Jesus, conceived by the Holy Spirit, is greater than he. Everyone who follows Jesus and accepts His salvation is privileged to be born of the Spirit too, and in that sense of privilege he is greater than John, for the New Dispensation is greater than the Old. Besides, Jesus Himself is the least in the Kingdom, by His own standards of humility and the greatest service (9:48, 22:27). Therefore John is a great prophet, but Jesus is greater. All those who accepted John's baptism were co-operating with God's plans for them, but by refusing to accept John's baptism the Pharisees *had thwarted what God had in mind for them* (7:30).

Jesus then turns to condemn His contemporaries for lack of sincerity and religious seriousness (7:31). In John they had refused to cooperate with the penitential preparation for the Kingdom of God, and in Jesus they refuse the joyful entry into the Kingdom with its forgiveness and healing. Since they refused John's baptism they have no authority or right to criticize John or Jesus (7:33–34). The Pharisees and lawyers who listened but did not obey either John or Jesus are the false disciples of 6:46–47 who are building their edifice on the sand of self-justification and criticism of others. They are like peevish, spoiled children who refuse to cooperate with the joy of a wedding or the sorrow of a funeral (7:32). To cover up their rejection of grace they now accuse John of being possessed (7:33), and Jesus of being morally lax (7:39). But they are blind, for even the Old Testament called the people who listened to and obeyed God's word the children of wisdom, and Jesus says here that *"Wisdom has been proved right by all her children"* (7:35). The two children of Wisdom in this context are Jesus and John, to whom the Word of God was given (3:2, 4:18), and through whom it was being preached to Israel. Proverbs 8:32–36 says that everyone is invited to be instructed by Wisdom. Those who find Wisdom find life; those who reject it are in love with death (Proverbs 8:35–36).

A Child of Wisdom is Born (7:36–50)

In this next section there is a delicate portrayal of how to switch from the critical, judgemental position of the Pharisee to become a beloved disciple and child of Wisdom, since Jesus is Wisdom Incarnate. He is the one who incorporates for us all the light and grace to change, heal and transform us. In 5:29–32 Jesus had table fellowship with tax collectors and sinners. Here he is at table with Pharisees, for Jesus as Saviour of all excludes no one (7:36). Jesus' response to the Pharisee and to the intruder who fell at His feet brings up the subject of His identity again (7:39, 49). We must look head-on at *why* He is the friend of sinners (7:34). Is it to leave them as He found them, or to make them children of Wisdom? This scene also brings up other favourite themes, the woman and the man, the sinner, younger brother of 15:13–24 and the elder brother (15:25–32), the love of His converts and the cold judgement of the Pharisees (7:42, 18:9–14), the rise and fall of many in Israel (2:34).

One of the Pharisees broke away from the usual hostility to Jesus by inviting Him to dine with other guests. His intention appears to have been a desire to check Jesus out as a prophet (7:39). During the meal they were interrupted by a woman, who had a bad reputation in the town, who came in and threw herself at Jesus' feet. Overcome by gratitude (7:47) she wept so much that she washed His feet with her tears, then to the shock of all present she let her long hair down and used it as a towel to wipe Jesus' feet before anointing them with the precious ointment she brought in her alabaster jar (7:38).

So far we have a delicate picture of gratitude and loving service rendered to Jesus for the gift of forgiveness and the Messianic peace which flowed from it. Both Jesus and the woman know what is going on, but has anyone else got eyes that see? The last section criticized the Pharisees for their refusal to open up to the work of God through either Jesus or John, yet the sinners did (7:29–30, 34). Could a Pharisee recognize the inner transformation that follows this opening up to God? That is the challenge here. Simon took the critical stance of judging that Jesus was no prophet if He allowed the likes of this woman to touch Him. After all a prophet was supposed to be able to read character at a glance (see 1 Samuel 16:7). Jesus replied by letting Simon know that He could read *him* rather easily (7:40–43)! Like Nathan the prophet, when he had to show king David his sins (2 Samuel 12:1–4), Jesus chose to use a simple parable which enabled the sinner to see himself objectively and thus pass judgement on himself. This was the only hope of repentance in someone who thought he was in the right.

The two debtors in the parable were the woman and Simon. She was a great sinner. No one disputed that. Could he see himself as a debtor, even a small one? Would he acknowledge any need of God? Was he not remiss in anything? Was he so self-deceived as all that? Neither debtor could pay, but the Creditor (God) pardoned them both (7:41). Since debt was a Jewish description of sin as we will see in the Our Father (11:4), Simon knows what Jesus is referring to, knows too, that forgiveness should be followed by gratitude. And yes, theoretically, he would concede that greater forgiveness would bring about greater gratitude (see Psalm 51).

Now Simon is called upon to look at the woman and himself, only to discover that in God's eyes right now she is in a better position than he is. Jesus, like the prophet Nathan, must spell out the sinner's shortcomings. Simon had omitted the usual courtesies to his honoured guest: no kiss of greeting, no anointing of the head with oil. In fact, he had shown very little love, and his omissions were supplied by this woman from the purest motives of grace (7:45–47). Simon must look at what his actions say about him to others, what they reveal. Jesus had seen so clearly, but the Creditor had forgiven him if only he could see. Then turning to the woman Jesus affirms her salvation before everyone making her forgiveness public just as her sins were (7:49). The messianic blessing of forgiveness is present in Jesus, and Simon can go away saved and at peace, like the woman, if he acknowledges Jesus as his saviour (7:50).

Some may worry that the woman's behaviour showed

excessive emotionalism. Would it last? Was this action a reflection of a moment or a life? This is answered in the next episode in 8:1–3 where Luke tells us of many women who offered heroic service to Jesus and the Twelve out of their own resources. They travelled with Jesus and His companions and took care of all their needs. The common denominator among them was that they had received great ministry from Jesus, and they were repaying Him by loving and devoted service, the unromantic drudgery of constant travel in poor conditions, and taking care of all their needs in impossible situations, and this for the whole length of Jesus' ministry right up to Calvary.

The Preached and Accepted Word of God (Luke 8:4–56)

The new community consists of Jesus, the Twelve, and the women (8:1–3), who find themselves surrounded by crowds who want to hear the Word of God, and become part of the Kingdom. Jesus responds by teaching in parables, a lovely teaching method whereby one captivates one's audience with a story which is true to life. Those who are sincere seek further clarification, while the insincere go away more puzzled than ever, but maybe disturbed enough to seek and find at a later date.

Jesus gave them the parable of the sower, which focuses on what happens to the Word of God once it is preached. He emphasizes the responsibility on the part of the receivers to take the Word of God to themselves and eventually bring forth a harvest (8:15). Jesus Himself, is the Sower: the seed is the Word of God (8:11), and the people are the soil (8:12). Like good disciples they must not be hearers of the Word only but doers also (6:47; James 1:21–25).

Through this parable Jesus challenges the superficial

adherence of the crowds and the disciples to His teaching. They listen, but do not comprehend its inner meaning (8:10). They look at Jesus without perceiving who He is or why He came. Jesus pleads with them to internalize the Word of God, and let it do its work quietly in them. Initial enthusiasm is not enough. Luke shows that the disciples during Jesus' lifetime did not grasp the inner meaning of the Kingdom of God. But Christians are to follow their example and go to Jesus in prayer seeking understanding (8:9).

The parable speaks of four different soils, representing the different responses we give to the teaching of Jesus. The picture of sowing in the parable comes from a time in the Near East when sowing was done before ploughing. The seed was scattered over the surface of the soil and afterwards ploughed into it. This meant that some seed fell on the path and was trampled underfoot, if the birds did not get it first. Some fell on rock which lacked moisture for growth, so that the seeds withered. Those that fell among thorns were choked, but those lucky enough to reach the good soil eventually brought forth a harvest, even as much as a hundredfold. Jesus pleaded with the crowds to *really* take in what He said (8:5–8).

The disciples asked Him publicly what the story meant, so it was not obvious to them, let alone the crowds. In reply Jesus spoke of those who were already in the Kingdom and those outside of it, who as yet have not heard the Word of God and responded to it. Using Isaiah 6:9, Jesus reminded them that the prophets of old suffered from the people's blindness and deafness to spiritual things. Luke does not quote the whole passage, which implies that hardness of heart is due to worldliness and sin. "*Go and say to this people, listen and listen, but never understand! Look and look but never perceive! Make this people's heart coarse, make their ears dull, shut their eyes tight, or they will use their eyes to see, use their ears to hear, use their heart to understand, and change their ways and be healed*" (Isaiah 6:9–10).

The fruitless preaching of the Word is explained here, but the text also carries the formula for healing. If the Lord opens the people's eyes and ears, and if the heart responds with repentance, then there will be conversion and healing. Jesus has already begun His part of this work by His healings and His planting of the Word in their hearts. Their work is to receive it and respond, for the mystery of the Kingdom of God is not forced upon us (8:10). It is revealed to all those who, like the disciples here (8:9) come to Jesus for enlightenment. If they listen to Him (9:36) they will come to full understanding.

Jesus explained that some people do not allow the Word of God any opportunity to change them. Their way of life is such that the Devil, or worldly forces that oppose faith, is free to come and snatch the Word from them, the net result being the same as if they had never heard (8:12). The second group live such a superficial life that the Word of God cannot penetrate deep enough into their personalities. They enjoy listening to it but when life challenges them they do not put it into practice (7:46–49), so they too produce no fruit. The third group are those allow the worries of the world and the happenings of everyday life to choke the Word. It does not occur to them to let everyday life be governed *by* the Word (1:38), so their lives are ultimately barren, not for want of hearing the Word but for failing to obey it. Those people *with a noble and generous heart* are the ones that persevere in daily life trying to live out the consequences of what they had heard. Despite their faults and failings persever-ance wins them a harvest in the end (8:15).

An overview of this parable shows that Jesus was very realistic about His followers. He could see their spiritual blindness and incomprehension, but He also knew the power of the Word of God. Like the seed, the Word could be seen as a "package" of divine energy, which when sown in the earth, would, ultimately, bring forth a harvest in the "now" and the "then" of history. Against all the odds, inside the disciples and outside them, in persecution from the forces of evil (6:22–23), the Kingdom of God would produce a harvest for God in every generation. Thus Luke consoles the struggling suffering Christians of his own day.

Parable of the Lamp (8:16–18)

Here Jesus goes on to show that once disciples have heard the Word for themselves, they have a grave obligation to share it with others. It would, He said, be absurd to light a lamp and then put it under a bed (8:16). It is utterly tragic to hide the light of revelation from others since their salvation depends on it. The believer becomes a lamp for others to find their way in the darkness of unbelief. They continue the work of revealing the mysteries of the Kingdom once Jesus has departed from them (8:10). Here in 8:16 Luke is probably thinking of the light which hung outside a Roman villa which showed the way for guests to enter the house. When the light shines it reveals what has been hidden from them (8:17). Jesus wants all that His disciples have heard privately ("secretly") to be proclaimed from the housetops when the time comes for the mission to all the world. Then, as Isaiah 9:1 foretold: the people that walked in darkness will see a great light . . . .

Jesus finishes with a warning about our responsibility to use what God has given to us for *"anyone who has will be given more; anyone who has not, will be deprived even of what he thinks he has"* (8:18). Superficially this sounds as if the "haves" are always given more, and the "have nots" continually lose out. But in this context Jesus is saying that when we use the revelation that we have been given to enlighten others, then we ourselves will be given more. The principle is that the more you give away or share, the more you receive. The other side of the coin is that we can lose what we have just by sheer neglect, so that it neither gives life to us nor anyone else. This amounts to a denial of discipleship, so Luke goes on to explain what constitutes "family" for Jesus. Those who have a true relationship with him *are those who hear the Word of God and put it into practice* (1:38, 8:21). Hence Jesus' mother and relatives are classed among the believers, or to put it another way, the old "natural" family are part of His new spiritual family of believing disciples (Acts 1:14).

The Gentile Mission (8:22–39)

The next two passages show Luke reflecting on the stormy passage of the Church from Jewish to Gentile territory. Jesus got into the boat with His disciples. Did this include the women (8:1–3, 23:55)? As they put out to sea He fell asleep, and even a sudden squall could not wake Him (8:23). Seeing themselves in danger the disciples woke Jesus up, amazed at His apparent unconcern for the fact that they were sinking! When He woke up He calmly rebuked the wind, just as He had rebuked the demons (4:35) and sickness (4:39), and the great sea became calm again. Then He rebuked His disciples for their lack of faith! Awe-struck they asked: *"Who can this be, that gives orders even to the winds and waves and they obey him?"* (8:25).

Initially this passage concerns the crossing from the Jewish west side of the lake of Galilee to the Gentile east side, where Jesus enters Gerasene country and delivers a poor man from the satanic grip of evil destroying his life. We have seen in 7:1–10 that the mission does include Gentiles, but Jesus must remove the uncleanness of evil from them first to make it possible for them to become disciples and so enter the kingdom of God. In the last section of 8:40–56 which parallels 7:11–15 Luke reminds us that the Jewish nation needed both healing and spiritual resurrection in order to become part of the New Israel. In other words *everyone* needed Jesus' power to open the eyes of the blind and set the captives free (4:18).

The Old Testament was quite clear that only God could control the sea and conquer the terrifying forces that governed the abyss. In fact, His ability to do that illustrated His awesome sovereignty over the universe (see Psalm 104). When travellers were caught in the terrifying power of the storm they knew that God alone could calm the sea, thus saving them from its terror (Psalm 107:28–30). When pagans found that prayer to their gods failed to calm the sea, they did not hesitate to offer the prophet Jonah as a sacrifice to the deep (Jonah 1:1–16). Jonah found that God alone could rescue him from the power of the abyss (Jonah 2:1–11). The parallel to this story continues when we realize that Jonah was sent reluctantly on mission to the Gentiles at Nineveh.

The early Church was reluctant too. The passage to Gentile territory was occasioned by persecution, and also turmoil within the community (Acts 6–15). This was the storm which overtook them after the Ascension of Jesus (24:51; Acts 1:6–11), and as far as they could see He was enjoying His peaceful rest in heaven, apparently not caring that "the boat of Peter" was going down! The community felt both threatened and frightened. Luke reminds them to learn from this incident to turn to Jesus in prayer and intercession, and he would then calm the storms of persecution. What He did for the disciples on the Lake of Galilee was a prophetic forecast of His handling of the storms of history later. For this the new disciples needed great faith and deep insight into the mystery of Jesus' identity. As Son of Man and Son of God (1:32, 3:28, 6:5) His authority extends to all creation, for He is the Creative Word of God (4:35, 39, 5:20, 6:8, 7:15, 49). If Jesus' followers would only call upon Him to calm the storms of life they will experience His presence among them in power as they journey through history. Unwillingness or inability through lack of faith to contact Jesus in prayer spells disaster.

They had now reached the opposite shore in Gerasene country (8:26). Here the disciples discover that the One who controls the wind and the waves is also Master of the uncontrollable and destructive forces of evil which attack and destroy human life. Here the Living One (24:5) meets a "dead" person and brings him back to life. The story which follows is a wonderful illustration of who Jesus is and why He came. Luke 8:27 says that the man is spiritually dead, full of demons and living in tombs, the symbol of death. His soul resembles the primeval chaos (8:29) where Jesus' creative and life-giving Word will banish the darkness, destroy the evil forces and bring about a new creation.

The poor man ran to Jesus and fell at His feet (8:28) in a position of pleading. He wanted to know what the Son of the Most High God would want with the likes of him. He could not endure any further torture to the hell he was already experiencing (8:28). Can the Sinless One do anything for the sinful one (John 8:46)? Can life do anything for death? Can the Holy Spirit residing in Jesus do anything about the evil spirits residing in their victim? What a challenge to the redeemer! The answers will be given gloriously on the Cross when a poor dying criminal will ask the same question and receive a resounding "Yes"

(23:39–43)! The Sinless One is here to take your sin away and free you from the bondage to sin and death (see Romans 8:1–49) so that you become free to become a child of God, a disciple of Jesus and a missionary for the Kingdom. What an unlikely candidate for mission this man is before his healing!

Just as Jesus had confronted and overpowered the devil in the wilderness (4:1–13) so He confronts and masters a legion of devils here by forcing them to reveal themselves (8:30). The devils pleaded with Jesus not to send them into the abyss, which was their place of destiny (see Revelation 9:1, 2, 11, 11:7, 17:8, 20:1, 3). This is the most eloquent comment on hell that could possibly be made, showing why we should lead the type of life that avoids the abyss where death and destruction hold sway.

Nevertheless, it was necessary for the salvation of the human race that the demons be banished to the abyss. They unwittingly brought this upon themselves in their request to be allowed to enter the herd of pigs. The Jews listed pigs among unclean animals (15:15; Leviticus 11:7–8). As such they make a more fitting dwelling place for unclean spirits than a man made in the image and likeness of God, one destined to be the dwelling place of the Holy Spirit (3:16). The destructive power of demonic influence is seen in the demise of the pigs, who fling themselves into the abyss, preferring death to the hellish presence of a legion of evil spirits. Thus, the twist in the story is that these unintelligent animals show more wisdom than the man, who is called *homo sapiens*, since the man tolerated all hell inside him. What a humiliation for that proud creature, Man, when even the dumb animals can teach him (8:32–33)!

The swineherds ran off to spread the news in the surrounding countryside (8:34). This brought the people out to investigate and they found the one-time demoniac sitting at the feet of Jesus, which is a description of a disciple (10:40), clothed and in his right mind (8:35). The man was so transformed that the people were afraid of such divine power. The swineherds' story put the place into a panic, so much so, that they asked Jesus to leave their territory (8:36–37). That country had now no demoniac, no evil spirits, and *no saviour*. It is a description of the empty house, a position of great spiritual danger, that concerns Jesus (11:24–26). He was the Good Shepherd who came to save this lost sheep, only to find that He Himself was banished as a result (15:4–7). This, too, is a forecast of the future, where the disciples will be persecuted rather than thanked for their good services (Acts 16:16–40).

This is the only incident where the people react to Jesus in such a way. The crowds normally respond with wonder and awe (4:36–37, 7:16). Here the fear is negative: it does not issue in faith or openness to God. The healed demoniac asked if he could stay with Jesus, and presumably travel with Him – the first Gentile to request discipleship (8:38)! Jesus did not need him at the present stage of the Jewish mission, but requested him to prepare the way for the Lord in his own land (8:39). Thus the healed man became an enthusiastic apostle declaring the wonderful works of God. This, too, forecasts the future where the Gentiles will be the enthusiastic missionaries of Jesus Christ to the ends of the earth, and the end of time, once they have been delivered from evil and saved themselves.

Jesus and the Jewish Mission 8:40–56

On his return to Jewish soil on the west side of the Lake of Galilee Jesus was welcomed by the people (8:40). They had been waiting for Him expectantly. Among them was Jairus, a synagogue official who threw himself at Jesus' feet pleading with Him to come down to his house where his only daughter lay dying. As Jesus followed Jairus he was almost stifled by the crowd (8:41–42). Compare this with text with 7:11–17 where Luke dealt with the son of a widowed mother: here it is a daughter and her father (Luke's balancing act). Just as the widow represented Israel, so the father represents the Jewish leadership who lacked faith in Jesus. Jairus only came to Jesus as a last resort.

Immediately one remembers the Gentile centurion in 7:1–10 whose request for healing so impressed Jesus because of his humility where he considered himself unworthy of Jesus' visit, and his understanding of Jesus' power (*dynamis* 4:14, 5:17) which he accepted could work at a distance. Jairus points to a more deficient faith which demands the personal presence of Jesus. It also lacks the understanding of the Person of Jesus, so he does not consider himself unworthy of the visit. The Jewish authorities were unwilling to accept the uniqueness of Jesus' person and mission. The same request is made here as is found in John 11, namely to save the girl *from death*. In both cases Jesus delayed long enough for the person to die (8:49), and John 11:5–12 says that the delay was deliberate. Here Luke says that it was the needs of the crowds pressing against Jesus that caused the delay. Physical death is not the REAL enemy, and Jesus decided to do more than was requested of Him (see Ephesians 3:21).

Sandwiched in the middle of this drama is the cure of the woman who suffered from a haemorrhage for twelve years. The little girl who died was also twelve years old (8:42). Somehow Luke wants to connect these events for the faith of the woman is greater than that of Jairus. She humbly approached Jesus, knowing that his power was such that she did not need personal attention from Him. She just needs to make contact for she is open to the new life that will flow from Him. Here she is a model of prayer which is more concerned about making loving contact with God, than in using words, however sacred.

Jesus was aware that salvific power went from Him giving life to someone. He insisted on finding who it was: *"Who was it that touched me?"* (8:46). Peter was amazed that Jesus could distinguish between those who tugged at Him physically, and this one person who made a faith-contact with Him as Saviour. It highlights the tragedy of the crowd who were so close to Him, yet did not allow him to save them. Their faith was even more deficient than Jairus'. At least he was willing to let Jesus touch his problem.

Trembling the woman came forward, fell at Jesus' feet and proclaimed to them all *why* she had touched Jesus and *how* she had been healed (8:48). This is a lesson for both Jairus and the crowd about accepting Jesus for who He really is and allowing Him to save them. Her fear in coming forward was due to the nature of her illness which made her ritually unclean according to the Mosaic law (Leviticus 15:25). Anyone whom she touched was rendered unclean also (Leviticus 15:19–27). This meant alienation from her family, synagogue and places of social contact. She had been a virtual outcast for twelve years! The Gentile demoniac was a social outcast due to demonic powers, but this Jewish woman suffered the same fate from the ceremonial law. Jesus came to set both these captives free (4:18) by removing *the cause* of the problem in both cases, thus becoming the cause of their joy and *the source* of their new life (see John 10:10).

Jesus lovingly affirmed the woman before the crowd. It was her humble faith, that is to say, her openness to let God work in her life, her openness to accept God's messenger, that brought new life to her (8:48). She could

107

go away now with the blessing of Messianic peace. In Luke's terminology this woman is saved. Can Jairus learn from this? Will he benefit from this lesson? He has witnessed an ordinary laywoman receive all that her heart desired from Jesus her Saviour. Will this increase his faith and expectation? Not at all!

Just then a messenger arrived declaring that the little girl was now dead (8:49), and added: *"Do not trouble the Master any further"*. Obviously they had faith in Jesus to cure sickness, but death was another matter altogether. Like most people, then and now, they accepted that "when you're dead: you're dead!" Death is the end of everything, also apparently of faith and hope. Jesus intervened, as He did in Lazarus' case (John 11:26, 40) *"Do not be afraid, only have faith and she will be saved"* (8:50). Jairus must put into practice what he has just learned from the healed woman. Faith moves mountains (Mark 11:23–25) and opens the way for the Glory of God to manifest Itself (John 11:40).

Jesus went to Jairus' house when it was too late. The funeral was already in progress (8:51). He desired the sign He was about to give be done in private, away from the prying eyes of those without faith, who could not understand the deep import of the miracle, and would only spread a spectacle story about Him. Jesus brought in the three disciples who would be privileged to witness His Transfiguration (9:28) and His agony (23:39; Mark 14:33), because this miracle was a prophetic forecast of His own resurrection, and also of the final resurrection of the dead (John 5:25–30). To soften the shock, and prepare them for the astounding revelation that death was *not the end* of anything, Jesus said that the little girl merely "slept", and he had come to waken her. This emphasized the re-awakening that resurrection from the dead would signify. The rest of the New Testament uses this metaphor for death also (see John 11:11; Acts 7:60; 1 Thessalonians 4:14–17).

Jesus took the girl by the hand, again ignoring the ceremonial law whereby one contracted uncleanness by touching a dead body. He spoke gently to her: *"Child, get up"*. The power of God went from Jesus to give life to this girl and she got up immediately (8:55). It was so simple, just one command, and death had to give up its victim, just as hell had done in 8:29, 35: So far Luke has shown Jesus as Lord of the Sabbath (6:5), of sickness (4:39–41), over sin (5:20, 7:36–50), over hell (4:31–37, 8:26–39) and now death (7:11–17, 8:55). He has proved that He is Lord, and that His Word carries power to save.

The girl's parents were beside themselves with amazement. Jesus ordered them to give her some food to strengthen her after her illness, but also to prove her return to life (8:56). It is noteworthy that this astonishment does not lead the parents to become disciples. They took their miracle, and went on living their old life -- not even someone coming back from the dead could change them if they would not listen to the Word of God (16:31). They were unfit to proclaim the secrets of the Kingdom, and Jesus ordered them to be silent (8:56).

Of course it would be impossible to keep the girl's miracle absolutely secret since half the town is outside the door waiting to get on with the funeral! Anyone who met the girl from this time onward would know what happened to her, so what was the secret? Was it the prophetic element that would only be revealed to the disciples present? If so, we have here an example of the mysteries of the Kingdom of heaven being revealed to them but not to those "outside" lacking gospel faith (8:10). At the Transfiguration these disciples will be further instructed regarding Jesus' *exodos* (9:31).

This incident foreshadows the inability of the Jewish nation to accept the claims of Jesus. They are willing to benefit from His powers of healing and exorcism, but unwilling to go any further. They will not accept the deep import of His resurrection, as the early Church well knew, even though He had eaten with His disciples after rising from the dead (24:28–31, 42–43).

The Mission of the New Israel (9:1–50)

Luke reaches the climax of the Galilean Ministry in this section. From 9:51 Jesus begins His fateful journey to Jerusalem, the city of destiny. Before that final movement of the gospel we witness Jesus send His New Israel out on mission (9:1–50), guided and supervised by Himself. He had already called (5:1–10) and appointed the new leaders (6:12–16) and their mission was to be intimately bound up with His own.

The several units of this section deal with the actual missioning of the Twelve (9:1–6), which raises the question of Jesus' identity (9:7–9). He then feeds the New Israel with the Messiah's abundant food (9:10–17). Peter responds by his confession of faith in Jesus as the Messiah (9:18–21), which leads to Jesus' further self-revelation concerning the true nature of that Messiahship (9:22) and its consequences for His missionary disciples (9:23–26). The climax is reached in the ultimate revelation of Jesus' identity on Mount Tabor (9:28–36) and the inadequate response of disciples to His call (9:37–43), their difficulty in understanding Jesus (9:44–45) and their own worldly thinking (9:46–50).

The Twelve, who are travelling with Jesus (8:1) are here sent out into Galilee on their first missionary experience without Jesus present. Like the healed demoniac they were sent to their own territory first. Jesus, therefore, supervises their transition from disciple (pupil) to leader (Master) which will be their position in the new community after His departure. He gave them His own power (*dynamis*) and authority over *all devils* and the ability to cure diseases (9:1). With this authority and power went the command to preach the Kingdom. Luke stresses that the Kingdom cannot be established by preaching *alone*. It must be accompanied by the signs that release the people to come into the Kingdom. There is abundant evidence in Acts that this was taken literally by Peter, John (Acts 2:43, 3:1–10, 4:15–16, 9:36–42); and Paul (Acts 14:8–10, 16) Philip (Acts 8:6), and the Church in general (Acts 4:29–31).

These men specially chosen by Jesus from the bulk of the disciples (6:13–16) are seen to be called to share in Jesus' own ministry. The secrets of the Kingdom of God have been revealed to them (8:10), and they were told to proclaim them at the right time (8:17). Their experience here prepares them for the Great Commission in 24:46–47 which will launch them on a universal mission for Jesus.

The instructions given to them allow them to experience complete dependence on God for all the necessities of life. This would keep before them that the the fruit of the mission lay in God's hands alone. They must abandon themselves to a life of trusting God for everything. Jesus did not allow them to bring money to buy their needs, nor a haversack containing provisions (9:3). They were to accept hospitality without choosing the best house to stay in. They were to accept what was given to them (9:4). This must have reflected the situation in Luke's church where travelling preachers, teachers, and prophets were given hospitality by the Christian community.

The Twelve are warned that the mission will not be

plain sailing, as was hinted in 5:1–10: Like Jesus they would experience rejection as well as acceptance, but Jesus indicated in 9:6 that He took their rejection as a serious matter. They were to give a sign to any area or town which rejected them. They were to shake the dust of that town off their sandals, thus throwing responsibility for their rejection of salvation back on the villagers (Acts 13:50–52). Since the Jews at that time considered even the dust of Gentile soil (or the presence of Gentiles in the market place) as unclean, they removed this dust before re-entering their own dwellings. For Jesus, the real uncleanness is sin (Mark 7:14–23), so those who reject the message of the Gospel remain in this uncleanness. The Apostles are warned not to become infected by such unbelief and the immorality that often accompanies it. It is interesting to note that *entering* a house of sinners would not defile them (5:29–32). The dust is only considered unclean if those sinners reject the healing and deliverance that enabled them to receive the salvation being offered.

Luke demands absolute commitment from the Christian missionaries, yet he will adapt the instructions for the missioning of the seventy-two in 10:1–16 and 22:35–38 to suit the changing needs of the times. Thus these instructions are meant to be seen as guidelines rather than absolute rules, as adaptability is essential for those who travel to foreign lands and different cultures. The self-sacrifice and trust in God would remain for these prophets like Jesus.

Herod's Anxiety (9:7–9)

The Twelve are travelling all over Galilee preaching and giving the same signs as Jesus. This naturally becomes a cause of concern for Herod, the Tetrarch. Everyone was asking who this man was, now that He had disciples working for Him. Jesus' identity assumes a more urgent importance. Not very wisely the people wonder if John the Baptist is risen from the dead (9:8). It is strange they should think this way before Jesus' own resurrection. Nobody assumed He had risen until He proved it! Perhaps it is the post-resurrection reflections of those who did not understand who Jesus was? Others suggested that Jesus was Elijah back from the dead, or even some other prophet – again back from the dead! Notice that they all accept there is something other-worldly about Jesus that they cannot accurately pinpoint. The very-worldly Herod dismissed all this as he himself had dispatched John in death (9:9). He correctly assumed that Jesus was different from these others, so the question of his identity is raised even more urgently: *"So who is this I hear such reports about?"*. The following sign answers the question if only Herod had eyes that see, and a heart that understood.

Feed the World (9:10–17)

On their return from the mission the Apostles gave an account to Jesus, who responded by taking them away for a rest from their labours. Thus He showed the pattern for their future activity was to be a balance of work and rest, apostolic activity and prayer. Total availability is impossible. But they were to understand that the power behind a balanced and fruitful apostolate lay in prayerful communion with God and each other. On the question of mission: were they to feed the people with the bread of God's Word *only?* Was there any other bread to feed the starving millions with? Jesus answers in the affirmative with a sign that reveals Him as the new Moses, and also *the source* of food for the new Israel. Having no bread or resources themselves (9:3), the Apostles are now com-

113

manded to feed the multitudes (9:13)! Like Jesus, their poverty is meant to enrich others (2 Corinthians 8:9).

As the crowds discovered, the hide-out was in Bethsaida which was outside Herod's territory. Jesus must have deliberately avoided him, since his desire to see Jesus had nothing to do with faith or any need of salvation (9:9, 13:31–33, 22:8–12). The hide-out was in a lonely place (9:13), but the people followed them out there. Just as Jesus welcomed the crowds in 8:40, so He welcomed them now, even though they intruded on His private time. He tended to their needs all day and cured the sick, until the Apostles interrupted to say that evening was approaching and the crowds needed food. Thus they were brought to see that preaching and healing are not enough. The people must be brought to the Table of the Lord to participate in the Messianic banquet also (9:12). Jesus replied: *"Give them something to eat yourselves"*.

There were only five loaves and two fish there for approximately five thousand people (9:13–14). Besides, with their limited resources they could not even buy the amount of food required. They are not being asked, however, to use worldly means, no matter how good, to feed God's people, for it was not material bread Jesus asked them to give, but the Eucharist – signified by this miracle. Watch the numbers here: there were five thousand people and Jesus ordered them to be put into table companies of fifty each to be fed on five loaves (9:14). Does five mean anything? It was the number for the Pentateuch, the Torah, which was the spiritual food of God's people. The Greek letters for "fish" spell "Jesus Christ, Son of God, Saviour", and it was used as a symbol in the early Church. 5 + 2 = 7, the perfect number. The combination of God's Word and the Eucharist is the perfect food that Jesus wants to feed the New

Israel with. This food is truly heavenly. The Apostles are commissioned to supply both to meet the spiritual needs of God's people.

Jesus also used the Eucharistic formula of the early Church as he *took ... raised his eyes to heaven, and said the blessing over them; then he broke them and handed them to the disciples to distribute among the crowd*. The source of this divine food is Jesus Himself. The Apostles collect and distribute it. In doing so they discovered that not only is there enough for the present congregation, but when they collected the scraps, they filled twelve baskets full of them. They had more left over than they had begun with! Luke uses the word *klasmata* for the broken pieces of bread, a word used by the early Church for the pieces of Eucharistic bread. The number twelve signifies the fullness of Israel with its twelve Tribes, God's own fullness, so the message here is that Jesus is providing enough spiritual food for all of God's people.

This miracle is a foretaste of the future Eucharistic banquet of the Church which fulfils the prophecy of Isaiah 25:6–9 which promised a Messianic banquet for all peoples, once the Lord had destroyed death forever and removed the shroud enwrapping all nations, when He would take away the people's shame and give them salvation. Jesus will provide the Eucharistic gift as He goes to fulfil this prophecy in His passion and death. After His departure it is the Apostles' on-going responsibility to feed God's people with both Word and Bread. Here Jesus succeeds in supplying a manna miracle greater than that of Moses, since Jesus' Eucharistic gift continues throughout the life of the Church and is a world-wide phenomenon. A flashback to the miracle of the abundant fish (5:1–10), should be a reminder that the entire mission is under the direct supervision of Jesus with

115

Peter in a special position of leadership (see Mark 16:29; John 21:1–23).

Jesus' Identity (9:18–22)

It is essential for their participation in the mission that the disciples and especially Peter as the leader, know who Jesus is. They cannot stay in the indecision of the people or Herod (9:7–9). Hence He was one day alone with them praying – a reminder from Luke that this is the context where God reveals Himself. So it is in prayer with Jesus that they receive a deeper revelation of who He is and why He came. In prayer God reveals Himself to us. It was also another opportunity to see Jesus in communion with God, but had they come to any conclusions? He challenged them to decision: *"Who do the crowds say I am?"* (9:19). Thus the argument takes up from 9:7–9.

From the answers – John the Baptist, Elijah or some ancient prophet revived, it was obvious that they did see something special in Jesus. They were prepared to label Him *a prophet* (see John 6:15). But when Jesus homed-in on the disciples he implied that a generalized "prophet" title was not enough to understand Him or be involved in His mission. *"But you, he said, who do you say that I am?"* (9:20). This was Peter's moment of grace, for he spoke up on behalf of the others that Jesus was *"the Christ of God"* (9:21). Peter acknowledged that Jesus was God's Messiah sent to Israel. This statement of his, given so simply here was destined to change world history.

Luke has already indicated to us, his readers, that Jesus is the Messiah. He was proclaimed such by the angel of the Lord in 2:11, by Simeon in 2:26, 29–32, and by demons after the struggle in the wilderness (4:34, 41).

Here we see the result of the slow process by which the disciples break in on the mystery of the person of Jesus. Once they acknowledged Him as Messiah Jesus enjoined strict silence on them (9:21), because the people's understanding of Messiah was too political, and the disciples were infected by the same thinking. Jesus immediately gave the first prophecy of the Passion (9:22) to explain the type of Messiah He had chosen to be. The Son of Man was a lowly suffering servant of God who would redeem them by His Passion, Death and Resurrection (see Isaiah 42:1–9, 49:1–6, 50:4–11, 52:13–53:12; Zechariah 12:10, 13:1, 7–9). From this point onwards Luke keeps this constantly before our minds showing what a struggle the disciples had to accept this aspect of the revelation concerning Jesus, and how abhorrent the whole idea of suffering is to human nature in general (9:44, 12:50, 17:25, 18:30, 24:7, 26, 44).

Discipleship and Mission (9:23–26)

The implications for disciples who follow a suffering Messiah are spelled out now. They must accept the mystery of the cross in Jesus' life, and in their own. A Christian without the cross is an anachronism (9:23). All disciples must embrace the *via dolorosa* in their own lives (see Romans 6:3; Colossians 1:24; Galatians 2:20; 1 Corinthians 15:31). Self denial must be in the heart of every follower of Jesus: *"Let him renounce himself, take up his cross every day and follow me"* (9:23). Jesus' thinking is so opposed to the popular notion of Messiah that it is easy to see why He silenced His disciples. He was at the height of His popularity with the crowds here, and it would be highly undesirable for the word to get out that He was claiming to be the Messiah, as this would arouse political ferment, and gather undesirable elements about

Him with disastrous results, as the Romans would ruthlessly suppress them.

The disciples had to be prepared for the opposite, that the nation would, in the end, reject Jesus, and hand Him over to be crucified. Yet this seeming failure would turn out to be the nub of the whole mystery. It is necessary for them to begin *to think* like Jesus, as there was a divine *must* about His Passion that indicated God's will in the coming events (9:22). There was, equally, a divine *must* about the cross in the Christian life, and in martyrdom for the sake of the Kingdom, and both would turn out to be all gain as they did for Jesus (9:14) They must also know that gaining power over the whole world, which was Caesar's position, was useless if it entailed the loss of the only thing we really possess, namely our own soul (or person, 9:25). A life lived for ourself is a life lost, but a life lost for Jesus' sake is a life gained. This is the fundamental paradox of the Christian life.

The world was going to give Jesus' followers the *same* response as it gave to Him. As they spoke up for God they too would be rejected and many of them martyred – as was happening in Luke's community at that time when the Church was undergoing severe persecution. If they were tempted to run away from suffering and the cross Luke gives them (and us) the solemn warning of Jesus: *"For if anyone is ashamed of me and my words, of him the Son of Man will be ashamed when he comes in his own glory and in the glory of the Father and the holy angels"* (9:26) Between the going of Christ in the Resurrection and His return in the Parousia or Second Coming, there was labour, suffering and the cross for all who work for the Kingdom of God (see Acts 14:22; 1 Corinthians 4:7–11, 16–18, 5:3–10, 11:22–29).

For the enthusiastic disciples fresh from their first experience of mission (9:10) and their first acknowledgement of Jesus as Messiah (9:21) this revelation would amount to a great shock and disappointment. What a bleak future awaited them! Surely they could be dead before the Second Coming (and they were). This left merely a life of hardship and suffering ... could they face it? Jesus promised that some of them were about to see a revelation of the coming Kingdom of God (9:27). He was referring to the privileged three, Peter, James and John who were going to witness His glorious Transfiguration. Most, if not all, of the disciples present would see Jesus in his Risen Glory after the Resurrection also (1 Corinthians 15:5–8).

Full Manifestation of Jesus (9:28–36)

The Apostles' faith in Jesus, and their understanding of His identity is crucial for their own mission. It is not enough to merely profess faith in Him as the Messiah, they need further revelation to see Him as the Beloved Son of God. It is to the first three disciples to whom He gave a special call in 5:1–11 that the full manifestation is given here on Mount Tabor. What they are about to witness we, the readers, have already seen at Jesus' Baptism (3:21–22), and both revelations were given while Jesus was at prayer (9:28). Both affirm the divine Sonship and the divine call of this specially chosen suffering Son of Man. The disciples are to *listen to him* (9:35) as He shows the way forward. Luke affirms that this listening and deeper understanding are done in prayer. The Christian who listens to God in prayer will come to know and understand Jesus and His mission to save.

About eight days later Jesus took Peter, James and John up the mountain to pray. This mountain is not named but traditionally believed to be Mount Tabor. As He prayed He was transfigured before them and the experience was so great that the Apostles were caught up in it to the extent that they, too, saw the vision given to Jesus (9:33). Moses and Elijah, two of the greatest Old Testament figures, were communing with Jesus. In the Jewish tradition both of these men were exalted by God. Both had divine revelation on Mount Sinai (Exodus 19; 1 Kings 19:9–18). Both were used by God to save their people at a crucial time in Israel's history. Both were taken up to God mysteriously in death so that both were considered to have been assumed into heaven (Deuteronomy 34; 2 Kings 2:1–18). Both suffered greatly from Israel (Acts 7:17–44; 1 Kings 19:10), and were closely associated with the Hope of Israel (Acts 3:22; Malachi 3:1, 4:5). Both had offered sacrifice for the salvation of the people (Exodus 12; 1 Kings 18:20–40). In the rabbinic tradition both were expected to appear at the end of time. Between them they represent the Law and the Prophets, or all that God had accomplished before the coming of Messiah. In this vision they were discussing Jesus' *exodos* or *passing* (9:31) where He would both fulfil and surpass all that has gone on before as His sacrifice is *the* sacrifice for the salvation of the world.

It is necessary that the disciples accept Jesus' departure for it is essential to the out-working of the Kingdom of God. Here Luke asks the early Church to try and cope with Jesus' physical absence from them. If they look to the first Exodus under Moses they will understand the definitive Exodus through Jesus (Acts 3:15, 5:31; Hebrews 11:22). The word *exodos* is used here and elsewhere by biblical authors as a euphemism for death (2 Peter 1:15; Wisdom 3:2; 7:6). The disciples are here challenged to see in Jesus the fulfilment of the Law and the Prophets, for He is the Hope of Israel.

During this manifestation of Jesus' glory, Peter and his companions were heavy with sleep, but managed to stay awake to see His glory (9:32), but they will fail to witness His deep struggle and final decision in Gethsemane (22:45). There, contrary to Jesus' own instructions they fell asleep until it was all over (22:40, 46). When Moses had been transfigured he came down the mountain *reflecting* the glory of God (Exodus 24:29–35), but here the disciples see Jesus' own glory and the glory of *his exodos* (Acts 3:13, 7:55, 22:11). They were willing to accept a glorious Messiah (John 1:14) but not a suffering one.

Peter, confused by all that he saw, said that he was willing to build three tents each for Jesus, Moses and Elijah, thus missing the point that these great worthies from the Old Testament acknowledged the supremacy of Jesus and his *exodos*. He, like Moses and Elijah, as the leader of the mission team to all the world needs a personal revelation from God on this holy mountain (2 Peter 1:16–18), so the Cloud of God's ineffable Presence descended upon them, covering them in its shadow (1:35; Exodus 40:34–38). They were now caught up in the glory of God themselves! The voice of the Father came from the Cloud revealing to them that Jesus " . . . *is my Son, the Chosen One. Listen to him*" (9:36). The symbol of the cloud is one that both reveals and conceals at the same time showing that even when the Father reveals Himself that He still remains shrouded in mystery.

Jesus is, therefore, that prophet like Moses of Deuteronomy 18:15–18, whom Moses predicted would come. Moses said that if the people did not listen to *him* they would be cut off from the people. Jesus is the fulfilment of all that Moses and Elijah stood for, and God wants us to listen *to Jesus only* now (9:36; Philippians 2:6–11). When the glory has gone, they must accept Jesus and *all* that He represents. It is *His* Kingdom they must work for. They were so moved by this revelation that, without a command from Jesus, they kept this vision to themselves until after the resurrection (9:36). They could now see that His Kingdom was not of this world (John 18:36). It had nothing whatever to do with power politics or materialism. *It was OF GOD*. The salvation of the world would be accomplished by a sacrifice of pure love on the part of the Father (John 3:16) and the Son (John 10:17–18). This was a shock to the materialistic and politically minded disciples who thought to use worldly power to spread the Kingdom of God. Knowing this ahead of time, Peter, James and John should realize that the death of Jesus was no tragic accident that dashes all their hopes, and the cross is no obstacle to spreading the gospel – quite the opposite in fact (see 1 Corinthians 2:2–5).

Problems of the Mission (9:37–50)

In the next four episodes, Luke deals with the failure of the disciples to carry out the task given them by Jesus (9:37–43), the reason being their failure to grasp the significance of the centrality of the cross for Jesus, for the Church *and* for the mission. The final two texts show some problems in the internal (9:46–48) and external relationships (9:49–50) of the community.

The New Moses descended the mountain only to encounter evil at work in people's lives at its foot (9:37; see Exodus 32:1–6; 34:29–35). The disciples cannot stay wrapped in glory on the mountain, for they must deal with the evil that destroys people's lives in the world. Here they failed to help the epileptic boy, and his father was distraught (9:40). The disciples must look to the Passion of Jesus as *the source of power over evil*. They were not given magic formulas to hand out, but the

122

redemptive grace and power released by Jesus' victory over death and hell. This is the revelation of Jesus' glory they will meet with throughout the history of the Church.

Luke's presentation of this story differs from the other synoptics. Here it is the only son of his father and the distraught man appeals to Jesus on the grounds that the boy is *his only son* (9:38). He went on to describe the child's symptoms as both epilepsy and demonic activity (9:37). Jesus' response to His disciples whose failure left both father and son in their misery echoes the impatience of Moses with Israel in Deuteronomy 32:5, 20, where, like Jesus here in 9:41, he called them a faithless and perverse generation. Jesus healed the boy and gave him back to his father and the crowds were awestruck by the greatness of God coming through Jesus (9:43).

Jesus can foresee failure in the mission if the disciples lose faith in Him. This will leave the seething masses of humanity without help or hope from those demonic evil forces that try to capture and destroy those destined to be sons of God, and for whom the Beloved Son gave His life. On the other hand, if the disciples are empowered by the cross and the victory of Jesus they will set the captives free and give God His sons back. The responsibility is very great! Jesus' anger with His disciples underlines this responsibility. Twice now they have shown a lack of faith in His provision for the mission. In 9:13 they baulked at feeding the multitudes and wondered how He could demand so much from their limited resources. Here they still show that they have not grasped that *He* is the source of the fruitfulness of the mission (5:1–11).

It is the Father of the Beloved Son who so loves the world of sinful and sinning human beings that He will give up His only Son for their salvation in order to heal them of all the perversity of unbelief and restore to them a true knowledge of the greatness of God. This is the gift that will overcome evil in the world and deliver the sons of God.

At this crucial moment when the people were full of admiration for all that He did (9:43) Jesus chose to instil the message of the cross into the disciples ... they were to have it constantly in their minds (9:44). Of course at this stage, the full meaning was veiled from them (9:45), but revealed to us, the readers. They were afraid to seek clarification from Jesus concerning it also, even though the secrets of the Kingdom of God were revealed to them (8:10). The next two episodes will explain why. Suffering is mysterious and frightening and only the Resurrection can reveal fully that it was part of God's plan for redemption (18:34, 22:14–18, 24:6–8).

In a world that worshipped the strong and the powerful, the notion of weakness and helplessness was abhorrent. A crucified Messiah was for them a contradiction in terms. They were still imbued with notions of a political Messiah, hence their preoccupation with prestige and precedence in the coming Kingdom of God. Power politics would destroy Jesus' community which was to be based on *agape*-love. Greatness in the Kingdom concerned great humility (like a child), and great service (like a slave) (22:24–27). The child had no rights in society in those days. It depended completely on its parents in love and trust. Luke has already told us that the Kingdom concerns the lowly in the Magnificat and the Beatitudes. The dispute here is about "the greatest" and "the least". Jesus' answer is: *"The least among you all is the one who is the greatest"* (9:48). As usual God's way of looking at values upturns our own (Isaiah 55:6–9). I suppose the question is more urgent now that they have been given power and authority by Jesus (9:1), and told that the rejection of the Christian missionary is a serious matter (9:3–5). Three of them were also singled out for special favour on Mount Tabor. Were they growing in a sense of their own importance? Only when the full self-emptying of Jesus on the cross breaks in on them will they understand God's notion of true greatness.

Intolerance of others who did not belong to their group was not accepted by Jesus, then or now (9:49–50). Even at this early stage the disciples came across people using the name of Jesus effectively to cast out demons! But because these did not join their ranks, the disciples wanted to stop them. However Jesus refused permission on the grounds that " . . . *anyone who is not against you is for you*" This is strange, coming as it does so close to the incident where the disciples themselves failed to cast out demons. They want to stop others even though they are effective! Such narrow-minded exclusiveness was not acceptable to Jesus. It probably reflected a problem of breakaway Christians from Luke's community, prepared to work for Christ, but not prepared to submit to the discipline of the community or its leaders. The future held a day when all hidden matters will be disclosed (9:23–26). For the moment the broad-minded view of acceptance is required. See 11:23 for the opposite statement: *"He who is not with me is against me..."*. Here the question concerns those who are *with you*, namely the community of Christians, whereas in 11:23 speaks of those who are *with Christ* or not. It is allegiance to Christ that is all important. Jesus allows no neutral position, yet enjoins tolerance on the Apostles particularly, as leaders of the community, even though tolerance is incumbent on all.

Here we conclude the Galilean Ministry of Jesus. From here on He sets out on the journey to Jerusalem, the city of destiny. He has revealed His personal identity, mission and Messiahship. He has called and trained disciples who must go forward despite the fact that their understanding of Him and how He will save them is deficient and infected by worldly thinking. There will be more teaching and revelation for them as they enter the final phase of Jesus' ministry.

Chapter Four
Evening Comes

We have reached the turning point in the gospel. Up to now Luke had described the *coming* of our Lord Jesus Christ into the world. Now he begins to present his *going* from the world, and shows us the stages of that going in the form of a journey from Galilee to Jerusalem. There He goes to the cross and passes on from human history to glory, and from there he will return to earth in glory again (9:51–24:53). It is from Jerusalem, after these awesome events, that the young Church which originated in the life and mission of Jesus, will begin its mission to the ends of the earth (Acts 1–18). Both Jesus' and the Church's destiny are *in God*.

As Jesus passes out into the presence of God, the Church is energized by His victory over death and hell and continues His struggle with evil throughout history. Jesus is *on the way* and the disciples must understand both their need to undertake the inward journey of true discipleship, and the outward journey of missionary endeavour. The New Exodus is under way, and the new People of God must follow their New Moses out of the Egypt of slavery to sin and darkness, and from thence on the spiritual journey to life, salvation and freedom (9:31). Luke has already prepared us for the journey by its foreshadowing in the infancy narratives (2:41–51), in the beginning of the public life (4:30, 42–43) and in the Transfiguration (9:31). He has also given two predictions of the Passion (9:22, 44), but told us that up to now the meaning was hidden from the disciples (2:50, 9:45). The meaning of Jesus' *exodos* will be explained on the journey to all faithful disciples.

Luke presents the journey in four major stages. In the first one, Jesus, like a new Moses, sets out the leadership of the New Israel with seventy-two new leaders (Numbers 11:16–30), and gives the basic instruction for all those who want to follow Him on *the Christian way to God* (9:51–13:21). The scenes in this section are situated mostly in Galilee. The second stage illustrates the journey of salvation and its implications for Eucharistic table-fellowship, discipleship and family; the proper attitude to wealth, and Israel's rejection of Jesus (13:22–19:48). This second stage moves from Galilee to Jerusalem. In Jerusalem the third stage deals with the reasons why various groups struggled with Jesus' claims and finally rejected them (20:1–21:38). The last stage culminates in the Passion, death and Resurrection of Jesus. What many people supposed to be the end of Jesus turned out to be the beginning, as Jesus journeyed on to God and glory (22:1–24:53).

The Journey to God (9:51–56)

The goal of the journey is presented first. Jesus is destined to be taken up to heaven in the Ascension (9:51). Luke presents Jesus' acceptance of His destiny in the firm resolve where: *He resolutely turned His face towards Jerusalem . . .* (9:52). This journey will take Him via Jerusalem into glory. This *ascent* of Jesus into glory is the opposite of His descent in the Incarnation (John 1:1–18; see 1 Timothy 3:16). The geographical journey to Jerusalem merely offers the appropriate setting for this more important Exodus-Ascension journey of the Messiah.

Jerusalem as a city has deep significance for Luke and

indeed for the Jewish nation. Apart from its being the capital city and the seat of the Kings of Judah, from whom the Messiah was to come, it was the city that housed the invisible Presence of God in the Temple. It was, therefore, the place where God lived among men, a unique privilege in the ancient world. God had sent a succession of great prophets to lead and inspire the people while preparing them for the coming of the Messiah. Jerusalem then, was the Messiah's own city where He ought to be acclaimed, crowned and enthroned as King. To present Himself as Israel's King, He would have to present Himself in Jerusalem (Zechariah 9:9).

However, Jerusalem's record for receiving the prophets was poor (13:34), so Jesus was realistic about His own reception there (9:22, 44–45, 12:49–50, 13:34–35, 18:31–34, 19:41–44). He knew, as did the people, that prophets perished in Jerusalem, and from the most amazing of enemies. It was not the evil, materialistic, or atheistic types who would kill Him, but those with the highest religious positions in the land. Those ordained to speak for God and discern His will would destroy the Son (20:13–15).

The journey of those who accompany Jesus here must be read on the deeper level of the road of discipleship, or the way of salvation. It is a path of commitment to the Lord and the Mission which has its own passion, death and resurrection cycle, for the disciples must become *like* their Master (6:40). The reader, too, is invited to join in on this journey. We are on life's journey already, one that passes inexorably from birth to death and beyond. Luke wants to show that that destiny in the "land of far beyond" may not be the same as the heaven Jesus entered. One's life determines whether the place of arrival will be the one planned by God, or not.

All of us will exit from this world, but many will be unprepared for heaven (12:16–21). Some will find heaven's door closed to them (13:25). Others who have lived in comfort and ease will find pain and suffering awaiting them there (13:28–30). For some the journey's end is the end of joy, but for others death brings eternal happiness (16:19–31). We are warned to get ready (12:35–48, 16:1–8), that our present behaviour determines our future destiny (17:9–10, 18:9–14, 19:11–27). We are encouraged to make sacrificial decisions that will ease our passage to our true destiny (14:11–14, 27–33, 16:9–15, 17:9–10). Let us now follow Jesus along His chosen path which passes through Jerusalem and Calvary before entering Glory. Luke shows us *en route* how the followers of Jesus may also pass that way, the Sacred Way of Isaiah 58:8–10, the way that only the redeemed can travel on before entering into Zion (symbol for both Jerusalem and heaven) with everlasting joy on their faces, now that sorrow and lament are things of the past.

An overview of the whole journey leaves us with a paradox, that the way of Jesus to His place at the right hand of the power of God (22:69) is through indescribable sorrow. The way up is down. ...*and the one who humbles himself will be raised up* (14:11, 18:14). The beginning of the journey brought Jesus and His companions through Samaria, which was notoriously hostile to the Jews, and a good symbol of the difficulty of the mission that lay ahead for disciples. They must learn how to respond to rejection. Calling down a destructive fire from heaven to consume the people was not the way to conversion, even if they could cite the great Elijah as their authority for so doing (2 Kings 1:10–12)!

The heavenly fire that Jesus wanted to send (3:16; Acts 1:5, 8, 2:3–4) down upon the earth was the Pentecostal Fire of the Coming of the Holy Spirit, a fire that would cleanse, heal and strengthen the disciples and anoint them for mission. Jesus had known rejection from the beginning of His coming on earth (2:7), so it is no surprise to Him to find no room in the village. The reason for His rejection now is the fact that He is on His way to Jerusalem (9:54), but they are unaware that He is going there to redeem them. The world comtinues to find the cross of Jesus a good excuse for rejecting Him even though it is the source of life for all.

Jesus rebuked His disciples for wanting to call down judgement on a village which acted out of ignorance and religious prejudice (9:56). It would be different if this rejection were given *after* the Christian missionaries had done their work there (10:10–16). We know from John 4 that Jesus did work among the Samaritans, and the disciples continued the mission after Pentecost (Acts 1:8, 8:5–25). This incident illustrates why James and John were nick-named Boanerges, sons of thunder (Mark 3,17).

In this first section the disciples are instructed to accept the hostility and rejection of the world with serenity, without feeling the need to avenge themselves. The second lesson prepares them for the hardships ahead. Like John the Baptist before them (7:24–28), they must sacrifice worldly luxury and comforts for the sake of the Kingdom of God (9:57–62). They will be homeless, like Jesus (9:58), constantly travelling, and finding a resting place in other people's houses, with no base to return to. Christian disciples find that "the world" is not their home as they journey spiritually to their home in heaven (2 Corinthians 5:1–10).

The disciple must leave the earthly family to cling to the new family (9:57–62). The three anonymous disciples here represent any person who wants to join Jesus during His lifetime, or that of the Church later. They must disengage from home (9:57–58), past responsibilities (9:59–60) and former relationships (9:61–62). Radical commitment is demanded as well as detachment from the world.

The urgency of preaching the Kingdom of God is so great and the labourers so few (10:2) that they must leave the spiritually dead to take care of the physically dead. The unbelievers were to be allowed to do what they could to help themselves while the disciples did what they could, empowered by the Holy Spirit, to bring New Life to them. The urgency and importance of the call is recalled in a reflection on the total sacrifice of Elisha of his old way of life (2 Kings 4:29). They are like soldiers called to join an army in time of war. The defence of their country then takes precedence over all personal ties and family relationships (14:25–27; see 1 Timothy 2:4).

Commissioning the Seventy-Two (10:1–16)

Like Moses before Him (Numbers 11:16–25) Jesus gathered a second layer of leaders about Him to augment His mission. The seventy were given a share of the Spirit given to Moses and a share in his authority to lead and guide the people of Israel. This prophetic spirit was also given to an extra two leaders who stayed behind in the camp (Numbers 11:26–30). This may account for the fact that some important manuscripts of Luke give seventy-two as the number while others give seventy. In any case Luke is pointing to the leadership of the Church especially in the post-apostolic era. He shows that their authority, like that of the Twelve, was grounded in the Person and Mission of Jesus (Acts 14:23). They, too, were endowed with the Spirit, and given a prophetic, apostolic, missionary role in the Church.

The field of missionary endeavour was so large that the labourers were too few, and prayer was needed to fill out the ranks of those willing to sacrifice all to serve the Lord in the Kingdom. In its original context, thirty-six pairs of disciples working in all the towns and villages, preparing the way for Jesus (10:1) amounted to a blitz campaign that awakened the whole countryside to the presence of the Lord and the urgency of His call (10:2). This was no mere apostolic exercise, but a major onslaught on the nation that might explain the reaction of the leaders and their desire to rid themselves of Jesus.

The Seventy-Two were to have no illusions about the spiritual warfare they were undertaking. In fact they would be like lambs among wolves (9:41, 11:29) under constant attack (10:4). Yet, far from protecting themselves, they were to face into the fray helpless and defenceless, without the ability to survive materially (10:5). Having neither money, clothes nor provisions, they needed the hospitality of the people (10:5–6), thus forcing decisions upon the villagers as to whether they wanted to accept or reject them. In simplicity and humility the disciples were to accept whatever was given, not worrying whether the food was clean or unclean (10:7; 1 Corinthians 10:27; Acts 10:25), and they were not permitted to choose the best lodgings either (10:7–8).

Their job was to bring the peace of Christ (10:6) and to cure the sick (10:9) while preaching the Kingdom of God (10:9). If they were rejected they were to give the sign of rubbing the unclean dust off their shoes (9:5,10:11) just as the Twelve were instructed to do, for then the judgement of the unclean would come upon them. In fact it would be worse than the fiery judgement of Sodom (10:12). In 9:55–56 Jesus rebuked His Apostles for wanting to bring fire down upon the Samaritans, because the fire of judgement is reserved to God at the end of the world (21:34–36).

The very serious implications of rejecting Christ and His missionaries is illustrated now with regard to the fishing villages in Galilee where Jesus had done so much work, and where He had been so well received (10:13–15).

The three towns of Chorazin, Bethsaida and Capernaum are uninhabited today, as is Sodom. Is this a warning to us at the end of the age? Sodom did not have the graces given to these villages. Likewise, the worldly Gentile cities of Tyre and Sidon (10:14) would have repented long ago if they had witnessed the miracles seen in these three privileged places. This gives a clear indication of the responsibility to accept and respond to graces given, for to whom much is given much is also expected (12:48, 4:26–27, 6:17). Capernaum had been privileged to witness such a great deal of Jesus' personal ministry that perhaps they thought they would be raised up to heaven without effort or change (10:15)? Had they forgotten that it is not the *hearing* of the Word but the *doing* of it that counts (6:46–49; James 1:21–25)? Jesus made it clear that we cannot make special claims on God because we were evangelized by a "special" ministry. The prophets of old condemned Israel for such arrogance (Isaiah 14:13–15).

Capernaum is warned that it will be cast down to hell. Here for the first time, we are confronted with the alternative destination to the one Jesus aims at, for there are serious consequences to the rejection of the Word, the missionaries and the Salvation of God. The missionaries must bear in mind that they are Christ's ambassadors, and the rejection of them is the rejection of Christ, and also the rejection of the Father who sent Him. This triple rejection excludes them from the Kingdom of God. On the other hand, those who listen to the disciples are listening to the Lord Himself (10:16).

The return of the Seventy-Two from their first missionary experience highlights a double movement associated with Jesus' "lifting up". His ascension into glory will occasion the downfall of Satan, who will fall like lightning from heaven (10:18). The spreading of the Kingdom of God is inexorably bound up with the downfall of evil in its many manifestations. The power given to the apostolic missionaries is power to *tread down serpents and scorpions and the whole strength of the enemy* (10:19). The people of Israel had marvelled at Jesus' power over demons (4:36, 41). Now the Gentile peoples marvel that such authority and power was given to the Christian missionaries (Ephesians 6:10–20).

All this would come to pass after Jesus had ascended into heaven (1 Peter 3:22) to sit at the right hand of God, *far above every principality, ruling force, power or sovereignty, or any other name that can be named not only in this age but also in the age to come. He has put all things under his feet, and made him, as he is above all things, the head of the church, which is his Body . . .* (Ephesians 1:21–22). The missionaries will have to battle with evil powers, but Jesus promised that they would never be hurt by them (10:19), and this because Christ's victory on Calvary would be decisive and complete (Romans 8:37).

The amazement and rejoicing of the Seventy-Two in the obvious power extended to them is understandable, but the focus of their rejoicing should be elsewhere, in the fact that they are already registered as citizens of heaven (10:20; Philippians 3:20). It is wonderful that here at the beginning of the journey Jesus allows His disciples to see its ending. The reward of heaven would act as a great incentive to them in their labours for the Kingdom of God. It is not difficult to see that Luke is both encouraging the leaders of the Church in the post-apostolic age, and also warning them against pride in the authority and power invested in them. The Church's triumphant march through the Roman Empire is due to Jesus' sacrificial death, and not to themselves.

The victory of the Seventy-Two (and the later Church) over evil causes Jesus to rejoice and to praise God for giving such revelation and power to "mere children" (9:46–50). The disciples were still so young and inexperienced spiritually, yet God permitted them to be effective witnesses for Him. God's love for the lowly or the little ones is such that He allows *even them* to pull down the mighty forces of evil (1:51–52). The learned and the clever in Israel then, and in the world since then, cannot understand God's wisdom or logic here, for it opposes the thinking of the world. Jesus rejoices in the Father's Will and the Father's way of accomplishing salvation (10:21; 1 Corinthians 1 and 2).

At this point Luke reveals one of his most important christological statements concerning the unique relationship that Jesus enjoyed with the Father: *"Everything has been entrusted to me by my Father; and no one knows who the Son is except the Father, and who the Father is except the Son and those to whom the Son chooses to reveal him"* (10:22; John 3:35, 4:46, 14:9, 17:10). In this context Jesus shows that He chooses to reveal such knowledge of the Father to His disciples and apostolic missionaries, who are being initiated into all the secrets of the Kingdom of God (8:10). We know from the Baptism (3:22) and Transfiguration (9:35) that Jesus is the Son of the Father. He alone can impart knowledge of the Father, and of the fulfilment of all the Old Testament prophecies and promises. Hence the disciples are truly blessed to see Jesus and to hear the secrets of the Kingdom (10:23–24; 1 Peter 1:10–12).

The Way to Heaven (10:25–37)

The revelation given by Jesus to the little ones, which was kept from the learned and the clever, is tested now by a lawyer (10:25) whose knowledge of the Law would be expected to disconcert Jesus and His unlearned followers. The tables will turn, however, when the lawyer struggles to cope with the wisdom of the simple (7:35). He produces chapter and verse from the holy books, but Jesus demands a life lived worthy of such knowledge. The parable which this test wrings from the heart of Jesus is all about life's journey, and each of the characters are judged, not by the letter of the Law, but by loving service to their fellow travellers (10:29–37).

The lawyer's question: *"Master, what must I do to inherit eternal life?"* refers to the understanding of the time that one was saved by the faithful keeping of the Law (10:25; Leviticus 18:5). Jesus responded by demanding to know what the Law laid down. Combining Deuteronomy 6:5 and Leviticus 19:18, the lawyer replied that the whole Law could be summed up in loving God with total commitment, the whole heart, soul, strength and mind, and your neighbour as yourself (10:27). Jesus agreed wholeheartedly with this interpretation of God's Will. All that remained was for the lawyer *to obey the Word* (6:46–49).

To love your neighbour as if he were your own self is a challenge to disconcert not only the lawyer in question, but all who want to journey into eternal life. All those present would have known the theoretical answer to this question, so the lawyer failed to reveal either learning or wisdom. He tried to escape his embarrassment by posing a further question as to *who* should be considered a neighbour. Who *is* this person to whom I should give such love to that it is the same as loving my own self? Surely they would have to be very special people (10:29)? Jesus did not answer the question directly, but replied in such a way that the lawyer was challenged *to become a neighbour* to others in need, without regard to class, colour or creed.

There are limitations to love in the lawyer's response.

137

He knew he had to love his fellow Jew, and Leviticus 19:34 demanded that he love the stranger (foreigner) who dwelt in the land also. But the mutual hatred of Jews and Samaritans, and Jews and Romans showed that the command stayed in the holy books. Jesus demanded that the law be *obeyed*.

The parable of the Good Samaritan is one of those immortal Lukan stories that captures the mind and the heart, while challenging the behaviour and lifestyle of the listener. Luke is so famous for his painting of word pictures, that the story carries visual appeal also. The present story follows the rule of three, where the emphasis lies with the third character, and the other two merely build up the story to the climax with the third. Jesus chose an everyday event in Palestine as the backdrop for His illustration of a neighbour.

The road from Jerusalem to Jericho passed through barren, desolate country, notorious for armed robbers, not only in Jesus' day, but right up to modern times. Since Jerusalem was about 800 metres above sea level, while Jericho lay 400 metres below sea level, the road went downhill all the way. For Luke, Jerusalem is God's city, and the city of destiny, through which all travellers must pass. Jericho, on the other hand, symbolized the worldly city, hot as hell in the summer, but the resort of the rich and the famous in the winter. It was the opposite of Jerusalem, the heavenly city. If the story is aimed at disciples in Jesus' time, and in the early Church, then Luke is saying that the man should not be travelling alone on the journey. He is also going in the wrong direction, and so falls victim to evil forces, and is left for dead. This is the spiritual condition of anyone who turns aside from *the way* to life that Jesus has marked out for us.

Three other travellers on the road encounter the dying victim, but two of them, a priest and a Levite, pass by on the other side of the road, obviously afraid of incurring ritual impurity by touching a dead body (Numbers 9:6–14), so they won't risk finding out if he is alive. These men can cite the authority of the Law for not serving their neighbour in his time of need (see Mark 7:8–13). This, notwithstanding the fact that the same Law required them to love their neighbour, so they are seen to pick and choose what they wish to obey at a given time. A Samaritan traveller came upon the victim, overcame all his religious and cultural animosity for Jews (see John 4:9), to love and care for this person as he would like someone do for him in the same situation. He bandaged the wounds, carried him on his own mount to the inn and had him looked after until he was well. Having paid for his keep, he was willing to take care of any extra expenses he may incur, thus he went way beyond what the Law required, and what would be accepted as *ordinary* service to a stranger. This is heroic love and service given to one's enemy (6:27–35).

This stranger was a hated Samaritan, an alien and a heretic in the eyes of the Jews, who considered them unclean and devil possessed (see John 8:48). He did not have the lawyers' learning, nor the dignity and status of the priesthood. Nevertheless, his love and service to the poor was kind, spontaneous, personal, disinterested and effective. Surely this is a reflection of Jesus' own ministry and that of His poor missionaries who will be strangers in foreign lands bringing the powerful love of God to people who were their natural and political enemies. The lawyer, like them, is challenged to live by the true interpretation of the Law, and to overcome his natural animosities in the service of others. The tables are turned completely when Jesus questions the lawyer about *becoming* a neighbour to others instead of selecting who will participate in his elite group (10:37).

The parable was so clear that the lawyer had to concede that the hated Samaritan (whom he refused to name!), proved by his actions that he was the true neighbour, the one who could be recognized by his fruits (6:43–45). Jesus gives the final blow when He challenged the lawyer to *"Go, and do the same yourself"* (10:37). This would involve a radical turning about in the thinking of the Jewish people towards the Samaritans and Gentiles, something that was both urgent and necessary for the Apostles and the Seventy-Two. This is the final answer to James and John who wanted to punish the Samaritans for their animosity in 9:51–56: Instead, they were to overcome their own nationalistic feelings and religious prejudice against them, and go and serve them as brothers instead. They did this after Pentecost (Acts 8).

Reading this story for the Christian disciple far removed from the Jewish-Samaritan problem in the twentieth century, the man on this journey represents the readers on their own life journey. If the pilgrims are freewheeling downhill, away from the place representing God's will and destiny for them, towards worldliness and sin, then they must not be surprised if they end up in trouble, and spiritually half-dead (see the demoniac and the prodigal son). The "Good Samaritan" who saves them from spiritual death is ultimately Jesus, whose perfect love (John 13:1, 15:13), heals, forgives and restores them. That love may be radiated by one of His disciples, and the person finds shelter and a home in the Church where the price of His salvation has been paid by Jesus Himself. We are all challenged to go and be such a neighbour and life-giver to some poor soul lost on its way through life.

Basic Priorites for Christians (10:38–13:21)

The last unit began and ended with a story about Samaritans, intended to open the minds and hearts of the disciples and missionaries. The next section begins in 10:38 *In the course of their journey* ... and deals with the centrality of our personal relationship with Jesus, the Word of God, and prayer as the motivating force of the Christian life.

It begins with a visit by Jesus to His friends Martha and Mary, who are already disciples of His (John 11). As hostess, Martha rendered the loving selfless service recommended in the Good Samaritan story, but Luke wishes to develop that theme and warn us that prayer and listening to the Word of God must not be sacrificed to such service. In fact prayer (11:1–13) and listening to the Word (10:39–40) are the power behind a successful apostolate. While Martha carried the burden of the work in caring for the special guest (or guests?) her sister, Mary, sat at Jesus' feet – which is the position of a disciple – listening to Jesus' teaching.

Martha's problem is threefold: she is overwhelmed by the demands of hospitality and table service. She has no help, and Jesus fails to notice her plight. She appeals to Him for fair play from her sister. As in the case of the lawyer Jesus penetrated to the source of the problem: "...*you worry and fret about so many things, and yet few are needed, indeed only one.*" Here He challenged Martha to see her priorities. If she gave time to prayer and listening to the Lord's Word, it would deal with the problem of being ... *distracted with all the serving* (10:40). Martha's fretting left her no time for the Lord Himself! Not that she didn't love Him, but there was no *time* to set aside to sit and listen to Him.

This reflects the Jerusalem community, gradually becoming overwhelmed by table service, due to the rapid growth of the young Church (Acts 6:1–6). The Twelve had no time for prayer and the Ministry of the Word, but they discerned the problem, took the appropriate action, and the Word of God continued to spread among the people (Acts 6:7). The lesson for pilgrims on the spiritual journey is to put Jesus in the centre of their lives and give priority to prayer and to the study of the Scriptures, so that their inner lives continue to grow and they have the strength and grace to deal with the pressures of the work they undertake for the Lord. There is also the fact that there are times – as in the Lord's special visit to this family – when we should go aside from the work to be alone with the Lord and with each other (9:10–11).

The Way of Prayer (11:1–13)

More than the other evangelists, Luke portrays Jesus as a man of prayer. He goes out of His way to show that prayer was the power behind Jesus' mission and miracles. He shows Jesus in prayer at all the significant moments of his life, for example, as a boy of twelve in 2:46–50, at His Baptism in 3:22, and in the wilderness in 4:1–13: Jesus attended synagogue services in 4:16–30 and 6:6–11: He gave priority to prayer every day (4:42–44). On occasion He spent whole nights in prayer to God 6:12–13, and kept some days for retreat 9:10: He was transfigured in prayer in 9:28–36, and rejoiced in God in ordinary things (10:21–22). Luke says that He would always be going off somewhere to pray in 5:16 and 11:1. He saturated Himself in prayer to prepare for the greatest test of His life in 21:37–38. He observed the liturgical feasts of the Jewish calendar in 22:7–20, and interceded for His disciples, especially Peter in 22:31–34: He agonized in prayer in Gethsemane and died in prayer and surrender to God in 23:33–46.

Jesus wanted His disciples to be photocopies of Himself (John 13:15–17), for He Himself is the model for prayer, service and obedience to the Will of God. If they are to take over the mission they need to turn to the source of power and authority in the spiritual life, namely union with God in prayer. Prayer makes it possible for us to become doers of the Word. The three fundamentals of the Christian life are thus introduced, namely active loving service, listening to the Word and personal prayer, because if life's first necessity is to listen to the Lord speak to us in His Word (10:38–42), the second is surely that we speak to Him in prayer (11:1–4).

After Jesus completed a period of prayer, His disciples requested that He teach them how to pray just as John the Baptist had taught his disciples (11:1). John's way of praying rested on the Old Covenant and is recognized as not adequate to express the inner life of the followers of Jesus, who, unlike John the Baptist, is *the Lord* (11:1). They have been shown (9:29–36, 10:17–24) that Jesus is the unique Son of God, as well as Lord, so they need a prayer-life that expresses this relationship of sonship and its responsibilities. Those who follow Jesus on *the way* need to pray for God's Kingdom to be fully revealed. Since they will be active missionaries there will be no time for lengthy or ostentatious prayers (see Matthew 6:5–6). The short prayer of Jesus' disciples contrasts with the empty and vain repetition of the pagan shrines they meet with on their journeys. Their brief prayer shines with simplicity and confidence before a loving Father. It seems obvious from the different formulations of Matthew and Luke that the "Our Father" was seen as a guide for "how to pray" rather than a fixed set of formulas requiring exact repetition: "You should pray like this" (Matthew 6:9).

In Luke's version of this prayer there are five requests, two reflecting God's interests, His Name and His Kingdom, and three reflecting our interests, namely daily bread, forgiveness and freedom from testing (temptation). Thus God's interests are served first as true priorities demand. Jesus prayed to God as Abba (my Daddy). This is the expression a small child uses for the male parent who is loving and gentle; the one who provides a sense of security, authority as well as the necessities of life. Jesus wants us to recognize our divine filiation when we pray. God is the Father of all people, but those who are baptized and filled with the Spirit (11:13) enjoy a special relationship with Him. Disciples can therefore, come boldly before the Throne of Grace (Hebrews 4:16). The fully mature response is given to this heavenly Father when Abba is combined with reverential awe and humility before God's transcendent greatness. This draws from us expressions of praise, gratitude, adoration and repentance before His awesome holiness.

Those who pray must remember the rules for proper relationship, and therefore put God's priorities for the Kingdom before personal requests. "Thy Kingdom come" says it all whether we are praying for the salvation of individuals or nations, for the process includes the healing and full growth of that person or nation. It also includes their happiness. Though Luke, unlike Matthew, does not include the formula "thy will be done", it is included with a proper understanding of the Kingdom. The coming of the Kingdom is God's Will, and the salvation of all nations is part of that great plan for planet earth. God will not force His Kingdom on us. It will come at our request! What urgency this puts upon the disciples of Jesus in every generation to love nations more than they love themselves. We pray for their highest good regardless of their personal or political hostility towards us (see Paul and Silas in Acts 16).

It is not enough that we respond lovingly to God as Father. God must be given first place in our lives and

His name reverenced and hallowed among us. Only then can we truly evaluate life's priorities and responsibilities. When God's name is devalued, when the sacred is dishonoured, then all other persons and relationships are devalued and dishonoured and life becomes cheap. When God's place is denied altogether, the sacredness of life, and the value of the person goes also, and we become "gods" of our own making, deciding who will live and who will die ... but let God's Kingdom be established in our hearts, homes, and nations, then God is given His throne and things return to normal, where the sacredness of each person is reverenced and society is restored.

Jesus' disciples, like Himself, are to become the solution to the needs of the human race. This they do by actively praying and working for God's Kingdom to be established in every age. If the Kingdom labourers (10:3) lose their fervour, anarchy follows eventually. This prayer of Jesus does not envision selfish interests, or a world centred on one's own family or "sphere" of activity. Like Jesus Himself we have to concern ourselves with others, and be missionary in our prayer as well as our work. Christians are essentially other-centred and their prayer gives life to others. They are aware that the coming of the Kingdom to their town and country will include them and their family. Elsewhere Jesus illustrated this: "*Set your hearts on his kingdom first, ...and all these other things will be given you as well*" (Matthew 6:33). If the disciples take care of God's Kingdom then God will take care of them, their families and all their needs.

Once God's priorities are seen to, the Christian community is allowed to request its own most important needs. The three requests which follow are all in the plural "us". The singular "me" is not considered. The daily needs of the community come under the heading of bread, the daily sustenance of the poor. Scripture

145

knows of three breads: ordinary bread (manna, Exodus
16), the bread of God's Word, and the bread of the
Eucharist (John 6). These are the breads that sustain the
community physically and spiritually. But as they move
out to the rest of the world on mission, the "us" extends
to foreign nations and peoples who also need God's
bread (4:4; Deuteronomy 8:3). When the Church gathers
to pray, one of the very necessary things (10:42) is that
we identify with the needs of the community in far off
lands, and pray for their daily needs so that the Kingdom
of God will be fully manifested to them.

We can now see that the prayer of the Father's unique
Son out on the lonely hillside morning and night, had to
do with "Thy Kingdom come... and daily needs for
everyone...". As we shall see in His Passover, the Kingdom came *through* Him, and the daily bread was provided
by Him. The forgiveness was His gift too, and He showed
the way to deal with the Tempter and to grapple with
evil. This prayer thus expresses a life lived for God and
neighbour. It is the Good Samaritan at the Inn of Prayer,
where healing is given to a broken and bruised humanity.
It is thus an expression of love for God, and the world
He wants to save (John 3:16).

The daily need for keeping personal relationships healthy
is the need to both give and receive forgiveness. Without
it the community will dry up (17:1–4), but in forgiving
others we are forgiven ourselves, and God's forgiveness
is manifested through us. We are all sinners, but in
imitation of Jesus we stand in solidarity with all who
repent and allow God's Kingdom to come into their lives
(5:27–32, 7:36–50).

The final request deals with life's testings. There is the
individual struggle to overcome sin and personal faults,
but there is also the spiritual warfare that the disciples
are plunged into for the sake of the Kingdom as they

come to grips with demonic evil in people (Acts 16:16–18), and the resistance to the gospel message from those who stand to lose power or position (Acts 14:19–22, 16:19–24, 17:5–9, 18:5–17). The testing that life sends is not meant to lead us into sin, but to make something great of us. It is under such pressures that the fruits of the Spirit develop – love, joy, peace, patience etc. (Galatians 5:20; see Sirach 2). The young community was expected to find its strength and inspiration from its fervent life of prayer just as Jesus did (Acts 2:42, 4:23–31).

The next two episodes deal with the perseverance required to pray and labour so continuously for the coming of the Kingdom and the conquering of evil. The prayer of the Church is so essential for the establishing of the Kingdom both for individuals and nations, that Jesus asked for persistence. His parable given to illustrate this speaks of a man who knocks up his friend at midnight because of his urgent need. In a one-roomed Palestinian village house the whole family slept on mats on the floor. No parent who had finally settled the children down for the night would be willing to step over them risking upset and the loss of a night's sleep for all, unless the knocking continued, and the lesser of two evils meant opening the locked door to answer the neighbour's need. The unwilling parent would give the person everything he wanted just to get rid of him (11:8)!

The lesson given is that disciples must persevere in prayer because God is very *unlike* our unwilling neighbours. He most certainly answers prayer: *"Ask, and it will be given to you; search, and you will find; knock, and the door will be opened to you"* (11:9). The problem of the one who prays is that God is unseen, and therefore we may doubt whether we are heard in prayer. Jesus gives assurance of God's loving acceptance of prayer for His children. For if a human father, weak, frail and sinful, will give the best he can to his children, then this is merely an illustration of the love the heavenly Father has, He who wants always to give more than we ask for (Ephesians 3:21). Instead of just giving us gifts, He gives us His Spirit who is the source of all the gifts and graces we need to further the Kingdom. Jesus wants His disciples to have the same anointing with power that He had Himself (3:22, 4:14; Acts 1:4–5, 2:1–4).

The problem of praying the way Jesus wants is that we may not see results soon enough, and give up in discouragement. Hence Luke emphasizes the persistence in prayer day-in and day-out, year-in and year-out. He will repeat the lesson in 18:1–8 using another parable. While disciples must persist in prayer for the Kingdom there is also the personal quest for God in their own lives, the asking, searching and knocking until one finds a deep personal relationship with God. In this context it is comforting to note Luke's emphasis that the searcher *always* finds, and the door to personal union with God *is* opened to the one who knocks sincerely and persistently. Revelation 3:20–22 gives the other side of the coin. Here it is the Lord who is knocking at the door of our hearts, seeking entrance. If this seeking and knocking is going on on both sides of the door there must be wonderful results!

The Lord's Power (11:14–36)

After treating of the Lord's Word in 10:38–42, and the Lord's Prayer in 11:1–13, we now focus on the Lord's Power, and finally on the Lord's Authority in 11:37–54. We, the readers, know from 3:22 and 4:14 that the Holy Spirit is the Source of this power, which enables Jesus to face and overcome the forces of evil at work in the world, and in individual lives. But Jesus' opponents do not accept this, as we shall see. As disciples, we must not only listen to the Lord's Word, but respond by speaking to the Lord in prayer (11:1–13), and by obeying the Word (11:28). Yet Satan keeps many people bound in their inner selves, unable to communicate with God, maybe not even believing in God's existence. They are like silent prisoners in a strong man's palace (11:21). Into this tragedy Jesus came, armed with the power of God, to attack and destroy the enemy's grip on the human race, and to expose and inactivate the tricks he uses to capture his victims (11:21–22).

When Jesus exorcized a dumb man, the people were amazed to discover that the departure of the evil spirit restored the man's speech. Their shock related to the revelation of the connection between the two things, and the fact that Jesus dealt with it with such ease. If the Devil could hold a man bound in this way, then Jesus could unbind him. In fact the whole ministry of Jesus can be seen as the unbinding of the human race from its chains of slavery. He unbound the sinners from their sins (John 8:34), the lepers from their leprosy, the demoniacs from their demon possession. He unbound the prostitutes from their prostitution, the tax collectors from their love of money, and the sick from their sickness. Even for those who were dead, he unbound the cords of death.

The interested onlooker has to see this as a work of God: *"You will be able to tell them by their fruits"*. Jesus kept His promise in 4:18 to set the captives free from whatever constituted captivity for them. We shall see the other side of the coin in the Passion as those who reject the power of God (the Finger of God) as the Source of Jesus' miracles become more and more aggressive in their opposition to Him. Here in 11:15 they want to attribute this power to Satan himself.

There, in the Passion, they will *bind Jesus* in arrest and physical captivity. Then they will further try to bind

Him emotionally by hatred, rejection and torture. It culminates with His binding to the cross, where He is bound in such a way that, humanly speaking, it was impossible for Him to break free from their fetters. At last they bound Him in death itself. They sealed Him in a tomb and, according to Matthew 27:62–66 they even put a guard on it to make sure He did not break free. Yet God raised Him from the dead, breaking the cords of death, and breaking the seal of the tomb. He unbound Jesus from every restriction of earth, making Him free from all limitations of time and space. It was then, from His glorious freedom in resurrection, that He bestowed the gift of the Spirit on the Church, so that it could begin its work of unbinding the nations from their slaveries of body and spirit.

The reaction of the people to this miracle is more important than appears at first sight. We are challenged to look at the reasons *why* human beings do not pray, do not turn to God for help, and we discover that the enemy has them bound to the wrong type of silence. We have just been told in 11:1–13 to shake the heavens with our cries for help, but this is not possible if a spirit of dumbness holds us bound. Disciples must set them free by "the Finger of God", an expression which means the Power of the Holy Spirit in a concrete direct intervention of God (see Ezekiel 8:1–13; Exodus 8:19; 1 Chronicles 28:12). People have to be helped to enter into a personal prayer life with God. The enemy is determined to keep them out of it by all kinds of tricks. Like Jesus we must be determined to set them free.

Another important aspect of the reaction is that we must not facilely accept signs and wonders as many appear to do today. We must penetrate the source of the power, and find out if it is indeed the Finger of God, or yet another elaborate deception to keep us away from the Kingdom of God. Jesus admitted that the Jewish exorcists had power and results (11:19), just as today with our deeper knowledge of the complexities of the human psyche, there are reports of healing coming from different sources. It was preposterous to claim that Satan might work against himself in Jesus' exorcisms, for that would destroy the hold he had over his own palace (11:21) and the kingdoms of the world (4:6), and would nullify Jesus' struggle with him in the wilderness. But if it really *was* the Spirit of God at work in Jesus, then the complete downfall of Satan was imminent (10:18) in Jesus' coming victory on Calvary. The prince of devils, properly called Beelzebub, would suffer a major defeat in the *exodos* of Jesus (11:21–22).

A solemn warning is issued to the opponents of Jesus that if they are so blind as to call Good "evil", and attribute to Beelzebub the work of the Holy Spirit (12:10), then they are against Jesus, and opposing God's plans for them personally, and for the salvation of the world. He would not allow them to remain "sitting on the fence". They must decide for or against him, and take the consequences of their decision. There can be no neutrality in the spiritual warfare between Jesus and Satan. He also issued a warning to those who are healed. It is not enough to have evil removed from your life and just remain empty. A basic principle of life is that nature abhors a vacuum. The refusal to change leaves an opening for an even greater infestation of evil (11:24–26). Jesus' healings and exorcisms are not magic, but require the active cooperation of repentance and a change of lifestyle.

As Jesus spoke a woman praised Him and marvelled at the mother that bore such fruit (11:27–28). But He replied that while His mother was indeed blessed, the real blessing was kept for *those who hear the word of God and keep it!* (11:28, 6:46–49). Hearing the Word was illustrated in the case of Martha and Mary (10:38–42) just as the doing of it was seen in the Good Samaritan (10:37). No matter how privileged were those in physical relationship to Jesus, *the REAL family in the Kingdom* consisted of people from every race and nation who were bonded spiritually by the listening heart of Mary (10:42) and the obedient heart of a true disciple (1:38). Since both of these qualities were present in Jesus' mother (1:26–38), she alone joins those truly blessed both by physical and spiritual relationship to Jesus.

Jesus' critics would do well to join the disciples instead of opposing Him, and testing Him by demanding a sign from heaven (11:16), as if the intervention of God in His ministry did not constitute sign enough! As the crowd has increased by now (11:29), Jesus addresses the nation rather than the small group, calling it a wicked generation (11:29), perversely demanding a definitive sign from heaven, thus testing God as their forebears had done in the wilderness. Disciples know that if they hear and obey the word of God, they will *produce* signs by the power of the Spirit working through them (9:1–3; 10:17). Jesus refused to give such a sign, for He never worked miracles for their own sake or just to impress (4:9–12). It was not God's way to force belief by the spectacular, the unnatural and the unnecessary. Jesus knew that people love spectacles. They enjoy them, are frightened, but rarely changed by them. When that spectacle is over they need another one, an even greater one, to impress them.

Besides, a sign had been given before, and it was still valid. It was the sign of Jonah the prophet. Just as Jonah *became a sign* to the Ninevites, so the Son of Man will *become* a sign to this generation (11:30). Jesus has already been presented to us as a sign by Simeon (2:35), a sign which would be rejected, and in which its rejection will expose the secrets hidden in human hearts. Jesus is already rejected by some here, but will be rejected by all in His Passion, which will expose the secrets of God's heart as well as ours. Jonah became a sign to the Ninevites by his miraculous deliverance from death after three days (Jonah 2:1), and then emerged to deliver a powerful message of ultimate judgement on the city, if it did not repent. But these Gentiles did receive God's (reluctant, in this case!) messenger. They heard and obeyed the Word of God and received deliverance and God's Mercy *en masse*. Now, a greater one than Jonah is here. They will witness His great sign in the Resurrection, but will the nation repent?

Luke, in keeping with his usual plan, now gives a female example to balance the story of Jonah. Both characters had to make a long journey, Jonah to preach the gospel, and the Gentile Queen of the South to come to Israel to hear it from an equally reluctant preacher, namely Solomon. Yet both the queen and the Ninevites received what God wanted to give them. God saw to it that they were not short-changed because of the weakness or sinfulness of the messenger. (We saw this principle in Elizabeth's case in 1:23–25). Since Jesus is greater than Jonah and Solomon (11:31–32) those to whom Jesus preached will receive a more severe judgement.

For, on Judgement Day, God in His justice will take into account the opportunities each person and nation had for hearing the Word of God. For those to whom much was given much was expected. The generation that refused to take God's Word from the greatest Witness of them all, the Son Himself, could expect the severest judgement. Israel never liked being reminded of her responsibilities, but she basked in her privileges, hence the prophets always had a rough ride. She would have to learn from history. Foreigners had recognized God speaking to them through human instruments before (4:25–27), and they would do so again through the Christian preachers.

153

Luke finishes this section by presenting Jesus as a lamp like those outside the doors of Greek houses, which shone on all who wished to enter (8:16). The light of Jesus Himself and His mission is clear for all to see. Neither He nor His message is hidden (11:33). Nevertheless, light is only useful to those who can see, hence the lamp of the body is the eye (11:34). If we still remain in interior darkness, prisoners of Satan's kingdom, we cannot perceive the light of Christ all around us. But if we allow Jesus to set us free, He will lighten up our whole being and the day of judgement can be faced without fear, for it will be a journey into the fullness of eternal Light (11:35–36).

The Lord's Authority (11:34–54)

Up to this point we have been shown that hearing the Word of God and putting it into practice is what constitutes true blessedness. Now Luke goes on to show that "doing" the Word, or obeying the Word, implies submission of the heart, not just an external observance. If external observance is devoid of internal content, it becomes empty legalism resulting in pride and self-righteousness. The setting of the scene is a meal, where Jesus is the guest of a Pharisee (7:36–50). Again He is criticized – in the last instance because of His exorcisms – and here for His behaviour at table, for He neglected the ritual observance of washing His hands before a meal (11:37–39). As Mark 7:3 tells us, this ritual washing was part of the tradition of the Elders, the Oral Law, which the Pharisees saw as just as binding as the Torah, the Written Law. Jesus ignored many of these practices to the chagrin of the Pharisees, who found here an opportunity to criticize Him for His unconventional and lax approach to matters they considered sacred and binding.

Jesus' response was a full scale attack on the dangers of the Pharisaic religion. Its strong emphasis on external observance held the danger of neglecting the inner spiritual dimension of life, as if the quantity of garden herbs offered in the Temple were an issue for God (11:42)! His attack was couched in six woes, three aimed at the Pharisees in general and three at the Scribes. The effect is cumulative and devastating, and offers a great contrast to the enlightened disciples (11:33–36), who are happy and free to obey God's Word (11:28). Disciples refuse to get tangled in such trivialities, while ignoring the issues of the Kingdom of God, such as justice and the Love of God (11:42), a reminder of the behaviour of the priest and the Levite in the parable of the Good Samaritan.

As religious leaders the Pharisees are full of pride and self righteousness (11:43–44). Their "light" was darkness, and they could not see the Light that was Jesus and His teaching. Their inner eye was clouded with greed, extortion and wickedness (11:40), so that their perception, let alone obedience to the Word of God, was also distorted. They reminded Jesus of those unmarked tombs that people accidentally walked on, thus incurring ritual impurity without adverting to it! They were unclean on the inside where purity really mattered, and this *was* an issue for God (11:39; Romans 3:9–18). They had neglected "the inside of the cup" in their zeal for external washing, but God wanted inner purity and holiness. External rituals were mere pointers to this (11:39).

The cure for this inner greed, extortion and wickedness was almsgiving, which demanded a flow of love from the heart to one's neighbour. Jesus says that this cleanses the heart, and therefore renders the external washing superfluous (11:41–42). In other words Jesus disregards these rituals whichever way the argument went, because they spent their energy on irrelevant matters while neglecting their duty of justice to their neighbour and their loving service to both God and neighbour. Jesus would not countenance their indifference to the rights of the poor.

The Scribes who were experts at the Law reacted to Jesus' condemnation of the Pharisees, for it was their casuistry that was responsible for multiplying so many of the regulations: "*Master, . . . when you speak like this you insult us too*" (11:45). Jesus rounded on them for loading heavy burdens of more and more regulations on lay people, but they had no compassion for anyone who broke under such stress (Acts 15:10). Their own skill in casuistry enabled themselves to escape these burdens while giving the appearance of exact observance (11:46).

Matthew 11:28–30 is Jesus' specific invitation to the poor, broken and heavily laden lay people to come *to him* and have their burdens lifted. The only burden He would place on their backs was that of loving God and neighbour. The lay people could not cope with these myriad regulations. One would need to be a lawyer, highly skilled at law, to even comprehend them. The people had to get on with daily life, so they unknowingly broke many of these laws and were despised by the Pharisees and the Scribes. John 7:48 says: "*This rabble knows nothing about the Law – they are damned*". Yet this same text goes on to show that they did not practice what they preached (John 7:49–52).

The outward exact observance is now compared to their refusal to hear the Word of God from any of God's prophets or messengers. It wasn't just Jesus they rejected. History bore abundant evidence of their refusal to submit to the teaching of the prophets. Even a cursory reading of the books of the Old Testament prophets reveals this (see 2 Chronicles 24:19–21; Acts 7:51; 1 Thessalonians 2:14–16). They thought that by building tombs to the prophets that they somehow made reparation for their ancestors' harsh treatment of them. They, like Christians today with regard to the saints, canonized the prophets when they were dead and no longer able to disturb their consciences. But no! Jesus claims that their attitude to religion is killing it, both for themselves and for the people. The tomb was a good symbol of that dead response.

The issue in religion, for Jesus, is that we must hear the Word of God *and keep it*. Both in the Old and New Testaments, God sent prophets and apostles to Israel (11:49-50), but they were all – including Jesus and His Apostles later – persecuted, rejected and killed (see Acts 7, 8:1-3, 9:1-2, 12:1-9). The present generation held more responsibility than all others because their prophet was Jesus, the Son of God, the long-awaited and prayed-for Messiah. To reject Him and His Word was equivalent to filling up the cup of iniquity of the nation in all of her history, which is a frightening concept (11:49-51). Perhaps Luke is saying that the coming of Jesus was the culmination of divine revelation for Israel and her rejection of Jesus was her definitive rejection of God's Word. The Wisdom of God had spoken through all the wise and holy men of old, but Jesus *is the Wisdom of God* (11:49). To reject that is to bring ultimate judgement upon themselves. Perhaps there is a hint here that Luke sees the destruction of Jerusalem in 70 AD as the end of Israel's "old" history in the sense of the Old Testament (21:32)?

The final woe to the lawyers is the most damning of all. Their duty was to unlock the secrets of God's Word for the people through their expertise, but Jesus claimed that they had taken away the *key of knowledge* altogether. Not only had they not entered into true knowledge themselves, but their casuistry prevented others from doing so either (11:52; see Isaiah 22:22; Revelation 1:18, 3:7, 9:1, 20:1). Jesus thus accuses the Scribes of preventing the people from entering the Kingdom of God, and of receiving true knowledge of God from the Holy Scriptures. Instead

157

of opening the Scriptures for the people, they had effectively closed them by an exegesis devoid of spiritual content. This is the frightening power of Scripture scholars which brings the judgement of God upon them. It is no surprise at all that the unrepentant Scribes and Pharisees attacked Jesus furiously after this outburst, and had it in for Him from then onwards (11:53–54).

Christians in the modern age would do well not to read this text as applying only to religious leaders in Jesus' time. Human nature is no different today, and we have reproduced the very same attitudes that Jesus condemned. Have we read the Word of God and put it into practice? Or have we gone in for rituals, laws and external observance which may be devoid of internal content? Have our scholars taken away the key of knowledge, giving lay people the impression that *they* would never understand the inner depth of the Word of God or its complexities? Has religion become so sophisticated that it is only for the rich? Will the accumulated sins of Christendom be visited on our generation? God never changes. He is the same yesterday, today and forever. It is a good escape route to round on the Pharisees of Jesus' time as the "baddies", when the Word of God is given to enlighten us, the readers, *now*. As the Queen of the South and the Ninevites will rise up to condemn Israel in Jesus' day, will the Third World rise up to condemn us for our international injustice to them, which shows how little love of God we Christians really have? I believe we have reason to tremble, for the written Word of God stands as a witness against us, just as it did for Israel (see John 7:45).

Readiness for the Coming Crisis (12:1–13:21)

Unlike the Scribes and Pharisees the ordinary people are so eager to hear the Word of God that they gather in

such numbers that they are treading on one another (12:1).
It must have been frightening for the disciples to experience
the rejection and fury of the leaders and the contrast of
the extraordinary enthusiasm of the crowds. If the leaders
had turned against Jesus then persecution and trouble were
inevitable. They were obviously afraid and Jesus addressed
them as "disciples" in 12:1 and "friends" in 12:10.

First of all Jesus warned His disciples not to copy the
evil influence (yeast) of the Pharisees, on the grounds
that one day everything will be uncovered, and all truth
revealed (12:1–2). Hypocrisy is utter folly when one
considers that God sees what we are like on the inside
anyway – and all the time! (see Psalm 139). Everything
is already open to God, but Judgement Day will open it
up to everyone else! What *is* this hypocrisy that Jesus
condemned? The Greek word for hypocrite is *hupokrites*,
and it means one who answers (or answers back?). Its
secondary meaning is an actor on stage. The Greek and
Roman actors wore large masks and spoke through mechanical devices to augment the voice, so the word came
to be used for a dissembler.

When Jesus used it He would never have experienced
Graeco-Roman plays, so it seems that He thought a
hypocrite was one more concerned with his image and
reputation than with truth and goodness. They want their
"holy" image to be appreciated by others, as in 18:9–14.
Hypocrite meant one who kept up the outward forms of
religion to the neglect of the inner reality, as described
in the last passage (11:37–54; see 2 Timothy 3:1–5). Isaiah
spoke about it in Isaiah 29:13: *"this people approaches
me only in words, honours me only with lip service while
its heart is far from me ..."*

For the disciples of Jesus, the Word of God tears the
masks of pretence from us, thus releasing us from false
security. But there is always the danger that we will

pretend in a different way – by refusing to share the light that is within us with others (12:3). This, too, is a denial of truth, for disciples must go public with the revelation of Jesus if the Kingdom of God is to be established. Lovingly addressing them as His friends, Jesus acknowledges their fear of persecution on account of the Word (12:4; Matthew 13:21). He knows that all authentic prophets are persecuted, and sometimes killed (11:47–51). He knows this fate awaits Him, His Apostles and thousands of His followers in every generation. Their fear is understandable, yet He begs them to take their eyes off themselves and look to God and His merciful Love towards all His creatures.

The persecutors can only kill the body. That is the limit of their power, but not the end of a person's life (8:52–56). The soul or inner person lives forever, and it is He who determines its ultimate destiny that should be feared, if there is a question of fear (12:5). Yet, the heavenly Father takes care of every hair on their heads, and every tiny sparrow, so there is no need to fear such a caring, loving God at all (12:6–7). This plea is for the disciples to find their security in God's loving acceptance of them.

Once they feel secure in their relationship with God, Jesus can challenge them to risk going public for Him. He declares that if they openly acknowledge Him before their generation that He, the Son of Man, will acknowledge them on Judgement Day. Their fate on that day is intimately bound up with their fearless confession or denial of Jesus on earth, especially at times of persecution. To be disowned by Jesus in the presence of God's angels as witness, would be too high a price to pay for dissembling in a human court. Perhaps Luke is here trying to motivate persecuted Christians to a steadfast confession of Jesus even at the price of their lives (Acts 14:22)?

Nevertheless the disciples remain weak and human with the distinct possibility of failing at the time of crisis. Would they be forgiven for denying Jesus? This is answered in the affirmative in 12:10, and later in the story of Peter's denials: *"Everyone who says a word against the Son of Man will be forgiven"*, but there is one unforgiveable sin, that of blaspheming against the Holy Spirit. This is a knowing denial of Jesus and the source of his life and ministry, namely, the Holy Spirit. It amounts to a radical denial of their own divine life and giftedness through the same Spirit (Romans 8; Galatians 5:22). This would cut a person off from his own divine roots, a conscious and wicked rejection of the saving power and grace of God towards humanity. Such apostasy is irreversible without a direct intervention of God.

The poor, weak, persecuted and frightened disciples will discover when put on trial for their lives that the Holy Spirit will be their Advocate, or defence lawyer (John 14:26). He will speak to them, enlighten them and teach them what to say (Acts 4:8–12). They will not need learned arguments or a well-worked out theology to defend themselves. The Holy Spirit given to them by Jesus after His resurrection, will give them wisdom to confound their judges, as illustrated in the case of Stephen in Acts 7:

The Problem of Security (12:13–40)

For those on the spiritual journey through life, as well as the actual missionary journeys, the problem of where you find your security is a big one, and needs to be settled if one is to be free to serve God. Jesus now challenges us all to hold life lightly, and keep our security in God. This section, like that of 10:38–42, begins with a family dispute. In that case, Martha asked Jesus to intervene in the proper distribution of work and responsibility within the family. Here He is asked to settle the proper distribution of material goods in an inheritance case (12:13). 11:31 presented Jesus as greater than Solomon, whose wisdom was so famous that his name was given to the whole Wisdom Tradition in Israel. This "Solomon" refused to settle the dispute. He was not called to be the judge or arbitrator of material things, but of the lives and destiny of the human race (see Acts 10:42). As such He is concerned with the roots of our being, and those things that we desire but can destroy us.

Jesus addressed the crowd: *"Watch, and be on your guard against avarice of any kind, for a man's life is not made secure by what he owns, even when he has more than he needs"* (12:15). The word he used for avarice is *pleonexia*, which means the desire to have more and more. Here the "more and more" refer to material possessions, but "avarice of any kind" covers the whole of life and the desire to have more and MORE pleasure, more and MORE ease, more and MORE power, more and MORE money and so on. It is something that can destroy life, and as such is condemned everywhere in the New Testament (Colossians 3:5; Ephesians 4:19, 5:5–6; Galatians 5:24; Romans 2:29; 2 Peter 1:19).

Disciples must grow into a true sense of values and recognize that their *real* life cannot be measured in terms of material possessions (12:22–34). The danger of having more than one needs is that it can insulate us from God and leave us poverty-stricken in the things that really matter. To illustrate the point Jesus told the story of a farmer who had bumper harvests and decided to pull down his existing barns and build bigger ones to store all this grain for the future. When the restoration was complete he settled down to a life of ease and pleasure saying: *"My soul, you have plenty of good things laid by for many years to come; take things easy, eat, drink, and have a good time"* (12:17–19).

This man is called a fool, which does not mean he is unintelligent, for the world would praise him for what he did. Psalm 49:18 expresses this: *"The soul he made so happy while he lived – 'look after yourself and men will praise you' – will join the company of his ancestors who will never see the light of day again"*. It shows him making *unwise* decisions, for he takes neither God nor his neighbour into account in his decisions, and he fails utterly in the great commandment to love. He is not only rich, but self-centred and greedy. Like the Pharisees in 11:37–54, he fails to release and cleanse his soul with almsgiving, which would have made him rich in the sight of God.

He is also unwise in not taking into account the shortness of life and its ultimate goal. He presumes that material abundance constituted security and happiness. Had he been given time to test out his theory of "eat, drink and be merry" he would have discovered that these, too, have consequences in this life as well as the next!

However, his life is cut short in sudden death (12:20), ensuring that the goods he so carefully guarded went into the hands of others *anyway*, but without benefit to his soul, as they would have had, had they been given in alms. The parable illustrates that to live for oneself is to arrive at "dead-end street" (12:21; see Revelation 3:17–18; 1 Timothy 6:17–19; Sirach 5:1–10, 11:18–20, and many psalms). This poor man *only* had material wealth, but nothing of any lasting substance, certainly nothing that could outlast life. He is one of the rich that are sent empty away (1:52). Material goods are given to us to be used wisely and responsibly. When we have more than enough we have the obligation to look after the materially poor (2 Corinthians 8:9–15).

Earthly Possessions vs. Heavenly Treasure (12:22–32)

Unlike the rich fool, disciples are not to be concerned about material things, for their security lies elsewhere, in their relationship with a loving Father in Heaven, who will take care of all their needs, as they work for His Kingdom. While the foolish of this world concentrate on "making their first million", and acquiring all the trappings that go with it, the disciples will tramp the highways and byways of the world for God and His Kingdom. Their two worlds are in stark contrast. Those on the side of Jesus must gradually learn to live a life of great simplicity, service and love. They will not spend their life's energy on food, clothes and material things, but on life-giving pursuits.

Through them the Holy Spirit's divine energy will be released on an unbelieving, materialistic world, to begin a process of growth and transformation that will eventually cause history to be rewritten (Acts 17:6). They will learn to be as free as the birds, to travel anywhere for God, unencumbered by the baggage of materialism and false security (12:23). Like the flowers in the field they will be clothed in the glory of the Lord, in the gifts and fruits of the Spirit (Galatians 5:22; 1 Corinthians 12–14), a glory that outshines the merely material and fading glory of the great Solomon (12:27–28; 2 Peter 1:3–11).

The mutual relationship that exists between the disciples and the Lord is that if they take care of His Kingdom and its needs, He will take care of them and their personal concerns. Oh wonderful exchange (12:31)! It is the outsiders, the unbelievers, who set their hearts on food and drink and allow worry over "making ends meet" sap their vital energy. Jesus warned that this was not to happen among them who were being cared for by the Loving

Father. As the Lord's little flock, the Father has promised *to give them* the Kingdom, which is their heart's desire, so they are guaranteed "job satisfaction" (12:32).

All this frees them to hold life lightly and get their priorities in the right order. *"If the smallest things, therefore are outside your control, why worry about the rest?"* So many of the daily events of life are outside our control. The weather cannot be guaranteed for that special day when you need sunshine. The road conditions may be icy the very morning you must travel. Traffic delays, storms, disasters, both political and economic, not to speak of earthquakes and famines ... It is senseless to worry when so much is beyond our control. Trust in God is the antidote to all anxiety and fear. When achieved, it results in tranquillity and peace. "All will be well" said the mystic Julian of Norwich, "and all manner of things will be well" (see Psalm 39:5–6).

The New Testament writers criticize those believers who hover between fear and hope, and never seem to find rest in God (see 1 Peter 5:7; James 4:4–10; Philippians 4:4–7; 1 Timothy 6:17–19). They are the Lord's little flock (12:32) weak, and few in number, facing the rich and powerful of the world. Their fear is understandable, but they must realize *who it is* that shepherds them (see John 10 and 21). They are like the remnant of Israel addressed by Isaiah 41:8–20 and 43:1–7: While unbelievers seek the kingdom, power and glory of this world, the Father bestows His Kingdom on His little flock, not because of their merits, but because of His great love (10:25; 23:51).

If the disciples are to be open to receive the Kingdom from the Father, they must sell their possessions and give alms, unlike the Pharisees who loved their money, possessions and power (11:41, 12:33, 16:14–15). This will give them treasure in heaven, free from both moth and thief, unlike the rich fool (12:16–21). Whatever it is we choose as our treasure, we give our attention and life-energy to. We put our hearts into it. It absorbs us. Jesus wants our life-energy to be given to things that outlast life, things that are life-giving so that we have a deep understanding that it is worth the effort.

Vigilance for the Master's Return (12:35–48)

Not only are the disciples on a journey with Jesus to Jerusalem and His *exodos* that will be accomplished there, but the pilgrim Church journeys through history to the Parousia, or Return of the Lord, and the individual makes the spiritual journey also. Like those who are involved in that first Exodus under Moses, these pilgrims must be constantly dressed for action, always vigilant and ready (12:35; Exodus 12:11; Mark 13:33–37). Hence they cannot be encumbered by attachments to material things. It is this journey and expectation of the Lord's return which puts material considerations into perspective (see 1 Peter 1:13). The Return is likened to a wedding feast where the servants keep the house prepared and lit up in expectation of the Master's return with his bride. They would be ready to open the doors for this joyous return.

A flashback to 11:5–10 will remind us that when we knock at the Lord's door in prayer He promises to open up to us joyfully in response to our real needs. Here we see the other side of the coin. When He knocks on the door of the hearts of disciples – individually and collectively – He expects us to be ready to answer His call (12:36), whether it be for mission or the Parousia. Thus vigilance, and listening to the Lord in prayer is essential to the work of the Church. If we fail in this, we may find ourselves locked out when the time for Him to open the *only door that counts* comes, like the Foolish Virgins in Matthew 25:1–13.

Using imagery similar to the washing of the feet in John 13:4–5, Luke says that the vigilant and ready disciples will be surprised to find their Master behave very differently to human lords. He will serve and honour them at the Messianic Banquet. Here the Master will gird Himself, sit them down to table and wait on them (12:37–38; 22:27). The problem is that the disciples do not know the timing of the Second Coming, so they must constantly remain prepared.

It could be late, as Luke uses the imagery of the second or third watch of the night to explain (12:39). The Jews measured the night in three watches, so the long night of waiting for the Master's Return could extend a long way into the future. Obviously the early Christians were impatient for the Parousia, but the final outcome of the Kingdom was still a long way off, and there was a long day's labour awaiting them in the Lord's vineyard (10:2). In the interval, they were in charge of the Lord's Household, and must remain in readiness for His return which will be as sudden and unannounced and shocking as that of an intruder in the night (12:39–40; see 1 Thessalonians 5:2–11; Revelation 3:3; 2 Peter 3:8–11).

Peter wondered if this teaching was meant only for the disciples and believers or whether it was for universal application (12:42). The Lord's reply makes it clear that those servants who have responsible leadership roles in the Church have the greater responsibility to be vigilant, prayerful and prepared. The greater privilege gives them greater responsibility before God for the flock. They are not lords, or owners, but stewards of the Master's property, committed to feed the whole of the Master's Household (12:42). Fidelity will be rewarded by greater responsibility over the Household (12:43; see John 21) But if, like the Rich Fool, they abuse their responsibility during the Master's long delay, particularly if they lose faith and resort to ill-treating others and behaving as the unbelievers *eating and drinking and getting drunk* (12:46), then their Master will find them unprepared for His coming and they will find their ultimate destiny among the unbelievers, because of their unfaithfulness (12:46).

While the main thrust of this section is for Church leaders, the followers of Jesus must realize that they are *all* stewards of God's gifts and graces, each one according to his own measure, and chosen way of life (see 1 Corinthians 4:1–5; Titus 1:5–9; 1 Peter 4:10–11). Each one is responsible for whatever part of the Lord's vineyard has been entrusted to him, just like the executive of a company has privileges to go with the grave responsibilities of his post. On a more general level, human beings are stewards of the planet entrusted to their care, and must take responsibility for their use or abuse of it. Like the Rich Fool we will leave Planet Earth as empty as we came to it. Earth's Creator will require an account from us. Earth's gifts were given for our use and we should have used them for the good of all.

With a sober eye to the future Jesus (and Luke) face the possibility of the loss of faith and love in a believer. If disciples are unfaithful to their trust and use natural goods and spiritual privileges just to indulge themselves, if they abuse power and responsibility, if they cheat in their dealings with others, if they oppress the poor and persecute the true servants of God – like the Pharisees and lawyers of 11:47–51 – then they *prove* themselves *unbelievers*, and they will be dealt with accordingly, because: *"The servant who knows what his master wants, but has not even started to carry out those wishes, will receive very many strokes of the lash"* (12:47–48).

Mention of the punishment which will be meted out at the Second Coming leads Jesus to state two principles on which the judgement will proceed. First, the more knowledge of the Lord's Will there was the more severe shall the punishment be. Second, the more entrusted to a person, the more will be demanded of him. Like our Jewish counterparts, Christians prefer their privileges to their responsibilities, and don't like the idea of a day of reckoning at all! Jesus in 23:34, Peter in Acts 3:17, and Paul in Acts 17:30 all speak of those who acted in ignorance, and therefore could expect mercy and forgiveness from the Lord. Yet Israel, as a nation, was one to whom much had been given.

A Sign of Division (12:49–53)

With regard to transitory material things Jesus refused to become judge or divider of property (12:14). Nevertheless, He is the ultimate judge and divider of the human race at the Second Coming (12:35–48). Here we see that this ultimate division begins in the here-and-now, as we take sides for or against Jesus, who *is* the sign from heaven (2:34). He Himself provokes the coming crisis by His person and mission. In order to cast the Fire of God's love, life and power upon the earth at Pentecost (Acts 2), Jesus must undergo a Baptism of blood martyrdom, the thought of which leaves Him anxious and distressed as He looks forward to His journey's end and life's goal (9:31, 13:32, 22:15; see John 12:27). He said that He came to cast fire upon the earth, and that He was anxious to see it blazing across the globe. Fire is a symbol frequently used by Israel's prophets to denote purification and punishment. It is also an eschatological symbol of judgement, where the good are cleansed and the wicked punished (see Isaiah 1:25; Zechariah 13:9; Malachi 3:2–4, 19).

The goal of Jesus' journey and His *exodos* plunge the disciples into the fiery furnace of persecution (see Sirach 2), while life's events accomplish this purification for

169

the individual cooperating with God's grace. John the Baptist had promised in 3:16 that Jesus would baptize His disciples – and therefore, His Church – with the Holy Spirit *and Fire*. We were guaranteed the cross of cleansing and purification, and if we cooperate with it, we should not need the fire of judgement (see 1 Corinthians 3:11–15).

Jesus came to bring the Messianic peace by reconciling the human race to God through His sacrifice on Calvary. But this does not mean the absence of struggle for either the individual or the world. Neither is it Utopia. In fact the peace aspect will remain unseen for the most part, hidden in the hearts of faithful believers. It is the divisions caused in families and society that will be seen and appear to contradict the promise of Jesus. The peace (2:14; John 14:27) is an interior grace given to those who hear the Word of God and keep it. But the tensions resulting from the rejection of Jesus and His Word will result in persecution (21:16), as Jesus, the double-edged sword of the Word of God (see Revelation 1:12–19, 19:13–16) is the cause of the fall and the rise of many in Israel and beyond (2:34). The social revolution caused by Jesus' Word can be seen in a simple illustration: His good news for the poor is bad news for the rich. As a friend of sinners, He was the enemy of self-righteous religious people.

Blindness to God's Signs (12:54–59)

The disciples in Jesus' time, and the Church today, must discern what is going on in the world, and make decisions that are relevant to God's Will. Jesus appeals to them to read the signs of the times in the same way as they read the weather (12:54–55). The farmers were always vigilant concerning the weather because of its effect on crops, but why not be concerned about the looming storm that will envelop the nation? If only they would look at *the sign*, Jesus in their midst (2:34), and the reaction of the leadership to Him they would know that a politico-religious storm was brewing. If they would discern God's ways with Israel from their history, they would know that the rejection of the prophet and his message occasioned judgement for Israel. They had demanded a sign from heaven, but their unseeing eyes could not see it was there with them in Jesus.

Jesus called them hypocrites for devoting their energy to the trivialities of everyday life and religious ritual (11:37–54) when "God's time" had come upon them. They were experiencing the greatest divine visitation in their history, but were blind to it. Luke uses the word *KAIROS* for time, instead of *CHRONOS*, which means measured time as we read it on a clock, and "chronology" which concerns one thing happening after another. *Kairos* is God's time, and here it refers to His timing of the Messianic fulfilment (see 2 Corinthians 6:2). This was, therefore, the most important moment in their history which it would be disastrous to neglect.

Because they cannot discern God's *kairos*-time, they consequently cannot discern God's Will for them at this moment. This discernment is the critical ability to distinguish from the relevant data what is required of us in terms of decision making (see Romans 12:2; Philippians 1:10; 1 Thessalonians 5:21). Jesus says that the people must judge *for themselves* what is right (12:57). They cannot wait for the leaders or anyone else. The case is too critical. They must decide for or against the Day of Christ, and take the consequences (see 1 Corinthians 11:31; 2 Corinthinans 13:5). They will not know what is the right thing to do if they do not decide for or against Christ Himself.

If only they could see that Israel, as a nation, was on

its way to judgement in God's Court of Justice. As they are still "on the way", there is time left for reconciliation and peace. But if Israel as a nation insists on going to court with God, then *"I tell you, you will not get out till you have paid the very last penny"* (12:59). If they demand justice for themselves, they will, unfortunately, get justice, and no sinner can afford this. What we need is mercy, forgiveness and reconciliation, the very things that Jesus pleads for.

The "court case" is Jesus' way of describing the impending crisis which will be a testing time for the disciples, a blood-baptism for Himself, and judgement for the nation. The nation's choice is either to align itself with God's purpose embodied in Jesus and His mission, or to choose the political path of nationalism, and enter into a collision course with Rome where she will be crushed. Jesus can see the shortness of time (*chronos*-time). Why will they not learn from watching people settle disputes on the very steps of the courthouse? To turn in repentance to Jesus would mean that God's highest purpose for Israel would come about.

If Luke's gospel was written after AD 70, when Jerusalem was destroyed and the Temple desecrated and burned, when the nation was cast upon the Gentile world to be abused and despised for so much of its history (although this anti-Semitism cannot be justified. There will be a court of justice for the Gentile nations too – see Matthew 25), then there is a special urgency for Christians to learn the lesson. The Christian Church is a pilgrim people on the way to God's judgement at the end of time. It is experiencing trials and persecutions, with the temptation to seek the secular city and to go the ways of the world. They are urgently asked to be reconciled with God before either personal judgement, as in the case of the Rich Fool, or national judgement, as in the case of Israel, comes upon them.

The Need for Repentance (13:1–21)

Two tragic events of recent history that everyone was talking about, are now used to reinforce the urgency of repentance on Israel. (These disasters are not mentioned by historians of the time.) The first one illustrated Pilate's hatred of the Jews, when he mingled the blood of Galileans with the sacrifices offered to God in the temple – an event that shocked the nation, and rightly so. In general, the Pharisees held that such atrocities were a punishment from God for sin (see Job 4:7, 8:20, 22:4; John 9:1; Jeremiah 21:19; Ezekiel 18:1–32). Thus it could be argued that victims of natural disasters could be considered to be punished for their sins, a fact that modern science disproved.

Jesus rejected this mechanical judgement and fatalistic view, but said that disasters should be read as warning signs, like the amber and red lights for the motorist today. If the nation, as a nation, does not repent, then disaster looms, not because of the punishing hand of God, but as a result of its own decisions or lack of them (13:2–3). Jesus reinforces the point with an example of His own concerning the collapse of the Tower of Siloam. Like the prophets of old, He considers disasters as invitations to *see, hear, understand, be converted and live* (Isaiah 6:9; Amos 4:4–12). Repentance was the most important and urgent part of the lesson.

This is reinforced by the parable of the fig tree (13:6–9). It speaks of a man who planted a fig tree which bore him no fruit. The owner wanted to uproot the tree, but the vinedresser pleaded for more time, another year, when he would tend it carefully and give it extra manure. If after this special treatment it still bore no fruit, then it should be cut down. The fig tree was an official symbol for Israel, just as the shamrock is for Ireland. We find this image of God and His vineyard in Isaiah 5:1–7: Here, too, Israel had failed to live up to God's expectations for her. The special care in the parable represents Jesus' ministry and intercession. Israel had been given every chance, but would be "cut down" if she finally rejected the Word. If the fig tree perishes it would certainly be a greater disaster than that which befell those poor Galileans, whose murder defiled the sacrifices.

Real defilement is to remain in sin (see John 8:21, 34–37). A flashback to John the Baptist's teaching reminds us that he warned Israel that her day of salvation was *now*, and that the axe was already laid to the roots of the trees (3:9). He had expected the tree to be cut down *then*, but now after three years of Jesus' ministry it was right to look for fruit. Israel had been given special care and attention by Jesus, but the Owner of the vineyard could still find no repentance. Not only were Jesus' contemporaries living on borrowed time, but so are we (see 2 Peter 3:9–12). The "repent or perish" message was sent out by the Risen Lord through His Apostles after Easter (24:47; Mark 16:16).

Healing The Crippled Woman (13:10–17)

Israel's spiritual bondage is graphically illustrated through an unknown woman who was bent double, unable to stand erect (13:11). She came to an unknown synagogue on the Sabbath day to hear God's Word and to seek God's help, but like all other sufferers who met Jesus, the Saviour and Lord, she received much more than she had ever expected (Ephesians 3:21). In this incident we meet Jesus on His last visit to a synagogue, and He leaves behind a sign, if only Israel can read it. It is late in the day, but whatever is holding the nation back from God's salvation, whatever is holding her bound, unable to stand erect as "God's first-born" among the nations (Exodus 4:23), can be released by Jesus. Even if Satan himself is holding her bound, she can be released by Jesus, who is stronger than Satan (11:20–22). Jesus must give this sign in the teeth of opposition from the leader of the synagogue.

Luke shows Jesus' freedom from social taboos in this healing when he illustrates Jesus' laying-on of hands on this woman, a thing not only frowned upon, but condemned by the Pharisees. Typical of Luke, Jesus did not wait for the woman to come to Him (7:11–17). He called her over and initiated the healing because God truly loves Israel, and salvation comes to her on God's initiative. God wanted His beloved bride to be gloriously free and glorifying God (13:13).

The woman's physical condition was, in itself, a parable for the One who came to set the captives free (4:18). God gave the human race dignity and freedom as His sons. They were to walk upright before His face, yet His people had bent their backs to the yoke of slavery in Egypt, but He came to deliver them. As Leviticus 26:13 says *"I, Yahweh your God . . . brought you out of the land of Egypt so that you should be their servants no longer. I have broken the yoke that bound you and have made you walk with head held high"*. (The NAB and the RSV both translate *"that you may walk erect"*). Deuteronomy 5:14–15 instructed them regarding the observance of the Sabbath: *" . . . but the 7th day is a Sabbath, . . . remember that you were once a servant in the land of Egypt, and that Yahweh your God brought you out from there with mighty hand and outstretched arm."* How many in that synagogue would know that their history was illustrated before their eyes and that Jesus does here what God did in the past when

175

He released this daughter of Abraham (13:16) from her yoke of bondage?

But, typically, the Pharisee ruler has no eyes for this wonder, but only for broken rules and customs. Not having the courage to criticize Jesus openly, he castigated the people – meaning the woman – for coming for healing on the Sabbath (13:14)! Jesus defended the woman, and accused the ruler and his ilk of hypocrisy, for having more love of animals than their neighbour (13:15). Animals meant money, so the leaders did not scruple to take care and water them, but they had no care for Israel's bondage, or her thirst for salvation (see Amos 6:1–7). Their excuse for watering the animals was that it was an act of mercy, but they had no mercy on Israel whom they overburdened with regulations that no one could keep (11:46; Acts 15:10). And now their legalism would even prevent her cure in God's *kairos*-time! The *chronos*-time for healing was between Monday and Friday, but God's *kairos*-time was *now*, on His own Sabbath day.

The result of this freeing was two-fold. The leaders were "covered with confusion", while the people rejoiced at *all* the wonders that Jesus worked (13:17). He had triumphed. His joy here is a forecast of the joy the Resurrection would bring when His *exodos* had freed all nations from their bondages (see John 16:20–22). What they were looking at now in this healing was like a mustard seed which is so small that one would find it hard to believe it could become a great tree, big enough to house the birds of the air (13:18–19). Jesus had come to unbind all nations from corruption so that they could stand erect in the glorious liberty of the sons of God (Romans 8:19–21). The Kingdom of God may have unremarkable beginnings, but it also has unimaginable endings. The image of the tree that filled the world and gave a home to all nations was not new. Daniel 4:7–14 gives the same image for Nebuchadnezzar's dream of world domination. Unlike Jesus this king would bind the nations into slavery, whereas Jesus' Kingdom will free the sons of God.

The work of God is hidden in people's hearts as the parable of the leaven explains. (Luke balances a parable about a mustard seed which a man planted, with a loaf of bread made by a woman.) Yeast was so powerful an agent that even a very small amount would secretly and mysteriously transform a batch of bread made from three measures of meal – which was a very large quantity, big enough to feed a hundred people (Genesis 18:6; Judith 6:19). The leavening was an overnight process. The people in Jesus' audience may not *see* the grace of God beginning its transforming work in the world, but Luke's church looking back was able to observe that it set in motion a chain of events that no one could stop. God continues to work away quietly in the hearts of believers transforming their lives and using them as "leaven" in the world. Jesus won for them the grace to resist all temptation to legalistic religion (see Acts 5:10). As Paul says in Galatians 5:1: "*Christ freed us, he meant us to remain free. Stand firm therefore, and do not submit again to the yoke of slavery.*"

The Destination that Awaits Us (13:22–17:10)

A new section of the journey is introduced at this point that deals with the ultimate destiny of all who undertake the journey. Will they all, like Jesus, attain their end (13:33)? We are about to see that this is not the case. The destiny one achieves is related to one's reaction to Jesus and the resultant repentance or refusal to change. The "all that glitters is not gold" principle will be illustrated

177

with surprising people suffering eternal frustration. There
will be an exclusion/inclusion principle shown here that
shocks, namely, that tax-collectors, sinners and Gentiles
get places reserved for Jews in the Kingdom of God.
How could such a shocking reversal of fortunes come
about? Let us see.

As Jesus was making His way to Jerusalem, the city
of destiny, He stopped in all the villages and towns to
teach, preach and complete the work He was given to do
(13:22). As part of their many discussions someone asked
the vital question: *"Sir, will there be only a few saved?"*
Typically, Jesus did not answer directly, but broadened
its scope to make it an urgent warning to "Come now!"
He said that entering into salvation was like going through
a narrow door *"because, I tell you, many will try to enter
and will not succeed"* (13:24). This parable shocks, especially in the light of 11:5–13, where we met a man
knocking on a closed door, in prayer, and due to his
persistence had the door opened to him. Besides, we were
told that *"the one who knocks will always have the door
opened to him"* (11:10–11).

What is the difference? In 13:25 Jesus says: *"Once the
master of the house has got up and locked the door ..."*
In the previous parable it was a normal family situation,
where the master locked the house after settling the family
down for the night. Here, the Master, Jesus, will not close
the door on Israel's Day of Salvation until AFTER His
Resurrection, after He has got up from the grave. Then it
will be the Day of the Gentiles, whereas now it is the
Jewish Day. If they come knocking after that, He will
disown them (12:8–9). There will be no point in claiming
that He, Himself, was their prophet and teacher, for that
was not the issue (13:26–27). If they read history, they
would know that Israel was not spared the Exile just
because she had the great prophets Isaiah and Jeremiah,

Amos and Hosea preaching to her. She would have been spared had she heard the words of the prophets and put them into practice. In other words if she had repented and allowed God to change her. Repentance is the issue for Jesus.

This is a warning for Christians too. Eating and drinking alongside of Jesus physically or in His presence socially, is not the same as eating and drinking with Jesus in fellowship, and being present to him in the Eucharistic Meal. The Christian equivalent would be: "Lord, we have received you in Communion: we had the Scriptures read in church: we had famous saints or preachers who evangelized us". It will be all to no avail. The person who reaches their true destiny is the one who enters by the narrow door of personal conversion, repentance of all one's sins and an intimate personal relationship with Jesus, which includes the daily following of the spiritual life in detailed obedience to the will of God. Otherwise, we will hear those dreadful words of rejection by Jesus: *"I do not know where you come from. Away from me all you wicked men!"* (13:27).

This rejection from the Kingdom of God is the ultimate frustration of the person called to intimacy with God. It is described as weeping and grinding of teeth, because those outside see themselves separated from their religious roots in Abraham, Isaac, and Jacob and *all* the prophets. Worse still, their places were taken by people from all over the globe who never had their spiritual privileges. This is a double blow. To be left out is one thing, but to have "unclean" Gentiles take your place is the last straw (13:28–29)! Jesus adds a proverb to ram home his point: *"Yes, there are those now last* (sinners and Gentiles) *who will be first,* (in the Kingdom) *and those now first* (Israel, Pharisees and other religious leaders) *who will be last"* (in the Kingdom) (13:30).

From this point onwards He illustrates this amazing reversal of fortunes for Israel, who will be horrified to find sinners and Gentiles come to experience the fulfilment of Biblical Promise while they, the "worthy ones", are left out (1:53).

Jerusalem Forsaken (13:31–35)

The exclusion of some Jews from the Kingdom makes shocking reading, but the "why" is made clearer now as some Pharisees – who were known to be in league with the Herodians (see Matthew 22:16; Mark 3:6) – told Jesus to get out of Herod's territory because His life was in danger (13:31–32). Herod's desire to see Jesus in 9:3–9 is now seen to have malicious intent. There was no way a man of his immoral life could comprehend who Jesus was or why He came (see 1 Corinthians 2:14–16). His lust for power and self-indulgence clouded his mind, and he had already murdered the Baptist in a fruitless attempt to block God's plans. Jesus sent him a sharply worded rebuke which illustrated the true prophet's fearlessness confronting worldly power.

He may have wiped out John the Baptist but did he know that John's blood baptism coincided with the inauguration of Jesus' ministry? He had no power to wipe out Jesus as *His* Destiny lay in Jerusalem far away from Herod's territory. Jesus' destiny lay in God's salvific plan for men, which is outside human power. Even so, Jesus' blood baptism would inaugurate the universal mission of the Church. How could Herod comprehend that the blood of the martyrs is the seed of the Church?

Besides, Jesus' ministry was following God's *kairos*-time, and his *exodos* would be on the third day as decreed (13:33), a fact that Jesus had already accepted independently of Herod. The fittingness of this plan could only be appreciated by those who had entered into the mystery of Jesus. The Son of Man was destined to die a prophet's death in Jerusalem, and this city and its leaders would have to take responsibility for that. Like a hen who calls and gathers her chicks under her wings for protection, the Messiah-Saviour had done that for this city so ultimately bound up with Israel's hopes. He had called and called, but they had refused to accept His salvation and the eternal protection it offered (13:34). They must now have the judgement of their Messianic Saviour given with a broken heart: *"So be it! Your house will be left to you . . ."* (13:35).

They have made their choice and Jesus respects that. Now they must live out the consequences, which is that the Lord will abandon Jerusalem and go seeking a people who will do His Will, and bear fruit (see Matthew 21:43). Again, if they read the history of the prophets leading up to the Exile, they would know that God did not have to punish Israel. He only had to remove His hand of protection from her, and she was automatically exposed to the might of her political enemies, who were quite happy to wipe her out. The prophets knew that the ultimate punishment was for the Lord to forsake the Temple, for this heralded the end of the Covenant relationship with Him, and disaster must follow according to the normal conditions of Covenant. Religion is an empty shell without the Lord's Presence.

One of the favourite images of God's protection in the Old Testament was that of the great bird sheltering his people under his wings (Deuteronomy 32:11; Psalms 17:8, 36:7, 57:1, 61:4, 63:7, 91:4; Ruth 2:11 etc). This presents salvation as coming from the loving, mothering, life-giving, caring concern of the Heart of God. To reject it is to choose non-life and ultimately destruction. Jeremiah 12:7 had clearly spoken on this subject: *"I have abandoned my house, left my heritage. I have delivered what I dearly loved into the hands of its enemies.*" Jerusalem faces certain destruction again. The "fall and rise of many" was to include the fall of Jerusalem.

Jesus finished with a statement that they would never see Him again until they , as a nation, would give Him the official greeting for the Messiah, taken from Psalm 118:26: *"Blessings on him who comes in the name of the Lord!" (13:35).* They will use these words briefly in 19:38 in His final and official entry into Jerusalem for His *exodos*, but that is not the sense intended. Until Israel recognizes and officially receives the Messiah God gave her, she can have her religion, her laws and her customs, but not Him! (see Jeremiah 7:1–15, 23–28).

Demands of Discipleship (14:1–35)

Chapter 14 develops the radical demands of discipleship for those who have joined Jesus on the journey to Jerusalem. The first section. (14:1–24) deals with the demands of table-fellowship, and the second unit (14:24–35) deals with the radical renunciation required of those who would persevere to the end with Jesus.

We have just considered the fate of those who had claimed to have eaten and drunk in the presence of Jesus, and who used this as an excuse to gain entrance into the Kingdom. Jesus' response may have seemed harsh in 13:26–27, but now Luke presents us with the true attitudes of many who did, in fact, eat socially with Jesus (14:1–6). One of the ruling Pharisees invited Jesus to a meal on a Sabbath day, but instead of friendly acceptance, Jesus found Himself closely watched by the hostile guests (14:2). The Pharisees maintained that to heal on the Sabbath was a serious breaking of the Law, and they wanted to see the evidence on their own premises!

This incident is very reminiscent of the healing of the

man with the withered hand in 6:6–11, and it is closely connected with the healing of the crippled woman 13:10–17. In each case Jesus was in a synagogue, and met with hostility and rejection from the leaders, who refused to look at the meaning of His action. In this case the man had dropsy, a disease in which the body swells up due to an accumulation of fluid formimg in the cavities and tissues. The Pharisees held that it was the result of immorality (see Numbers 5:21–23). If this was so then why did they have an unclean sinner in their midst? Did they forget about ritual defilement in their anxiety to trap Jesus? Whatever about us, Jesus would not have missed this point! Perhaps they thought that as a layman Jesus would not defy them to their faces?

However, Jesus took the challenge, and the stigma that went with it, and showed Himself fearless before them. He challenged *them* to answer if it were allowed to cure a man on the Sabbath day or not. They refused to be drawn, perhaps because they knew His thinking already on this subject (14:4)? Jesus healed the man and sent him away to enjoy his new life without condemnation, and also without seeing the price, even in the here-and-now, that Jesus had to pay for his healing (14:5). Then Jesus challenged His opponents on their reading of Scripture: *"Which of you here, if his son falls into a well, or his ox, will not pull him out on a sabbath day WITHOUT HESITATION?"* When this question is read in the Aramaic that Jesus spoke, there is a pun on the words son (*bera*), ox (*beira*), and well (*bera*), which accounts for variations in the translation. Jesus knew well that the Pharisees' practical course of action in an emergency would be inconsistent with their theoretical position on the matter, so He placed them in a position whereby if they replied to His question they would stand accused (14:6).

Jesus is aware that self interest catapults them into

action. What about the unbinding and releasing of human beings, which is the concern of God? This is God's Will, and love of neighbour demands action, but they remain silent, confounded but not repentant. Should they be permitted, therefore, to enter the Kingdom just for eating and drinking in Jesus' Presence (13:26–27)? Here Jesus demonstrated that their meticulous keeping of the Law was, in fact, circumventing their obedience to God's commandment to love God with their whole heart, soul, mind and body and their neighbour as themselves (see Mark 7:8–13).

As far as Jesus was concerned, the healed man was *only* sick. His sickness was a parable on the spiritual, pathological state of the Pharisees, bloated as they were with pride, self-importance, and a swollen sense of religious achievement, a condition far worse than dropsy, and much more difficult to diagnose and heal. The shock for the Pharisees who do eventually knock on the door of the Kingdom of God is, that they find that Jesus *is the Master of the House!* Yet, thankfully, the Acts relate how many of them did subsequently take their places in the Kingdom of God (Acts 2:37–41, 3:17–24, especially 6:7).

Teaching on Table Fellowship (14:7–24)

Turning now to the guests (14:7–11), the host (14:12–14), and to all present (14:15–24), Jesus sets out in parables what the situation will be in the Kingdom of God. As so often happened, He chose what was to hand, and used that as His illustration. It was the man with the withered hand in chapter 6, the woman bent double in chapter 13 and the man with dropsy here that provoked discussion on the Sabbath. Now Jesus uses the guests and the host to illustrate that things will be very different at His Messianic Banquet. He likened *his* feast to a wedding which was a typical Messianic symbol (see Isaiah 62:4, 54:5; Hosea 2:7; Jeremiah 2:2).

When the guests filed in to the dining hall Jesus noticed how they took the places of honour at table (14:7–8). This was dictated by their own sense of self-importance. Even in a social context this leaves them open to humiliation if the host is forced to ask them to give up their place to someone more important than they. Embarrassment will then send them to the lowest place (14:9–10). The position of a humble person is very different, as he will choose the lowest position anyway, and then find himself honoured before all present when the host insists on bringing him higher. *"My friend, move up higher"* draws the attention and admiration of all present, while the proud one is covered with confusion. For even in worldly circles, and not taking the Kingdom of God into account, it can be demonstrated that the self-exalted will be humbled, while everyone loves to honour the simple freedom of the truly humble person, in touch with the reality of things (14:10–11).

When we take this meal into the context of table fellowship at the Messianic Banquet, humility becomes all important. Jesus' guests, whom we will discover in a moment (14:22) are the poor, the crippled, the blind and the lame, and sinners in general (5:27–32, 16:19–31, 18:13–14, 19:1–10). These people will know how to take the lowest place, so grateful are they to be present at all! They are excluded from all worldly banquets, only permitted to stand around watching the rich and the privileged dine (7:36–38), allowed to listen to their erudite discussions and know themselves as the world's "have-nots". But in the Kingdom everything is reversed. They are guests at the table, and they discover that their Host is the humblest of all (12:37–38, 22:17), and their privilege was sung long before now by His humble virgin mother in her Magnificat: *"he has routed the proud of heart . . . pulled down princes from their thrones and exalted the lowly. The hungry he has filled with good things, the rich sent empty away"* (1:51–53).

Thus it is a fulfilment of Jesus' promise in His inaugural address at Nazareth (4:18–21). The Pharisees caught up in seeking earthly honours (11:43–44) do not even hear the invitation to the Messianic Banquet, while the others are eager and willing, and many have already responded (14:15–24). Luke warns Christians to keep this lesson on humility alive and not fall into Pharisaic attitudes (see 1 Peter 5:5; James 4:6; Philippians 2:5–11).

Turning to the host, Jesus remarked on the guest list which consisted of friends, family, relatives and rich neighbours in that order. Each one would feel the obligation to return the invitation (14:12). Following His own teaching in 6:33 that we should give with no expectation of recompense, Jesus challenged His host to invite the poor, the crippled, the blind and the lame, as He Himself was doing for the Messianic Banquet (4:18–19, 7:29). The fact that they *cannot* pay you back makes you blessed in Jesus' eyes, for recompense will be given where it counts most, namely on the last day *"when the virtuous rise again"* (14:14).

One of the bystanders at the meal, thus one of the poor, on hearing Jesus speak thus to the host and guests said: *"Happy the man who will be at the feast in the kingdom of God!"* (14:15). Knowingly, or not, this man is the voice of the poor, longing to be included in God's plan of salvation, weary of being excluded from all the privileges of life. This wrung from Jesus the parable of the Great Supper, which he addressed to him, personally (14:16), and to all whom he represented. It concerned a man who gave a great banquet, but when he sent his servant to call the guests, he found they all made excuses not to come. One had just bought a piece of land while another had purchased some livestock. Yet a third had just married and was otherwise occupied. Each one used their normal life commitments as the excuse not to respond (14:17–19).

The host was very angry at these unfounded excuses and ordered the servant to go quickly into the streets and alleys of the town and bring in the poor, the crippled, the blind and the lame, but they did not *fill* the house. The servant was then dispatched to go to the open roads and the hedgerows to force the people to come in to make sure that the house *was full* because the host was determined to bar the original guests from his banquet (14:21–24).

This story may not have originated with Jesus. It may be part of His use of everyday events to teach people deep truths. Professor J. Jeremias in his book *Parables of Jesus* (London 1963) quotes a story about a rich tax collector called Bar Ma'jam who arranged a banquet for the city councillors, but they all refused to come, so he gave orders that the poor should come in and eat it, so that the food would not be wasted. The story would have been told far and wide, and lend immediate understanding to Jesus' point. They would clearly see that the Jewish leaders were treating the Lord with the same contempt as the aristocracy had shown to this nouveau riche tax collector.

The Jewish people were the first to receive the invitation to the Messianic Banquet in the Old Testament, and through the ministry of John the Baptist. But by the time Jesus came to announce that the time had arrived, the nation was too engaged in its political, economic and family affairs to be bothered with the good news. In spite of this the banquet went on as scheduled, and the nation had to watch, to its chagrin, the most unlikely people participate in it. However, they had been warned about this more than once (13:28–30; see 1 Corinthians 1:26–31).

The Cost of Discipleship (14:25–35)

We have just looked at who will get into the Kingdom of God, and who will be left out. Now Luke reminds those inside that there is no room for smugness, as the cost of discipleship is high, and there always remains the problem of persevering to the end of the journey. The Pharisees refused the cost of accepting the invitation to the banquet, but disciples may be tempted to underestimate the cost of discipleship, and embark on a course which is beyond their ability. Great crowds accompany Jesus, both on His journey to Jerusalem, and on His journey through history (14:25), but their enthusiasm must be tempered by the realities of the situation. If they are to persevere as true followers of Jesus, then they must take into account the cost, in terms of loss of family ties, loss of income, and maybe even loss of life in martyrdom.

Jesus demands complete commitment saying: *"If any man comes to me without hating his father, mother, wife, children, brothers, sisters, yes his own life too, he cannot be my disciple"* (14:25–26). To hate, in Jesus' language, that is, Aramaic, means "to give second place to". It does not mean psychological and emotional hostility to one's family. It is, instead, a radical demand to put God *first* in one's life, and *all* other matters, including one's family, second, as He had done Himself (8:19–21, 11:27–28). Natural ties must take second place to those ties that bind us all in one body at the Messianic Banquet, and on this journey. The pilgrims are following a Crucified Lord, and it is essential to master the lesson of total renunciation and total self-giving (14:27, 9:23–26).

With this total commitment to the Lord and the mission, the followers of Jesus have the function of salt in the world. They preserve it from corruption, while giving it good "taste". They give meaning and purpose to the lives of millions lost in the darkness of unbelief. Without this total commitment disciples are useless for the furthering of God's purposes. They have reverted back to being part of the problem, instead of remaining at Jesus' side, part of the solution to the sorrows and brokenness of the human race. That's about the sum of it: we can be part of the problem or part of the solution. There is no middle ground for armchair Christians. Hence the urgency of the call to free oneself from whatever keeps us back from service.

Moreover, Jesus does not want rash disciples, making decisions in the heat of a fervent moment, decisions that cannot be lived out in the cold sober conditions of everyday life, (14:28). He wants them to assess the situation fully, like a builder beginning a new project. He would be a laughing stock if he poured money into a job that he could not complete (14:29). Better to hold on to your money if you could not complete it. Luke 18:18–23 will give an example of a man making just such a decision. To reinforce the point, Jesus speaks about a king preparing for war. He would be completely mad to expose his army to annihilation if the enemy were more powerful than he (14:31–32). Disciples are facing a greater battle than any of them could anticipate, a battle that would cost them dearly in terms of personal conversion, repentance and spiritual warfare as they face the forces of evil in the world, and in terms of martyrdom as they are called one after the other to lay down their lives. When the storm breaks during the Passion of Jesus even the Apostles will have casualties (22:21–23, 31–34; see Matthew 27:3–10; Acts 1:16–20).

Lost and Found (15:1–32)

This chapter forms one self-contained and artistically con-
structed unit with a single theme, even if it is removed
altogether from its context. It is one of the most wonderful
pieces of writing ever to emerge from the human mind.
Like Psalms 23 and 51 it touches such a deep chord in
the human heart that it can be variously explained, but
never surpassed. It is one of the clearest pictures of the
tender mercy and loving kindness of God our Saviour in
the Bible. It consists of an introduction (15:1–3), and two
short parables (15:4–7 and 8–11) given as preparation for
the great parable of the Prodigal Son in 15:11–32. In
this, Luke continues to show us that things are not what
they seem: one sheep is as important as ninety-nine, and
the good son is not as good as he seems, while the bad
son is not as bad as he looks. Even worse, God loves
them equally!

Now that the invitations to the Kingdom of God have
gone out the tax collectors and sinners were *all* seeking
Jesus' company, eager to hear His teaching and eager
to join His Kingdom (15:1). The Pharisees and Scribes
– whose true attitudes to Jesus are open knowledge
now – criticize Him again, this time for receiving the
unclean tax collectors and sinners, and even eating with
them (15:2–3). As we have already seen, their ideas
of immorality and his were very different (Luke 6, 12,
11:37–54). They could not accept that Jesus was not
lowering His moral standards by joining them, but that
they were leaving their old sinful ways to join Him
and His banquet. They had begun the repentance that
would lead them to the Father's House and Home.

The first two parables form a typically Lukan pair of
a man and his sheep, and a woman and her coin to make
the same point. All three parables deal with two categories

of people in Jesus' immediate environment, namely, the tax collectors and sinners who are well known to us now in the gospel. They represent all religious outcasts, and become a type or symbol of all others referred to in 15:1: The second group are the Scribes and Pharisees, whom we know equally well as symbols of self righteousness. They represent people both in Jesus' day and in our own. The interesting thing is that Jesus was a welcome guest in the houses of *both* groups! (5:29, 7:36, 11:37, 14:1). The Pharisees, who were known for their exclusive ways socially and religiously, objected to this (15:2). When they said that Jesus "welcomed sinners" they meant that He offered them hospitality at His table. There is a note of horrified contempt in their description of Him as *"this man"* (15:2) which we will find again on the lips of the elder brother as *"this son of yours"* in 15:30.

Because it is not so much the question of Jesus as guest that is at stake, but Jesus as Host, we can conclude that Luke is thinking of the situation in the early Church with Christians gathered around the table of the Lord, where openness and universality of table fellowship continued to challenge the self-righteous, who protested at the presence of sinners. These parables need to be read, therefore, in the context of Jesus' day, and in the prevailing situations in the Church today.

The first parable concerns a man who abandoned his ninety-nine sheep in the wilderness to go after one which was missing. He searched until he found it, and then returned joyfully with the sheep on his shoulders. On returning home friends and neighbours were called to rejoice, because, he said: *"I have found my sheep that was lost"* (15:7). Jeremiah 31:10–20 and Ezekiel 34:11–16 give the background to the image of God's people as "sheep", and God Himself as the loving Shepherd. John 10 presents Jesus as the fulfilment of this. This picture of a loving shepherd (see Isaiah 40:11, 49:22) seeking out his lost sheep presupposes two things: first, that the ninety-nine are left in the care of another person, for it would negate the caring image to abandon the whole flock for the sake of the endangered one. Of course this is a hypothetical situation, for there are no ninety-nine who don't *need to repent!* (5:32; Romans 2:23; 1 John 1:8). Second, it would have been in the evening when the shepherd counted his sheep before penning them down for the night (see John 10:1–5) that he discovered the missing one.

The conclusion drawn from the parable is that there is *"more rejoicing in heaven over one repentant sinner than over ninety-nine virtuous men who have no need of repentance"* (15:7). This clearly refers to the distinction between the sinners and the self righteous who *thought* they had no need of repentance. The refusal of the latter group to accept the invitation into the Kingdom of God and its consequent refusal of conversion and repentance would certainly cause no joy , but much suffering to Jesus, the Shepherd. The contrasting humility and openness of the other group would make anyone with a shepherd's heart go after them! In the same way the helplessness of a child in danger makes a parent go to any length to save it. It was a great triumph for Jesus, the Shepherd and Guardian of our souls (1 Peter 2:25) to bring into God's Kingdom those that once were held captive by Satan and the forces of evil in the world. His rejoicing victory will be seen in the post-resurrection era.

In contrast to the man with a hundred sheep, the woman has only ten drachmas, but, like him, she is prepared to leave the nine drachmas to diligently search for the lost one. The drachma was a Greek silver coin roughly equivalent to the Roman denarius, which was a working man's day's wages. Many believe that the ten silver coins formed part or all of the woman's dowry, which was worn as part of her headdress. To lose such a coin was a great loss for a poor woman. Since she lived in a peasant's house with a low door, and probably no windows the search through the dirt floor had to be diligent. The rabbis circa AD 200 had a parable similar to this about a man who loses something valuable in his house and lights many lamps in order to find it. Their application was that they ought to search the Torah, the written Word of God, for the hidden treasures there. The woman invited her friends and neighbours to rejoice in the same way as the angels of God rejoice when a sinner is found (15:8–10).

The Lost Son (15:11–32)

The previous two parables have prepared us to enter into this one with understanding. The caring shepherd and housewife are now replaced by the loving Father who obviously represents God. There is great celebration when his lost son is found and returns home. However, there is an unexpected twist in the parable to intrigue and captivate us. The rejoicing in heaven does not have its counterpart on earth among the older brothers who want nothing to do with these wastrels. The parable throws out the challenge to the "virtuous" to accept the repentance of confessed sinners, but no response is heard. So it is ultimately concerned to justify the attitude of God to sinners, and therefore the attitude of Jesus who acts as God's representative in forgiving them (5:20–26, 7:48–50). As far as the Pharisees were concerned it was unthinkable that Jesus would go *searching for sinners*. They believed that God loved sinners *after* they repented, but not before (see Isaiah 55:7; Jeremiah 3:12 and compare with Ephesians 4:4–16).

God has two types of children, as shown here. Both are sinners, but only those who openly rebel come to face their sinfulness and repent. The other group, the religious ones, tend to hide the wickedness of their hearts behind an exterior of exact obedience to the Law. But, as in the case of the sinful woman in chapter 7, it is the condition of the heart that determines who we are in God's sight (7:36–50, 16:19–31, 18:9–14 and Matthew 20:1–16, 21:28–32).

The younger son in this parable demanded his third of the inheritance (since the Law laid down two thirds should go to the first born) from his father. The father responded by making over *all* his property to his two sons (15:31), with the understanding that he is in charge until his death. Handing over the property implied moral obligations for the younger son. But he despised all obligations to family, religion, and country, cashed-in his portion and emigrated. He left *for a distant country where he squandered his money on a life of debauchery* (15:13). His sin alienated him from his family, religious community and God. He was a spiritual leper (see Sirach 9:6; Isaiah 1:2–9, 16–20), and another example of a rich fool, a person who does not handle life or its resources wisely. Luke will give instruction on the right use of money in the next chapter (16:1–15).

This young person was unwilling to reflect on life's realities until he had gone through his fortune and was left in the gutter, with nothing but his memories to keep him warm (see Proverbs 19:3, 29:3). Then, to compound the situation, the country itself fell on hard times, and famine reared its ugly head (15:14). Starvation made him do something which violated his sense of Jewishness. He took a job on a Gentile farm feeding pigs, an occupation considered unclean by the Jews (see Leviticus 11:7). To feed swine was about as low as a Jewish youth could go, but to desire to eat their food was the nadir of degradation. He had reached rock bottom: the only way out was up!

(15:16). He had been freewheeling downhill until he is now left for spiritually dead. This is the condition of the victim in the parable of the Good Samaritan. This boy needs a Saviour more than anything else.

One of life's bitterest realities hits him now: when you are down, nobody wants to know you. It is here that a true friend would be seen, but none of his former associates came near to that description. He is now both poor and destitute, spiritually and temporally. Proverbs 19:7 fits well now: *"The poor man's brothers hate him, every one; his friends – how much the more do these desert him!"* Unfortunately this man waited for disaster to teach him, when the ordinary events of everyday life are sufficient. However, pain, isolation, hunger and loneliness brought him to his senses (15:17). Reflection led him to see that even the paid servants in his father's house were in a better position than he, who should have been a son in that household. In other words, he began to realize that it was better to be a floor sweeper in the Kingdom of God than to be an emperor in hell. Those servants had all the employment, security, love and fellowship that he lacked right now. He had made himself an outsider, an alien in his own home (see Ephesians 2:11–22).

His long journey back to the father, which symbolizes the sinner's return to God, begins now. The first step was to come to his senses and meditate on life. The second was a decision to do something positive about it. He decided to leave that place, go home and confess that he had sinned against heaven, because of his hedonistic lifestyle, and against his father, because of his neglect of his duties and the commandments of God, and also because of the disgrace and heart-break brought to the family. The youth realized that he had forfeited sonship, both by his declaration of independence at the beginning, when he demanded to leave home as an independent adult, but also by the fact that his behaviour brought disgrace upon his father's name and the family's reputation. This new self-knowledge paved the way for real humility, confession and reconciliation afterwards (15:18–19). The third stage of his recovery is that he put his resolve into practice. It changed from being a good intention to a good action.

So far we have watched the change of heart in the young man, but what made him so sure that his father would receive him? Why was his return home so confident? Was his share of the estate given with resentment or forgiving love? We shall see that now, for the story takes up what was going on in the father here: *While he was still a long way off, his father saw him and was moved with pity* (15:20). The son had gone away from the father but this was not reciprocated. The father's heart had remained loving, caring, forgiving, and open to reconciliation. The wretched condition of the son did not fill him with hate or loathing, but with compassion, much as the sight of a severe illness does not fill us with loathing, but moves us to compassion for the sufferer. The spiritual malaise of the boy touched the soft "daddy" in the heart of the father, who did not wait for the boy's arrival, but ran to meet him, *clasped him in his arms and kissed him*, all signs of loving forgiveness for this wastrel of a son (18:13–14, 23:39–43; Acts 20:37).

This loving acceptance made it possible for the boy to move on to the next stage of recovery. There, in the safety and security of his father's love, he confessed his sins openly and honestly without excuse or subterfuge (15:21). But the father had no ears for a long list of misery and failure. His son was back from the dead, and this was a matter for celebration! Instead of a lecture on wasting his life and opportunities, the son hears his excited father order a celebration for his homecoming, a response beyond his wildest dreams (sée

Ephesians 3:21). He was to get the *best* robe, not just a robe, a ring on his finger and sandals on his feet (15:22). The father ordered his son to be fitted out *as a son* not as a servant or a slave. Full sonship is restored to him. The ring signifies authority in his father's house (see 1 Maccabees 6:15; Esther 3:10, 8:8). The shoes signify a freeman, not a slave or a guest, for in the house shoes were worn only by the master and his family. Guests removed their shoes at the door. Having been fully reinstated, it was time to celebrate. The motive for the feast was the grace-filled reformation of the son, which was compared to a resurrection, or to a precious object once lost but now found (15:23). So far the movement of the story has gone from death to life, and one is caught up in the excitement and joy of the re-creation of this young life and the marvel of the grace that achieved it. If the story ended here it would be all joy.

But what about the dutiful elder son, who never disgraced the family? One who never descended to an immoral life, a young man who spent all his life in the company of *this* loving father? Surely, he must be happy and contented, and free? But no! The real shocks begin now. Somehow the sinfulness of the good person is more devastating than the crimes of the bad one. How can they miss so much? This boy returned from the field to hear the celebration in progress (15:25–26). Instead of automatically presuming that he should be part of it, he made enquiries from a servant as to what was afoot, only to hear that his brother was back, safe and sound! (15:27). Instead of loving acceptance and forgiveness, there arose anger and resentment in the heart of this boy who refused to participate in the feast.

This brought the father out to where he was isolating and alienating himself from all that was happening at home. The poor father had to search for this "sheep" too, one who didn't know he was lost! Yet, on the principle that out of the abundance of the heart the mouth speaks (see Mark 7:21), this boy is a long way from union with his father, let alone his brother. In anger he retorted to his father: *"All these years I have slaved for you and never once disobeyed your orders, yet you never offered me so much as a kid"* The boy does not address his father as "Father", but in the irreverent "look here ... you" language. The younger one remembered his dad, and showed respect and reverence in his conversion. It seems that the boy's self-righteousness destroyed love in his heart, for everyone. Therefore, a wrong type of religion can insulate us from loving both God and neighbour.

This son reveals himself more than he knows when he speaks. His service of his father has not been free, but very grudging. He expects such meticulous observance to be rewarded. One hears the martyr complex here too: "Nobody understands all the work I do around here"! He seems to have forgotten that he owns the place. He was given twice as much as his brother originally. All he has is criticism both of his father and of his brother. This "son of yours" is a rejection of blood relationship and fellowship because of his misdeeds.

The list of sin seems endless: anger, resentment, bitterness, unforgiveness, self-pity ... he is totally negative, and has not at all profited from his supposed goodness. The father's final plea to his son is very sad, and carries Jesus' own plea to the Pharisees and Scribes represented in this boy's reaction: *"My son, you are with me always and all I have is yours"*. This boy needed no permission to celebrate. He could have done so any day but celebration dies in a sour heart, caught up with self-pity and legalism.

This parable is a pathetic cry to the leaders of Israel

to see things from God's point of view. What was going on in Jesus' acceptance of sinners was a miracle of grace and transformation. If only they would join in and experience the joy of the Lord and the fellowship of the redeemed, but their self righteousness blinded them totally. The Eucharistic table fellowship in the Church is meant to reflect this joy and celebration, where the redeeming, transforming grace of Christ binds all into the family of God.

The Proper Use of Money (16:1–31)

Having just emerged from the story of the Prodigal Son who wasted his inheritance in riotous living, Luke now gives a whole chapter on the right and responsible use of money. Running through this gospel is a theme that almost appears like an apology for rogues. Luke loves using "baddies" in his stories. Perhaps, like most of us, he really appreciates an original "character" who has the guts to break rules, and yet is a lovable rogue behind it all. We have already met a disobliging neighbour in 11:5–9, and we are about to meet the crafty steward in 16:1–8. We will meet the unjust judge in 18:1–8 and Zacchaeus in 19:1–10, not to mention all those tax collectors and sinners dotted all over the place, who don't feel like scoundrels in Luke's delicate rendering of the tale.

Even the Passion will have its own quota, in Peter 22:54–62 and the good thief (23:39–43), who makes everyone green with envy just because he got a bright idea at the last moment, and ended up first into Paradise! No wonder the Pharisees were jealous. Aren't you? These rogues live life fully and end up getting the best of both worlds! Jesus didn't seem to be able to resist them at all. It makes one suspect that there must be a "rogues' gallery" in heaven. There wouldn't be much fun there if only Scribes and Pharisees got in! Of course the Old Testament abounds with lovable rogues too, like Jacob, Rahab, Judith, Jonah and David, to mention just a few. It certainly illustrates that God is a friend of sinners.

Jesus addressed this parable to His disciples about a steward who wasted his master's property. Palestine, as a whole, and Galilee in particular, had many large estates owned by absentee landlords, who entrusted their property to stewards who had full authority to run the estate. It was a situation open to embezzlement of funds and all kinds of underhand dealings (12:43–48). The charges here were taken seriously by both master and servant, a fact that indicates they were correct. The master acted quickly in dismissing the steward, but demanded an account of the state of the property before he left. Up to date accounts were needed by his successor, and the steward's actions are consistent with this.

Reduced to poverty overnight, the man wants to ensure that help will be available from grateful clients and customers, so he alters the accounts in their favour (16: 5–7). Once he leaves this job he will be unemployed, and he could not face the shame of begging (16:4). Many scholars suggest that the reason why the steward could cut down the bill of the first customer by fifty percent is that he *had* been dishonest in getting around the Jewish prohibition on usury, and charging excessive interest (see Exodus 22:25; Leviticus 25:36; Deuteronomy 23:19). The customers would be utterly grateful, and the steward would, accidentally, have done his master a good turn by giving him a public reputation for generosity! That was certainly an astute move, which even his master appreciated (16:8)!

Jesus asked his disciples to take a leaf from the steward's book and apply practical prudence in their everyday affairs. He did not want followers who were so heavenly-minded that they were no earthly use! The "children of light", a term he used to describe those who joined the Kingdom of God, needed practical wisdom to run the affairs of the Church, but not dishonesty! The Lord had put them in charge of the Master's House (12:35–48), and they were to run it His way (see John 12:36; 1 Thessalonians 5:5; Ephesians 5:8).

If the parable is read from the angle that the Pharisees and Scribes could be dishonest stewards running God's House in Jesus' day, then it is an urgent call for decision to make friends where it matters, for they are soon to be unemployed! Jesus says that *all* money is tainted, because so much dishonesty is associated with financial matters, and especially the acquiring of vast wealth. The only way that money could win you the type of friends that would welcome you into the tents of eternity is almsgiving – Luke's favourite use of money (16:9; 1 Chronicles 29:14). By a strange twist, the steward in this parable found that money was only useful to him when he gave it away!

This forms an excellent introduction to the story of Dives and Lazarus in 16:19–31. Jesus goes on to ask for responsible stewardship in money. By comparison with eternal riches and heavenly graces it is indeed a small thing, but one that affects us all, and deeply, in everyday decision making (16:10–12). Jesus wonders if we cannot be trusted to deal honestly and wisely with money, what would we do with His Church? His people? His mission? the gifts and graces of the Holy Spirit? the spiritual life, or even life itself? In all these things we are responsible stewards involved in authority and administration, decisions and consequences. The most intimate possessions a person can have lie in the spiritual sphere which is affected for good or ill by all other decisions. Astuteness and wisdom are urgently needed here (see 1 Timothy 3:5, 6:6–8).

"No servant can be the slave of two masters: he will either hate the first and love the second, or treat the first with respect and the second with scorn. You cannot be the slave both of God and of money" (16:13). This is the conclusion of the parable, and makes the whole point clear to us. The Aramaic word for money is "mammon", which usually stands for money gained dishonestly, yet the literal meaning is "that in which one puts one's trust". So Jesus is telling us about our tendency to trust money and what it can buy, so it can take the place of God in our lives very quickly. Love of money is the quickest way to kill the spiritual life, for it insulates a person from God and blocks the first Beatitude "Blessed are those who know their need of God".

The Danger of Loving Money (16:14–31)

The ever-present Pharisees in Jesus' audience laughed at His teaching on money. They were known as money lovers (16:14), and, moreover could cite the Law against Jesus here. Deuteronomy 28:1–14 promised wealth as a divine reward for keeping the Law, and besides being meticulous keepers of the Law, the Pharisees also practised almsgiving. Jesus was not impressed by their ability to justify themselves in the eyes of the people. They can be deceived by appearances, but God reads the heart and the motives that govern one's life (11:41, 16:15; 1 Samuel 6:17; Psalm 139:1–12). And Scripture gives abundant evidence that God hates the proud, arrogant and self-righteous, and exalts the lowly (1:51; Romans 12:16; 1 Timothy 6:17; Proverbs 16:5, 21:2). They should learn to fear God who has the power to reverse the fortunes of people after death (12:4–5, 16:19–31). These law-abiding, well dressed, and well-heeled hypocrites, will now be given enlightenment in the story of Dives and Lazarus, to warn them that they may find themselves outside of Abraham's banquet and the neglected poor inside (13:28–30).

Moreover, Jesus reminded the Pharisees that they were in a new era with regard to the Law. The Mosaic law and the teaching of the prophets lasted up to the time of the Baptist, who had the privilege of spanning two eras in his own lifetime. John's ministry completed the Old Testament period and inaugurated the era of the Kingdom of God (16:16). Since John's time the Kingdom of God has been preached, and only those who make real efforts at repentance and conversion are going to enter it, as has been abundantly illustrated in previous chapters (13:24). If the Pharisees remain looking on, they will be left out. There are no complimentary tickets being issued to the Messianic Banquet. What is happening under their very eyes does not nullify the Law and the Prophets. No! Anyone who truly understands the significance of Jesus' person and ministry realizes that He brought the Law and the prophets to their true fulfilment (16:17; Acts 15:21, 21:21).

To illustrate the point Jesus cites the law on divorce, and shows that His interpretation of it was stricter than the strictest Jewish interpretation of that time. The freedom that Jesus brings is the freedom to behave fully as sons and daughters of God, freedom to do God's Will on earth as it is done in heaven (6:46–49; Matthew 6:10). The Pharisees followed the teaching of Deuteronomy 24:1–4 on the question of divorce. This permitted a man to divorce his wife *for some impropriety in her*. The liberal school of Hillel, to which many of the Pharisees belonged, interpreted this "impropriety" as *any* fault displeasing the husband, even down to the triviality of burning the dinner! The strict school of Shammai demanded that this "impropriety" had to be infidelity to the partner. Jesus put both partners in marriage on the same footing with regard to both privilege and responsibility. In those days it was unheard of that a woman could divorce her husband. That was seen as a male preserve. Here, unusually for Luke, he cites only the male side of the issue, perhaps because it *was* only the man who divorced at that time (16:18; see Mark 10:11–12; Matthew 5:32, 19:19)?

For Luke's readers, there is the reminder that they are still "on the way", and must not get attached to wealth for fear that it would prevent them from entering into the eternal banquet of heaven. They are the privileged disciples of the New Era but they must fight valiantly to enter by the narrow gate (13:34), for fear that worldly laziness cause them to lose their place in heaven. They are still obliged to obey God's law, and the new stricter interpretation of marriage that Jesus gave them. There is no room for complacency on this pilgrimage at all. The story of Dives and Lazarus is for them in their time, as it was for the Pharisees in Jesus' time.

Dives and Lazarus (16:19–31)

The story which follows is a shock to those who follow the "prosperity gospel", who believe that wealth is a blessing, even a reward from God and a guarantee of God's blessings. In a few haunting phrases Jesus challenges the money lovers of all generations to wake up to the consequences of their actions, decisions and life style. *"I will tell you whom to fear: fear him who, after he has killed, has the power to cast into hell"* (12:5). When this story is read on a national and international level, it carries a great warning to the rich, overfed and indulged West (Dives), where the starving and sick Third World is Lazarus sitting at our feet looking at us from our TV screens while we eat.

The rich man is not condemned for *having* money,

204

but for its selfish use. The man is described as spending
it all on himself in luxurious clothing and food, in
total disregard for the poor man, Lazarus, whose name
means "God is my help". The poor man is literally at
his gate in great need, so sick and hungry that he
would gladly have taken the place of the house dogs
to catch the scraps of food that fell from the rich
man's table (see Mark 7:28; Proverbs 27:7). His poverty
and sickness put him in the same plight as the Prodigal
Son in 15:16. Even the dogs had pity on him, thus
highlighting man's inhumanity to man (16:28). Obviously
Lazarus *had* turned to God as his help, and somehow
in the dreadful crisis had never let go of his faith and
trust in God, because when he died he was *carried
away by the angels to the bosom of Abraham*. Then
his misfortune changed for now he participates in glory.
By contrast, *the rich man died and was buried* ... in
hell as we discover (16:22).

The great divide that separated Dives from Lazarus
in their lifetime cannot be compared with the gulf that
separates them permanently after death (16:26). Dives
is now a long way from his father Abraham's home
(15:13), but he can see Lazarus enjoying his company.
Being a son of Abraham, he cried to him for pity,
obviously not seeing the injustice of asking Lazarus to
do for him in death what he refused to do for Lazarus
in life, namely, to show compassion and alleviate his
suffering (16:23–24).

The Baptist had clearly warned Israel in 3:8 not to
presume on physical descent from Abraham as an automatic
ticket into the Kingdom of God. If they were to show
themselves true sons of Abraham, they should show their
faith in God by producing the fruits of true repentance,
which they consistently refused to do. Now Dives finds
the fruit of gluttony in a tortured tongue in Hades (16:24;

see 6:24–25). Lazarus' enforced fasting is being rewarded at the banquet in the Kingdom (16:26). The hungry are being fed with good things while the rich are sent empty away, but now it is permanent, and that is the tragedy (1:46). On earth there was always the possibility of repentance and conversion of heart.

At this point a new element comes in where Dives begs Abraham to send Lazarus as a missionary from the dead to warn his five brothers to repent before it is too late. Since five represents the Torah, or the Law, it possibly stands here for *all* Israel, and the request is to send Israel someone back from the dead in order to *make* them believe (16:27–28)! By the time the gospel was written, Israel had received the resurrection of Lazarus of Bethany (John 11) and that of Jesus, yet neither had the effect of converting the nation. All the gospels attest that miracles do not *produce* faith, and may not even increase it. Israel, and through her the rest of the world, had been given the Scriptures (Moses and the prophets), which they must listen to and obey (16:29–30).

Revelation is offered to everyone, but salvation depends on our response to the revealed Word of God. It is not *having* the Scriptures, but *obeying* them that makes the difference. For Dives, it would have demanded that he love his neighbour (Leviticus 19:18), and take care of the needs of the poor (Deuteronomy 15:6–11). If he had listened to Jesus (16:16) he would have become a Good Samaritan (10:25–37). His present position illustrates that he had not *behaved as a son of Abraham*. His selfish indifference to the plight of the poor was clear disobedience to God's Will as revealed in Scripture. If he was not open to God's Will or to loving concern for others he would also dismiss any extraordinary manifestations from God, as history has often shown (16:31).

Luke here warns his own community and us, the readers,

to put the story of the Crafty Steward (what to do with money) and the story of Dives (what not to do with money) together, and learn from them. Unlike the Crafty Steward, Dives did not use his wealth to win him friends who would welcome him into the tents of eternity (16:9). Lazarus would have made a useful contact "on the other side", but Dives did not cultivate his friendship! The mammon of iniquity would really have been useful if Dives had "cultivated" Lazarus by taking care of his needs and leaving him indebted to him (16:1–9). The community had hard lessons to learn from the tragedy of Ananias and Sapphira in Acts 5:1–11, but a shining example was given in the generosity of Barnabas in Acts 4:36–37.

Sin and Reconciliation (17:1–10)

Jesus was very aware that His disciples were new to the challenge he presented, and that true conversion of heart is a slow, agonizing process that takes years to accomplish, even amomg those who are honestly trying (13:24, 16:16). Hence he addressed what he knew would be the factual situation among His disciples in any given period. There would be sin, and erring disciples leading to scandal, lack of forgiveness and loss of faith as a result (17:1–3). The community must learn how to deal with these on-going crises. The vulnerable members, the "little ones", were especially to be looked after, those who might suffer a loss of faith due to the sinfulness of a person in authority. Human nature being as it is such things will happen, yet Jesus makes it clear that we are responsible for the results of our actions. He said that it would be better to die than to become a stumbling block to another, so fearful is the ensuing judgement (17:2).

Each one had the duty to watch his own step (17:3), but there was a community duty to correct one of the brethren who was seen to be going in the wrong direction (10:29–37, 17:4). If they repent they are to be forgiven, even if the process is continuous. Sinners in the community are to be forgiven each time they repent, no matter how often they sin (17:3–4). Continuous forgiveness is such a challenge that the Apostles feel their faith-level is too low, and so they request an increase of faith from Jesus, only to be told that minimal faith is enough (17:6)! Using the image of the mustard seed again Jesus says that the tiniest amount of faith is capable of great deeds because it is openness to the creative work of God in and through us (see 1 Corinthians 13:2). Since it allows God freedom to act, tasks, which seemed impossible when left to human resourcefulness, are now not only possible, but easy.

Although demanding great works from His disciples, Jesus warns them in another very Lukan parable not to seek reward in the way they observe among the leaders. Using an image from the world of slavery, which was considered normal at that time, Jesus speaks of a servant (the usual translation for *doulos*, a slave) working hard in the fields all day ploughing or minding sheep. When evening comes he still has household chores to do before he can rest, and still he can expect no thanks from his human master (17:7–9). Like the case of the Crafty Steward, Jesus is unafraid to use images from the harsh realities of everyday life to illustrate a point.

The Apostles and disciples are merely servants of God and it is their privilege to work in the vineyard (10:2). They are not to seek positions of authority and power like the Scribes and Pharisees (11:43), or to think that they are clocking up merit that will gain them a higher place in heaven. The Jews thought at that time that good works gave one a claim on God for due reward. Jesus repudiates this claim because creatures cannot put God in their debt. To be sure, this does not mean that God is mean (19:21), offering no reward to His faithful servants. We have already noted in 12:35–37 that He will not only be their Host at the Heavenly Banquet, but He will serve them! What is being corrected here is that proud, arrogant, self satisfied attitude of one who deserves 'B' for doing 'A', and therefore can perform the good for all the wrong motives (see 1 Corinthians 9:16). As sinners, constantly in need of divine grace and forgiveness we are to give thanks instead of seeking thanks. When the Pharisees had carried out all the "orders" of the Mosaic law what credit was due to them? God is entitled to our total and unending service. We are merely servants, that is, totally in God's service (17:10). Any reward comes from God's loving generosity and abundant grace.

The Coming Kingdom (17:11–37)

At this point Jesus and His followers were travelling along the border between Samaria and Galilee (17:11), making for the Jordan Valley and eventually Jericho (18:35) before beginning their ascent to Jerusalem and all that awaited them there. Mention of Samaria reminds us of the alienation and separation that existed between the Samaritans and the Jews, who hated them (see John 4:9). Besides, the ten men who came to meet Jesus here were alienated and separated from society by the dreadful disease of leprosy, which united the group of nine Jews and one Samaritan (17:18). The Samaritans were considered unclean by the Jews anyway, but the dreaded uncleanness of leprosy made other barriers disappear.

The Law forbade lepers from approaching healthy people, so they called from a respectable distance for Jesus to pity them and heal them (17:13). Unlike the healing of the leper in 5:12–15 Jesus did not approach them or touch them. He stood His ground and commanded them to go and show themselves to the priests as the Law required (Leviticus 13:45–46), for the Temple priests were like health inspectors (Leviticus 14:2–32) who could restore them to their village c_ mmunity. This group were challenged to believe on the Word of Jesus, something the Jewish nation found very difficult. They were to walk away believing, and as they did so, they were healed (17:14). As with Namaan the leper in 2 Kings 5:10–15, the healing was not immediate, but a journey was demanded as a test of faith. As with Namaan, the foreigner returned to give thanks for the healing (2 Kings 5:15; 17:17–19).

At this point there is an interesting development in the story. One of the ten, the only Samaritan in the group, when he realized he was healed, turned back from his journey in order to give thanks to Jesus. The other nine proceeded on to the Temple as instructed. Nowhere else does Jesus make an issue of anyone having to render thanks to Him for their healing, although Luke remarks on their exuberant praise and thanks to God. However, we have just come from the text where the servant was to give absolute service to the master (17:10). The servant is not to expect thanks from the master, but the master does expect thanks when he renders service to the servant (17:17). We have no right to God's mercy towards us and so we have a duty to render thanks. A wrong type of thanksgiving will be seen in the Pharisee's prayer in 18:11. Jesus ruefully remarks that no one came back to give praise to God except this foreigner (17:18).

The Samaritan threw himself at Jesus' feet in utter gratitude and praise. All alienation and separation that existed between him and Jesus at the beginning, either socially or religiously or from his disease, had now vanished. He wasn't satisfied to just thank God privately and go away to begin a new life. He came back to Jesus to render public thanks and associate himself with his healer/Saviour. Jesus commanded him to stand up as a new son of God, and begin his new spiritual journey as his faith had brought him salvation (17:19).

The sadness of this episode is that ten were healed, but only one allowed Jesus to become his Saviour. This person was the foreigner, the Samaritan. This healing, therefore, turns out to be a reflection on the response of Israel as a whole to Jesus. She was willing to accept healing but not salvation, yet Jesus came to bring salvation, not just healing. Those nine healed Jews would one day leave their bodies behind in death. What then? By contrast the Samaritan allowed himself to be healed body and soul. The healing should have pointed them to Jesus as their Redeemer. The foreigners and Gentiles in general would accept this. It is late in the story when Luke presents the hero as another Samaritan (17:16), not just a Good Samaritan whose charity was greater than that of the Jewish priest and Levite, but even worse, one who suffered a loathsome disease that was popularly seen as a curse from God.

To those whose eyes of faith are opened, this healed Samaritan is a sign that the Kingdom of God is a present reality among them, and that it comes in the person of Jesus. In spite of that the Pharisees ask Jesus when the Kingdom was about to manifest itself (17:20)! They are so blind to the mystery of the person of Jesus that they seek for the Kingdom of God everywhere except in front of their eyes. Jesus replied that they were not going to see the establishment of the Kingdom in the way they expected, for it was among them already (17:21). He had given them many signs which should have pointed to Him (10:21). There was no point in talking about the future manifestation of the Kingdom when they had not entered into it by faith and conversion of heart. The realization of the Kingdom would only occasion judgement for them.

However, there is still a future dimension to the Kingdom which Jesus went on to explain to His disciples (17:22). There was to be a long period between the departure of the Son of Man in His Passion and death, and His return in the Parousia. He has already given instructions for the behaviour of the disciples during that time (12:35–48). During the long night before Jesus' return (17:34) the disciples, under pressure from trials and persecutions (6:22–23, 12:11–12), will long for the days that will inaugurate the Second Coming (17:22). Nevertheless, it is as senseless to ask for the map of where it will occur as it is to ask for the timetable. Neither will be given (17:23–24). When the time comes, the Parousia will be as universally obvious as lightning flashing across the sky at night (17:25). It will be impossible not to see it. Disciples should be wary of *all* claims of "sightings" here and there, for such will surely come. However, we must put first things first. Jesus' departure must happen before this subject can become a reality. Jesus *must suffer greviously and be rejected by this generation* (17:25).

On the pre-Calvary time scale this refers to the rejection by the Jewish nation, but to a reader of the twentieth century it is plainly obvious that every generation has had to examine Jesus' claims to be the Messiah, and the majority reject them, as happened in His own day. This leads into the next section where Luke explains that the Parousia will find us unprepared, that it will be the day of the great divide when God will discriminate between those who are faithful and those who were not. Hence it will not be a day of rejoicing for many (17:31–37).

Jesus cites two examples from the Old Testament history to drive the lesson home. During the days of Noah (Genesis 6–8), the people rejected the word of this "preacher of righteousness" (2 Peter 2:5), and carried on their daily lives as if Noah's warnings contained no reality. This continued even up to the day when Noah entered the Ark and the Flood came and destroyed them all, except those who had obeyed God's Word (17:26–27). He also cites the case of Lot, who was saved from Sodom, when God rained down fire and brimstone destroying the five cities of the plain who had carried on living in total disregard to God's Will for them (Genesis 19:1–29). In both cases the judgement of God took everyone by surprise.

Unfortunately for us, human nature has not changed. Jesus had warned us that the Parousia will take the unheeding world by surprise too, when it is too late to repent (17:30; see 1 Thessalonians 5:3). And it will be a day of apocalyptic judgement (2 Thessalonians 1:7–9, 2:8–12). The amazing thing is that the reason for unpreparedness given here is not the awful sinfulness of the people in Noah's day (Genesis 6:11–13) or in Lot's day (Genesis 19:1–11) but their preoccupation with ordinary everyday life to the total exclusion of God and His Kingdom. The problem is the fact that their lives are God-less and their attachment is to the things of this world, as was the case of Lot's wife who looked back longingly to the life she had left behind so reluctantly, and in doing so perished (17:32).

Since human nature does not change, many will want to save their possessions. Jesus warns that when the Parousia comes, there will be no point in going back to salvage one's possessions. Attachment to material things then would cost them their lives (12:15, 16:13, 15). There will be no escape from judgement (17:33). Moreover, just as the judgement at the time of Noah and Lot discriminated between the good (those who listened to and obeyed the Word of God), and the wicked who rejected God's claims on their lives, so it will be when the Son of Man appears. Then the discrimination will even separate man and wife who will be dealt with separately (17:34). Luke says that of two in one bed, one will be taken and one will be left.

The disciples wonder *where* this discriminating judgement will occur, only to be given the enigmatic reply: *"Where the body is, there too will the vultures gather"* (17:37). A dead body can be tracked down in the desert by the vultures gathered overhead. The sight of the scavenging vultures is not pleasant, but they do the necessary job of removing masses of decay and putrefaction from the earth. The subject of judgement is equally unpleasant, but the day will come when Christ will come *to destroy those who are destroying the earth* (Revelation 11:18).

There may be a painful reminder here of the encircling Roman standards during the long siege of Jerusalem. The Roman standards had the sign of the eagle on them, and the encircling army must have appeared like vultures to the doomed city. Just as their presence signalled judgement for Jerusalem in AD 66–70, so the general judgement of the nations will be evident to all at the end of time.

The Need For Prayer (18:1–14)

For the ungodly and the unprepared, the Coming of the Son of Man will be a disaster, but for the believers, the interim period will be very difficult. They have to deal with evil within themselves and in the world, with the consequence of trials and persecutions. God's elect must endure all kinds of suffering and injustice that will be very severe (see Matthew 24:21–22). Jesus told them that during this time they must *pray continually and never lose heart* (18:1). Prayer is the source of their strength and supernatural joy, patience and long–suffering. It is the source of their inspiration and hope as they sense the nearness of the Lord. It gives the ability to forgive continually, as they have been told to do (17:4). It is the source of fraternal love, the bond that binds disciples into a community of love. The early Church leaders greatly emphasized the need for constant, persevering prayer (Romans 1:10,12:12; Ephesians 6:18; Colossians 1:3 etc).

The story concerns a poor widow and an unjust and corrupt judge. A Jewish judge was seen as the protector of the poor, the helpless and the oppressed. The widow was a symbol of all those he was pledged to serve, but this judge had no fear of God or man in him, which means that he had no concern for God's judgement, on him or anyone else. Hence he represents the unbelieving and corrupt judges the disciples will face on their mission, from whom they can expect no justice. Since the widow has no money, and therefore cannot bribe the judge, he has no interest in her case whether it is just or otherwise. Her only hope is to sit on his doorstep and persevere with her request until the very sight of her depresses him (18:3–5). Then he will deal with the case just to get rid of her.

Again we have Luke using a scoundrel to teach us a lesson, for if the widow can get her just rights from an unrighteous man, how much more will God listen to the persistent cries of His chosen ones, who cry out to Him day and night, even if He delays to help them (18:6–8; see Revelation 6:10; Romans 8:33). The big problem in prayer is the long delay in receiving an answer which tests the perseverance of the pray-er. Justice will be done, Jesus says, when the Son of Man returns (18:8), but will the elect persevere that long? He wonders will there be ANY faith left on earth when He returns, or will everyone have given up?

This parable is similar to one about the friend at midnight in 11:5–8, and is given here to strengthen the young community of Christians in the face of a period of persecution and suffering. Just as there was "a day" for Israel, so the church must persevere in hope until *the age of the pagans is completely over* (21:24). Then, as Israel received judgement, so will the Gentile nations, and from the same impartial judge. When the time for judgement comes, after the long delay, it will be as sudden as it was for the Flood and for Sodom (18:7).

Right and Wrong Ways to Pray (18:9–14)

Having brought up the subject of prayer, Jesus reminds us again that our inner attitudes make all the difference. Persevering prayer does not just mean words uttered in God's presence with no corresponding inner conversion of heart. There is yet another group who will be unprepared for the Parousia. This surprising group are very religious, and externally look ideally prepared, but unfortunately their religious observance has filled them with self righteous pride and this is one of the greatest obstacles to our conversion.

Jesus gave this teaching to *some people who prided themselves on being virtuous and despised everyone else* (18:9). The two men who went to pray in the Temple embody attitudes we have frequently met in this gospel. One is the self-righteous Pharisee who saw no need for repentance, for he kept the Law fully, and the self-abasing tax collector, whom everyone knew needed to repent. The first group held the second group in contempt. The Pharisee stood before God pompously unaware of any debt on his side. Indeed he could boast of his religious observance. In the eyes of the people as well as himself, he was loaded with virtues, the best that Israel could produce, whereas the loathsome tax collector was at the other end of the scale, working for the hated Roman occupation, with a career that spelt corruption and avarice. His very job denoted uncleanness and sin. These men stand apart.

The Pharisee feels free to go up to God's presence in a strong position, for he went beyond the prescriptions of the Law in fasting twice a week (5:33–35). He was only expected to pay tithes of his major crops, but he tithed everything (11:42, Numbers 18:21; Deuteronomy 14:22). He appears to be unaware that his religion is a combination of works of supererogation (what the Law did not require), and what he is not, what he did not do, what he kept away from ... he was not grasping ... adulterous ... (18:11). Yet he did not scruple to judge *the rest of mankind* as adulterous, and the tax collector as grasping and unjust, one who dared to pray in a holy place in his unclean condition! There is a conspicuous absence of love, justice, or mercy from this list of "goodness" (11:42).

By contrast the tax collector stands at a distance, possibly in the outer court of the Temple where the Gentiles were allowed to gather, *not daring even to raise his eyes to heaven* (18:13; see Psalm 123:1). Instead, he beat his breast with grief, the sign of one longing for forgiveness. He accepted the condemnation of his neighbour, but did not judge him in return. Instead, with a humble and contrite heart (Psalm 51:1, 17) he threw himself on God's mercy and begged forgiveness, making no excuses, and no claims to good works in his life. Reading the hearts of both of these men, Jesus said that the latter went home justified in God's sight, while the former did not, because, as we have already seen in the Magnificat, and in 14:11, God exalts the lowly but resists the proud of heart.

Entry into the Kingdom of God (18:15–19:10)

Since 17:20–37 we have dealt largely with the Second Coming and the preparation for it. Now Jesus deals with those who enter the Kingdom of God in its present phase. So, who may enter, and what are the conditions for entry? The first story concerns mothers who took their children to Jesus to bless them, for a mother's instinct is to give her child everything that is good, and every opportunity for development. However, the disciples thought this was a waste of Jesus' time since He was on His way to Jerusalem to accomplish great things. There was no time for this type of piety. *But Jesus called the children to him* (18:16), saying that the Kingdom of God belonged to them and to others like them, and they were not to be prevented from coming because of adult misunderstanding of their place.

They represent the poor, lowly ones of the earth, all those who, like children, will receive from Jesus love, forgiveness, protection and salvation, without reflecting whether they deserve it or not. Jesus says that *"anyone who does not welcome the kingdom of God like a little child will never enter it"*, thus making their attitudes of humility and openness to God and life, models for adults (18:17). Like the grateful Samaritan (17:11–19), the widow (18:1–8) and the tax collector (18:9–14), they must receive the Kingdom of God with faith, grateful praise, persistence, and the unpretentiousness of a child (18:17), if they wish to enter it on the great day of the Son of Man (17:22–37).

Luke now presents an example of one who did not enter the kingdom like a child. A member of one of the leading families came to Jesus. Being one of the aristocracy he was very rich (18:23), and so enjoyed all that money could buy. He was also a good man by the standards of the Law, which he kept meticulously (18,22). He addressed Jesus respectfully: *"Good Master, what have I to do to inherit eternal life?"* (18:19). His question is the same as the lawyer's in 10:25, yet Jesus deals with it differently, because of his ability to read hearts. Perhaps this man wants to enter the final stage of the kingdom without having to go through any change, and feels that he is ready for it?

It was most unusual to address a rabbi as "Good Master" since this term was reserved to God alone (see Psalms 106:1, 118:1, 136:1; 1 Chronicles 16:34; 2 Chronicles 5,13). The reader, who knows that Jesus is the Son of God recognizes the irony in Jesus' question . Had the man recognized Jesus' divine sonship, he could call Him good. Otherwise it was just empty flattery. Jesus pulled him up on this, reminding him that ultimate goodness was an attribute of God alone (18:20). Perhaps Jesus meant to stir his conscience with some remembrance of shortcomings? As Paul reminds us in Romans 3:23 *all have sinned, and lack God's glory.* But as we have seen before, the meticulous keeping of the Law can cloak a sense of sinfulness, which is needed as the first requirement for entrance into the Kingdom. If there is no sense of sinfulness no need of a Saviour will be felt.

Since this man is from one of the leading families, Jesus can presume knowledge of the Law: *"You know the commandments"* (18:20) The Decalogue of Moses was a summary of our relationship with God and neighbour. The first four commandments pertain to our relationship with God, and the last six to that with our neighbour. Since the man presents himself as a keeper of the commandments Jesus homes in on the second half of the Decalogue: *"You must not commit adultery"* he said to a man who thought he was good. *"You must not kill"* he said to a keeper of God's law. *"You must not steal"* he said to a rich man. *"You must not bring false witness"* he said to one who considered himself upright and truthful.

219

"Honour your father and mother" he said to one who was good and therefore, would see to his social obligations.

Throughout this examination the man felt unchallenged for he had kept them all – and from his earliest days! This was no wild youth kicking against the traces. He was a good man, and his very goodness was his problem. He could not see that he lacked anything, or that his religion was negative. "Thou shalt not . . ." He had kept away from evil, but had he done any good? The great "Thou shalt . . ." of the Mosaic law demanded love towards God and neighbour, as the lawyer in 10:25–28 well knew. The present young man is caught on legalism in religion, and the love of riches (see Philippians 3:6–7). He is not aware of this until Jesus asks him to open up his wallet and his heart to become a giver of life to others. *"Sell all that you own and distribute the money to the poor, and you will have treasure in heaven; then come, follow me"* (18:22–23).

Love is a free gift from the heart, unsolicited, utterly other-centred. It is the most divine energy within us, and life's greatest challenge. Even when expressed on the material level of sharing one's goods, it gives life to the poor and needy. This is where Jesus asks the man to begin to develop treasure in heaven. All he has is on earth now, subject to both decay and theft. If he transfers to the heavenly bank his treasures will be eternal, and his heart in the right place (12:34). Learning to give on the material level is a good training ground for learning to give on deeper levels of one's being, so that others can receive life in all its abundance (John 10:10). Detached from earthly possessions, he would then be free to follow Jesus on His way to God and eternal life in the Kingdom (18:22). If only he knew what a treasure the Kingdom was, he would give everything just to have it (see Matthew 13:44–46). Unfortunately the man is attached to his wealth and goes away sad. Perhaps he could not let go of the

Old Testament idea that wealth was a sign of God's blessing? If so, Jesus' challenge was too radical and too great. What the young man refused to do was normal practice in the early Church, as Peter was quick to point out (2 Corinthians 6:10, 8:9; Acts 2:44–45, 4:32–37).

Jesus looked at the man sadly, for He knew better than he what had occurred. This man would be the first of millions, who, when they compared the Kingdoms of this world with the Kingdom of our Lord and of His Christ, would choose the former, where they had power, influence and everything that mammon controlled. In the end they reject God for mammon, for they, like the Pharisees and the Sadducees, do not succeed in serving both (16:13).

Jesus' comment was that it was hard, indeed impossible, for one given to riches to enter the Kingdom. It is as hard for them as it is for a camel to go through the eye of a needle, which is impossible (18:25). Since it was ingrained in the popular mind that riches were a blessing from God (see Deuteronomy 28:1–8; Job 1, 42:10–17) and equally, since everyone depends on money for so much that life offers, the listeners asked Jesus if anyone could be saved? (18:26). Jesus' reply throws us back to the Annunciation to Mary in 1:37, and to Genesis 18:14, where we see that what is impossible to limited human beings is possible to the creative power of God (18:27). Grace can work a miracle in the heart of a rich man, as shall see in the case of Zacchaeus in 19:1–10:

Peter reminded Jesus that he and the other disciples had given the response demanded of the rich man (5:11, 18:28). Was there to be no reward for their renunciation? Was there no advantage to joining oneself to Jesus' group? In His reply, Jesus listed the various personal sacrifices they had made. Many had left wife, brothers (relatives), parents, or children for the sake of the Kingdom. Jesus promised that they would be rewarded in kind both in this present stage and in the final stage of the Kingdom (see 1 Corinthians 9:5). Self denial for the sake of the Kingdom will be vindicated. Notice the absence of material possessions here.

The emphasis is on the sacrifice of family life and its comforts, and may reflect the divisions in families in the early Church, as someone left all to follow Jesus (12:51–53). As the Jerusalem church lived in community groups (Acts 2:42–47, 4:23–37, 5:12–16), they quickly learned about the new brothers, sisters and family that Jesus promised. Those who travelled on missionary work also found the hearts and homes of many in foreign lands open up to them as the family of Jesus grew. Here they learned the humility of the child (18:17) and, unlike those who cling to material possessions and earthly values and relationships (17:26–31), they joined Jesus in accepting suffering, rejection and renunciation (17:25, 18:28–30).

With a jolt Jesus brings the Twelve back to the reality of the journey and its goal, with His third official prediction of the Passion, although it is Luke's seventh reference to it (5:35, 9:22, 43–45, 12:50, 13:32–33, 17:25, 18:31–34). Everything that will soon happen has been predicted by the prophets (see Isaiah 52–53; 50:4–9; Psalms 22, 30, 88 etc). For the first time Jesus indicates that he will die at the hands of the Gentiles (18:32–33), but He will rise triumphantly on the third day. Luke emphatically states their complete incomprehension of this message: *But they could make nothing of this . . .* (18:34). They also felt no desire to ask for clarification either. Not until they meet the Risen Lord will the pattern begin to unfold. Like the nation of Israel, they are blind, partly because of their mind-set regarding Messianic expectations. Their idea of a Messiah did not include rejection, maltreatment, suffering, death, and an other-worldly kingdom, so Jesus is speaking from an incomprehensible position.

A Blind Man who Could See (18:35–43)

Just at this crucial point in their journey they reach Jericho, with the long climb to Jerusalem ahead of them. Here in this city, where the Israelites first entered the Promised Land to experience the fulfilment of all God's promises to them through Abraham and Moses, Jesus is addressed as Messiah (18:39) by a blind man, Bartimaeus (Mark 10:46–52), who allows Jesus to do the impossible for him. He lets Jesus remove the obstacle that blindness made to his entrance into the Kingdom, so that he, too, could follow Jesus on His journey and experience all that God planned for him (18:43). Here he is presented as a model for the Israelites and disciples alike.

Luke, who alone relates the story of Zacchaeus' conversion, gives an interesting triptych here, beginning with the healing of blind Bartimaeus in 18:35–43, as Jesus enters Jericho. Then the conversion of Zacchaeus in Jericho (19:1–10, and finally, the parable of the pounds as the group leave Jericho (19:11–27). It is a fitting climax to the journey motif and preparation for the Jerusalem ministry.

Bartimaeus (Mark 10:44) was a blind man whose disability condemned him to begging at the side of the road. Having enquired about the crowd that was going past, he was told that Jesus of Nazareth was there (18:37). Obviously this was what the people called Jesus, especially all those who had not penetrated the mystery of his person and mission. Yet the unseeing eyes of Bartimaeus did perceive what those with physical sight missed. He called on Jesus as the Davidic Messiah: *"Jesus, Son of David, have pity on me"* (18:38). Jesus was on His way to Jerusalem to declare Himself for the first time the Davidic

Messiah (19:28–40), and here the blind man is His fore-runner and proclaims this truth. The crowd, with its lack of perception, tried to drown this prophetic voice but could not, as Bartimaeus raised his voice above the din until Jesus heard him (18:39).

Here he typified the persistent prayer of all true disciples (11:5–8; 18:1–10) who continue until the Lord gives them their heart's desire. Like children, who are models for disciples (18:15–17), when his prayer is not heard he raises the volume rather than lengthens the prayer (Matthew 6:7–9). Jesus stopped and ordered the man to be brought to Him. There, standing before a blind man Jesus asked: *"What do you want me to do for you?"* (18:41). This request is a little puzzling if one presumes one knows what the beggar wants. Love does not presume, so Jesus allows the man to express the desire of his heart. Barti-maeus replies that he wants the gift of his sight, namely the ability to live a full life. He does not ask for short-cuts or hand-outs. From someone else he would merely ask for money (Acts 3:5), as they could not save him from his situation. But Jesus is different. He is the Davidic Messiah, so he requests salvation instead.

Jesus gave him his sight and assured him that his faith, his openness to let God work in him, is what saved him (18:42). Instantly the man could see, and the first object he ever beheld was his Messiah and Saviour (see Ephesians 3:21). He followed Jesus as a disciple, praising God that the Messiah had come his way. Here, in one simple movement of grace, Bartimaeus experienced all that the Scribes and Pharisees could not comprehend because of their unbelief, and the fact that they felt no need of Jesus or why He came.

Bartimaeus, unlike the Apostles, the Scribes, Pharisees and the Jews in general, was not scandalized at the appearance of the Davidic Messiah as a dust stained traveller on the

Jericho road, nor indeed, as a humble servant of God, ready to hear a poor man's cry. Perhaps if he followed Jesus to Jerusalem, he was not scandalized by the Passion either? Did he perceive that if the King did not come close enough to His subjects to be rejected, scourged and killed, that He might not have come close enough to heal the suffering poor either? Did he know what Luke's community and we, the readers, know about Jesus the King? That He could not only serve them and suffer for them on earth, but also serve them in glory (12:37, 22:27)?

Meanwhile those who follow Him along the road to glory, are challenged eventually by Peter (who did not understand at this stage) to follow Jesus on the path of innocent suffering for the sake of the Kingdom and the salvation of souls (1 Peter 1:6–12, 2:18–25). Paul said the same when he told his converts that entry into the Kingdom lies through many trials and tribulations (Acts 14:22). Jesus made Himself poor to enrich us, who are poverty stricken beggars in spiritual things, so that through His poverty we might become rich (2 Corinthians 8:9). Because of this we should be willing to suffer with Him now before entering into His glory (Romans 8:17).

A Rich Man Enters The Kingdom (19:1–10)

The final act of Jesus before the Jerusalem ministry begins concerns the dramatic conversion of a rich tax collector, who was well known, since he was the chief tax collector in the fertile oasis of Jericho, which was on an important trading route through the Jordan valley. Since he was in charge of all taxes, customs and excise, Zacchaeus would have been a household name, as well as being hated by everyone. On top of that he was short in stature, a fact that would go against his social acceptance, where he would be unable to tower over others either physically or psychologically. He was known to be a wealthy man, most probably through extortion, bribery and corruption. The synagogue despised him, and the people hated him. As such he was a man whose wealth could not procure for him what he most needed, namely, acceptance in the community and love. He was a lost sheep of the House of Israel, who desperately needed a shepherd "to seek out and save that which was lost" (15:4–7, 19:10).

As Jesus' last great act before entering Jerusalem, the saving of Zacchaeus is a commentary on the whole mission ahead for the disciples. Zaccheus was anxious to see Jesus, and, as we shall see, this indicated not just curiosity but a heart open to God's salvific action, to conversion and to the challenge of a new life. Nevertheless, he could not presume on acceptance by Jesus since he was rejected by everyone else. So he forgot his wealth, his dignity, his high office, and climbed a sycamore tree to catch a glimpse of Jesus as He passed by. In his own way, this showed a childlike disposition that indicated he was not all bad (19:3–4).

The surprise in the story is that the initiative is taken by Jesus. Zacchaeus did not presume to come to Him (7:1–10), so He came to Zacchaeus, and invited himself to his house as a guest that very day, so there was no time for delay. The mission was urgent and the conversion of sinners was not to be delayed. They must come into the Kingdom now, while there was still time, for a decisive confrontation between God and Israel is imminent just then, and there will be one for the Gentiles and God before the day of the Son of Man. Conversion is urgent for all.

Zacchaeus accepted Jesus joyfully, and the salvation that He brought. In that moment of confrontation with Jesus, he discovered his long-lost dignity as a son of Abraham, and a member of God's Household. He was a man loved by God with an eternal love, so great that He sent His Son to seek him out and find him, and rescue him from slavery to sin, and to the god, mammon. Here the Saviour of all the world stood in his own house and invited him personally into the Kingdom. Outside, everyone complained that Jesus went into a sinner's house – thus defiling himself (19:7). They had no perception that we are all sinners and every house Jesus entered was a sinner's house. But he entered it as Saviour, not as one in solidarity with evil. Zacchaeus understood this.

The criticism and condemnation of the crowd did nothing to change Zacchaeus' heart, in fact, it would only harden it (19:7). The acceptance and love of Jesus released the vice-grip of money on him, and he was a free man, free to give a response to Jesus that would shame the Pharisees, for he decided to give half his wealth to the poor, just to begin with! The rich young man would have been amazed (18:22–23). From the other half, Zacchaeus promised to repay fourfold anyone he had cheated. This went way beyond what either the Jewish or Roman Law required. Only in extreme cases was fourfold restitution demanded. Jewish law required one plus one-fifth (Numbers 5:7) unless for very serious theft (Exodus 21:37–22:3).

Since Zacchaeus generously decided to love his neighbour without counting the cost, Jesus did not ask him to sell all and give to the poor. No doubt this first stage of giving set him on the road to more generous service for the Kingdom later. Jesus stood there listening to this marvellous confession of sin and repentance, and pronounced that salvation had come to the whole household; that a lost sheep was restored to the fold. The early Church had to follow in his footsteps, in accepting Gentile sinners into the fold in the teeth of opposition (Acts 10, 11:14, 16:15, 18:8). They too had to learn that entering a Gentile household was not a defilement (Acts 10:15–16, 20–21); see Galatians 2:11–14).

The final statement before they set out for Jerusalem

is a fitting commentary on the whole ministry of Jesus and a declaration of the fulfilment of His mission programme at Nazareth (4:18): *"the Son of Man has come to seek out and save what was lost"* (19:10).

The Road to Jerusalem (19:11–27)

As they travelled the uphill road from Jericho to Jerusalem the people accompanying Jesus discussed His teaching concerning the coming of the Kingdom (18:31). Listening to them, Jesus realized that they thought the Kingdom was going to manifest itself then and there on their arrival in Jerusalem. So He set about correcting this false notion (19:11). Their misconception was understandable given the proclamation of Jesus as the Davidic Messiah by Bartimaeus and His own explanation of His mission in terms of seeking out and saving the lost. Not understanding the predictions about the Passion and Resurrection (18:32–34), they did not grasp that it is the Risen Lord who will be their King. Their idea of the Kingdom is too worldly and limited. The parable of the Pounds needs to be read in this context, for, typical of Luke's presentation, it looks both backward and forward.

Jesus, the Messianic King and Son of David, is about to make His official Messianic entry into Jerusalem to offer a peace that will be rejected. This begins a process that will end in the destruction of Jerusalem and its famous Temple, which was one of the wonders of the world at that time. The people were full of political hopes and frustrations, and it would be disastrous for them to interpret the coming events of the Jerusalem ministry in political terms. Luke has told us often enough that the Kingdom is a present reality with a final stage to be manifested in the Parousia. The parable fits this in-between stage, which is the time of the Church (9:27, 22:69).

As they were leaving Jericho the home of Archelaus, son of Herod the Great, Jesus told His story based on a journey that Archelaus took in 4 BC to have his kingship confirmed by the Roman Emperor. His father had left him Judaea and the title of king, but this needed to be confirmed by Rome (19:12). Since the Jews hated him, they sent a delagation to oppose his mission (19:14), and succeeded in persuading Augustus to give him only half his father's kingdom and the title of "ethnarch", a fact attested to by Josephus in his Antiquities. He turned out to be a bad and cruel ruler, who, according to Josephus, was eventually deposed and deported to Gaul and replaced by a Roman Governor.

This appears to be the historical background to a story about Jesus' Kingship which will be bestowed on Him after His ascension to glory (24:50–53) and His eventual return at history's fulfilment (Acts 3:20–26). Jesus is, therefore, the nobleman about to go to a distant country to be appointed king, and afterwards return in the Parousia (19:12). He calls ten of his servants and shared out ten pounds equally among them. This small sum was a test of faithfulness in the servants (16:10), to see if they could be trusted with greater things (19:17). The servants are expected to prove themselves worthy of this greater trust by a master who offered equal opportunities to his servants. Discrimination will only come at the judgement when the master returns.

Thus the parable is aimed specifically at Christians who live their lives between the First and Second Comings of Jesus, between the Ascension and the Parousia, and it highlights their responsibilities and problems during the long delay. Besides, Jesus the King will be rejected by His people and persecution will be the norm for His loyal subjects (19:14, 23:1–25). The Church will be persecuted by those who reject the present reality of the Kingdom in their midst.

After this introduction, the parable focuses on the king's return, and the day of reckoning for his servants (19:15–25). It will be a day of slaughter for the king's enemies too (19:27; see Revelation 19, 20 and 21), but the king's servants need not focus on this, as they have their own duties and responsibilities to see to. The Lord Himself will deal with others for "Vengeance is mine, I will pay them back" says the Lord (Romans 12:19; Hebrews 10:31). The servants must not remain passive in the Lord's absence. They have received a trust which must be developed according to their ability. If they neglect this mission they will have no place in the full manifestation of the kingdom (19:15–25). Furthermore, they will be punished (12:35–48), for they received a serious commission which had everlasting consequences for themselves and others, and they must come to terms with this.

Like the Scribes and Pharisees in Jesus' day, who must look on as the tax collectors and sinners take *their* places in the Kingdom, unfaithful Christians will also see their places taken by others (19:24–25), for God is an impartial judge. At the Last Supper we will hear that those who *have* remained faithful, will join Jesus as judges when the kingdom is fully manifested (22:30).

The parable makes it clear that each servant will be interviewed (judged) by the king. There will be no hiding behind the community and its good works. Each one must render an account of his stewardship alone, and hear the king's personal judgement upon him. The king sent for the servants *to find out what profit each one had made* (19:15). Like Israel (the fig tree), fruit was expected and judgement pronounced in its absence (13:6–9). Only three responses from the ten are given as examples. (Ten is a number denoting the fullness of earthly things, so here it represents all that the servants were doing on earth). The first servant had done well and made ten pounds from the one given. The master's "well done!" was accompanied by giving the servant responsibility over ten cities! The image of the manifestation of the Kingdom is thus not the end of the world, but of the Reign of Christ (see Revelation 20). The second servant did well but not as well as the first, and he was rewarded with five cities (19:18–19).

The third servant, on the other hand, shows what happens to the lazy and wicked servant who did nothing and excused his behaviour on the grounds of fear of judgement! He also, like the elder brother, judged his Master as unjust (19:21, 15:29–30). This one displayed neither love nor loyalty to the king, and is condemned out of his own mouth (19:22). He had to stand there and watch his money being given to the servant who had worked hardest (19:25). On a monetary level this would appear strange, but on the level of work for the Kingdom, it means that some of the work was left undone, and the king gave it to the competent and generous servant to do. The text does not imply that the wicked servant was excluded from the Kingdom (see 1 Corinthians 3:15), but that he has done no work for the Lord.

The parable finishes with the proverb that completed the parable of the Lamp in 8:18: *"to everyone who has will be given more; but from the man who has not, even what he has will be taken away"* (19:26). This has been illustrated in the first and third servants, and Jesus explains the loss as that person's own fault. It is our own responsibility if eventually we stand empty-handed of all good deeds before the Lord on that Great Day of Reckoning. The graces and opportunities were given equally to all, but the responses were different. The lazy servants must come to see that "having a good time" may go sour on them someday. It is better to spend one's life-energy on what will outlast life.

Chapter Five
The Jerusalem Ministry

Entry into Jerusalem (19:28–48)

At last we reach the climax of this long journey to the city of destiny. As they neared the city Jesus went ahead of them, His mind occupied with matters they could not grasp. He was going to receive His Kingdom (19:12) by the extraordinary means of the Passion, death and Resurrection (19:12, 14, 27). There are three stages to this final and official entry of the Messiah King into His own city (19:29–46). First, the descent from the Mount of Olives (19:29–40), from which He will ascend to the Father later, in His resurrection victory (24:50–53; Acts 1:12). This is the official entry and exit of the Messianic King and Son of David from His own city under the uncomprehending gaze of His subjects. The second stage is 19:41–44, as He drew near to the city from the Mount of Olives and its wonderful panoramic view of Jerusalem that so moves pilgrims even today. It moved Jesus to shed tears over it, and its rejection of God's plan. 19:45–48 is the third stage when Jesus enters the Temple and takes authority over the Household of God. Here the focus is Jesus' daily activity in the Temple and the reaction to His teaching.

Jesus carefully planned His descent from the Mount of Olives. As He alone knew what the future held, He requested that the disciples bring Him a colt that no one had ever ridden. Its owner would release it upon learning that the Lord wanted it (19:30–34). Obviously he was a disciple and understood the Master's need to commandeer the donkey for a while. A disciple would also appreciate the necessity of putting one's possessions at the disposal of the Kingdom of God. Jesus was right. It happened just as He said.

The choice of the donkey was a symbolic message to the leaders of Israel, who would interpret an entry on horseback as a symbol of war (see Acts 9:1–9), but the donkey was a symbol of peace. To add to the significance the disciples threw their cloaks over the donkey's back for Jesus to ride on, and the people spread their cloaks on the road in front of the donkey. This was an overt conferring of kingship on Jesus, a gesture known from earliest times (see 1 Kings 1:38; 2 Kings 9:13). The whole scene evoked the prophecy of Zechariah 9:9–10: *"Rejoice heart and soul, daughter of Zion! Shout with gladness, daughter of Jerusalem! See now, your king comes to you, he is victorious and triumphant, humble and riding on a donkey... He will proclaim peace for the nations. His empire shall stretch from sea to sea, from the River to the ends of the earth."* The prophet goes on to say that this person will be (1) rejected, and sold for thirty pieces of silver (11:11–13) and killed (12:9–11), (2) the fountain of forgiveness (13:7), (3) the Lord who will be King forever (14:9) on the day of His Visitation (14:5), and there will be no traders in the Temple afterwards (14:21).

This entry also evokes Judah's rule over the twelve tribes in Genesis 49:10–11: The fact that a colt which was never used before was always chosen for especially holy sacrificial purposes (Numbers 19:2; Deuteronomy 21:3; 1 Samuel 6:7). Here it signifies, not only the holiness of Jesus, but the sacrificial nature of what was to take place on Calvary. There is the added fact that His rule is a completely new phenomenon in salvation history. As King, and leader of a new Israel, Jesus fulfils and transcends Old Testament expectations of Him.

As Jesus slowly descended the Mount of Olives with the magnificent panorama of the city and its Temple before Him, the whole group of disciples joyfully began to praise God at the top of their voices *for all the miracles they had seen*. They also cried out: *"Blessings on the King who comes in the name of the Lord! Peace in heaven and glory in the highest heavens!"* (19:38; Psalm 118:26). Here Luke has us recall the whole ministry of mighty works before the sun sets on Jesus' ministry with such speed. They acclaim Jesus as the blessed king without associating it with His death, as the reader should (13:35). This tiny crowd is not representative of the Jerusalem leadership or people who will shortly reject Jesus officially and finally.

Nevertheless, the crowd unconsciously proclaims the truth and the deepest meaning of the events that are taking place. The day has yet to dawn when Jerusalem accepts her Messiah King. As the angels proclaimed at his birth (2:14) he is the king of Peace and He alone can bring true peace and reveal God's glory to Jerusalem and everywhere else. To reject His person and His peace is to sign one's own death warrant. Jerusalem means the city of peace. For her to reject her king of peace was to court disaster (19:2, 41–44, 21:5–28).

Some Pharisees who have not been privy to Jesus' forecast in 13:33–35 demanded that Jesus check His disciples (19:39). No doubt they feared trouble from political elements who could stir up an uprising (23:16–25). From a religious point of view they rejected the idea that an itinerant preacher would allow himself to be acclaimed as a king who came in the Lord's name. Jesus replied that there was no silencing the truth (19:40)!

As He drew near the city the wonderful sight that had moved thousands of pilgrims to tears of joy each year, moved Jesus to tears of sorrow and lament. This great city refused to recognize who came to her in the person of Jesus. She was blind to this greatest of all divine visitations in her history. As predicted (11:47–51), she was about to reject this last and greatest prophet sent to her, and she must live out the consequences. The great prophet Jeremiah (chapter 7) had told Jerusalem in his day, that she would be destroyed and her Temple reduced to ruins for her refusal to hear God's Word through the prophets. It was no different now. The long sight of Jesus, their prophet, could already see the invading armies of Titus, even though these events lay forty years into the future. He could see the wanton destruction of this beautiful city and the murder of its citizens. There would only be silent stones left to give testimony to an amazed world as to why the daughter of Zion had been brought low. She was warned (19:42–44)!

To refuse to hear and obey the Word of God has serious and permanent consequences for us all. It meant destruction for this city. What will it mean for the individual soul (see Mark 8:36)? Jerusalem needed the faith of Bartimaeus and the openness of Zacchaeus. Otherwise the truth would be hidden from her. Since she was blind to what the ordinary people of Nain could see, that God had visited them (7:16; 1:78), she would be destroyed, and there would not be one stone left upon another.

Jesus in the Temple of God (19:45–21:38)

The third and final stage came with Jesus entering the Temple in Jerusalem. Apart from being one of the wonders of the Near Eastern world at that time, it was the centre of Jewish worship, for it housed the Presence of the God of Israel in its inner sanctum, the Holy of Holies. Of course there was nothing to see, as the Emperor Titus mockingly related on entering it in AD 70, for God is a Spirit. All Israel understood this spiritual Presence, and revered, not only the Temple, but the city that held such a treasure. Malachi 3:1–5 had predicted that first the Lord would send a forerunner to prepare Israel for His coming. Then the Lord Himself would suddenly appear in the Temple to purify it and its sacrifices. Malachi viewed this as a judgement on all evildoers. The rest of Malachi's prophecy deals with the discriminating judgement on the day of the Lord (Malachi 3:13–4:3; 17:20–37). But for those who turned to the Lord in repentance there would be healing (Malachi 4:2), and a revived Elijah would turn the heart of the nation back to God (Malachi 4:3–6).

In this context Jesus' cleansing of the Temple was certainly *according to scripture* (19:45), for this cleansing was expected at the end of time (Malachi 3:4; Zechariah 14:21; Ezekiel 40–48). It is a definitive Messianic sign to Israel, whose significance no one would miss. At the time of Christ the outer court of the Gentiles, (the only part of the Temple where non-Jews could pray) was turned into a market for buying and selling animals for sacrifice. The highly unpopular Sadducees who controlled the markets, refused to accept animals brought by the people from their farms, and insisted that they buy animals specially reared for the Temple at exorbitant prices, thus exploiting the poor. And of course there was the money changing for all those travellers from abroad who came to Jerusalem for the feasts. Every Jew had to pay Temple tax also, and it was payable only in shekels, the only coin with no image of a king on it, but the money changers charged for their services and for the exchange.

Quoting both Isaiah 56:7 and Jeremiah 7:1, Jesus took over, and threw them all out, on the grounds that God's House was meant to be a House of Prayer for all peoples, and they had prevented any non-Jews from having access to the presence of God by turning this outer court into a market place. Jeremiah (7:11) had spoken these words as a prediction of the destruction of the Temple. Jesus was opening a way for tax collectors, sinners and Gentiles to find a place in the Household of God. That new and sacred way that only the redeemed could walk upon (Isaiah 35: 8–10) was the one He was carving out on this fateful journey to Jerusalem, through Calvary and on to glory, where all nations would be redeemed and find everlasting joy, and where there will be no need of a temple of stone, since the Body of Christ will be a living Body (see John 4:21; Acts 7:48; 1 Corinthians 12).

Jesus had come to the Temple on other occasions as a private worshipper (2:41–50, 21:37–38), but now He took authority there and taught daily (19:47) in the last lap of His public ministry. Thus having taken the Chair of Moses, He restored the House of God as a place of prayer for everyone. And also as a place where the Word of God could be authoritatively preached and heard, as was fitting in God's House. The people sensed that something special was afoot and *hung on his words* (19:48). The people as a whole listen to Him attentively and are shocked at His death in a few days (23:48), in contrast to the leaders who plot his demise (19:47). Clearly Jesus was not a nationalistic Messiah, but the Lord visiting His people and His city, seeking to purify the hearts and fulfil God's promises to them. But as we have already seen Jerusalem is both unready and unwilling to receive Jesus as a divine visitation.

Hurricane in the House of God (20:1–21:38)

Since Jesus has taken the Chair of Moses and dares to teach in the Temple without authorization from the Sanhedrin, the leaders can no longer ignore Him. They must do something (6:11), so a hostile confrontation ensues in which Jesus is asked to defend both His actions and His teaching. This time He must produce His credentials. A wandering country rabbi, who has not passed through "the system", cannot presume the right to teach in the pulsating heart of Judaism. Yet history shows that the prophets did just that, claiming that their authority came from God.

Jesus is questioned by the chief priests and the Scribes, together with the elders (20:1). The priests referred to here are most probably Sadducees whose work was associated with the Temple, whereas the Pharisees were associated primarily with the synagogues. In Luke's account Jesus has no further dealings with this latter group. The Scribes come to the fore now, for they were the recognized teachers of the people (20:19, 39, 45–47). Like Jesus they, too, taught both in the synagogues and in the Temple.

They demand to know by what authority Jesus has acted, especially in cleansing the Temple, for its prophetic significance would be clear (20:2). In reply Jesus posed a real dilemma for them. He asked for their official discernment on the case of the last prophet, John the Baptist. It was their duty as leaders and teachers of the people to discern the difference between a true and a false prophet. To fail to do this is a declaration of incompetence for the position they hold vis-à-vis the people of God (20:3–4). In discussing the subject among themselves they acknowledge the dilemma, because if they accept that John's authority was from God – and Jesus was aligning himself with John – then there is the obvious problem of why they neither accepted John's baptism nor repented, for they had refused to believe in him (20:5–6).

On the other hand, they dare not say "from men" for they knew that *vox populi* – the discernment of the people of God – was that John did come from God, and the people could put Deuteronomy 13:1–11 into effect. The penalty for a false prophet was stoning, and this could be used on those who deny the legitimacy of a true prophet. Here the people are the representatives of the True Israel having to deal with unworthy leaders. The result was that they refused to commit themselves and took refuge in ignorance. Because of their insincerity and untruthfulness Jesus did not respond to their question either. It was obvious that they were at variance with the people in this case also (20:7–8).

Jesus' Killers will be Destroyed (20:9–19)

Having caught the leaders in an embarrassing dilemma, Jesus turned to the people who had discerned both John and Himself correctly. He told them the history of Israel's leaders in running the Lord's vineyard and their involvement in the death of Jesus, God's Beloved Son (20:13). The people must be put into a position where they can discern for themselves concerning *the stone rejected by the builders* of Israel (20:17). As for the leaders who are obviously included, they hear that their rejection of both John and Jesus will bring about their own ruin (20:16, 18–19), so they, too, are given an opportunity to repent.

Again this parable was drawn from everyday life in Palestine, where absentee landlords demanded a percentage of the crop as rent from local tenants, whose smouldering anger would often make them refuse to pay. The servants sent to collect such fees must have been often mistreated. The parable is also based on the idea of Israel as the Lord's vineyard (Isaiah 5:1–7

Jeremiah 2:21, 12:10; Ezekiel 15:1–5, 19:10–14 etc).
He was the invisible (but not absentee) Lord, who had
placed the leaders over the people in His name *for a
long while* (20:9–10). The story relates God's patient
dealings with Israel and her constant refusal to accept
the authority of His servants, the prophets, who, like
John and Jesus, were sent in His name to demand the
fruit to which He had a right (11:42, 13:6–9, 20:11–12;
see Amos 3:7; Revelation 10:7; Acts 7:52).

After persecuting and mishandling the prophets, the
owner of the vineyard (God Himself) decides to send His
only Son with His authority and power to deal with the
situation. In the human context, if the tenants killed the
son and heir, there was a chance that they could claim
ownership of the land under Jewish law. They would see
it as taking back the land that the Lord gave to Israel
from their oppressors. In the context of God's Kingdom,
it meant that the Jewish Messiah was speaking to His
own murderers, letting them know their responsibility
before God. Luke is also saying that this confrontation
with the Jewish establishment brought about the death of
Jesus, and that they must bear the consequences of their
actions (20:13–15).

Now comes the judgement: since the story is given in
parable form, Jesus asked His audience for their judgement
on the situation. What would an absentee landlord do to
tenants who killed his son and heir? The people answer
correctly that he would come himself and make an end
of those tenants and give the vineyard to others. This
refers to a divine visitation in judgement, and the giving
of the Kingdom of God to other nations (see Matthew
21:43; John 12:48). Those who would destroy Jesus (19:48)
would themselves be destroyed (20:16–19). No wonder
they exclaimed: *"God forbid!"* for the leaders knew that
Jesus spoke the parable against them (20:19), and it spelled

the destruction of Jerusalem and its glorious Temple – and also the end of their vice-grip on the nation.

Jesus appealed to Scripture for confirmation of His point. Quoting Psalm 118:22, He asked them for an exegesis of the text concerning the stone rejected by the builders. The leaders were the builders of Israel, and Jesus was obviously the rejected stone who was the keystone on which the Kingdom of God hinged (Acts 4:11; 1 Peter 2:7; Romans 9:32–33; Ephesians 2:19–22). In saying this Jesus *looked hard at them* hoping to penetrate their closed minds. Judgement is then pronounced in an enigmatic proverb: *Anyone who falls on that stone will be dashed to pieces; anyone it falls on will be crushed* (20:18).

The imagery is that of a clay pot falling on a stone being dashed to pieces on the one hand, or on the other, the stone falls on the pot and pulverizes it. It recalls the judgement text in Daniel 2:34–45, which speaks about a mysterious stone crushing earthly kingdoms while God sets up His everlasting Kingdom. It also evokes Isaiah 8:14, where the Lord Himself becomes *a stone of offence and a rock of stumbling* for Israel (see 2:34, 22:34), where He demands a definitive decision on the part of the people for or against Him. Jesus is the stone of offence on which many – including the Apostles – will stumble (Romans 11:11). Nevertheless, He will go on to victory and glory despite His rejection.

The stone will not be broken, but they themselves. Those who plot the destruction of the stone will be pulverized themselves. During the Passion they will stumble on that stone which will be passive, but in the Parousia the stone, now active, will fall upon them. This entire passage is a dreadful warning to all those in every generation who oppose the work of God and His Church. Thus we stand with the Jewish leaders in saying: "God forbid that stone should fall on us" (12:5)!

Tribute to Caesar (20:20–26)

The authorities had failed in their attempt to intimidate Jesus. Instead they brought down upon themselves the unanswerable attack which must have embarrassed and discredited them in the eyes of the people. Unwilling to risk humiliation a second time, they awaited their opportunity, then sent spies posing as devotees of the Law to try and trap Jesus on the explosive question of the yearly taxes to Rome (20:20). This second deputation had the specific aim of persuading Jesus to say something incriminating, which would form the basis of an accusation against him to the Roman Governor.

This Roman tax of one denarius per year per adult was levied when the Romans installed a procurator in Judaea, Samaria and Idumea after AD 6, when Archelaus was deposed. It had to be paid in Roman coinage, just as the Temple tax had to be paid in shekels, the Jewish coinage. The denarius was a silver coin with the emperors head on one side bearing the words: "Tiberius Caesar, son of the deified Augustus". The other side bore the figure of the emperor's mother, Livia, as an earthly incarnation of the goddess of peace. The coin therefore, symbolized not only the political power of the emperor, but also his religious claims which the Jews held to be blasphemous. The coin itself was a graven image, and as such, forbidden to the Jews (Deuteronomy 4:16; Jeremiah 8:19).

These men approached Jesus with flattery, acknowledging Him as a true teacher of righteousness, who showed no partiality in pointing out the ways of God to the people (20:21). Yet under this guise they try to force Jesus into a position of partiality with the question as to whether they should pay the taxes to Caesar or not (20:22–23). It was a subtle trap, for Jesus who would be in trouble whether He said "yes" or "no". His "yes" would bring problems with the Jewish authorities, and His "no" would get Him handed over to the Romans as a subversive. Luke is anxious here to show that Jesus was innocent of the charges they eventually brought against Him in the Passion (23:2; Acts 5:36–37).

Jesus saw through their cunning and asked *them* to show Him a coin! This, of course meant that they were already trafficking with Caesar. Since the coins they were using belonged to Caesar and his reign, he had a right to have them back (20:24–25). The wisdom of Jesus not only penetrated the subtlety of the question, but the hearts of the questioners. He said that they should not only give back to Caesar what belonged to *him*, but also they should give God his due. Each one of them was made in the image and likeness of God, and they owed Him the gift of themselves. Thus Jesus showed that their characterization of Him as impartial in teaching God's ways was indeed well founded. The trap had failed to close on its prey.

On the question of Church and State, Jesus appears to be saying that each has rights in its own sphere. Clearly all of us owe allegiance to the political order, which of necessity is imperfect, but absolute obedience which denies God His rights is not permitted. Peter and the early Church understood this to mean that "obedience to God comes before obedience to men" Acts 5:19 (Acts 4:19–20), showing where the priorities lie.

Will the Dead Rise? (20:27–40)

Having escaped the trap set to discredit Him in the eyes of the people, and to get Him into trouble with Rome, Jesus was approached by some Sadducees who posed a mocking question intended to ridicule His teaching about the Resurrection (14:14). They were a group whose members were drawn mostly from the the priestly class, but also included some aristocratic laymen (20:27). As far as doctrine was concerned, they held the opposite position to the Pharisees, believing neither in the resurrection of the dead, nor in angels or spirits (see Acts 23:8, 4:1–2). They tended to be fundamentalist in their approach to the Scriptures, holding tenaciously on to the books of Moses (the Pentateuch), but rejecting developments in doctrine found in the later books, especially the doctrine of the resurrection in Daniel 12:2 (Isaiah 26:19; Psalm 16:9–11).

The question they raised concerned the levirate law, which may not have been practised even in Jesus' day (Deuteronomy 25:5; Genesis 38:8). According to this law a man was obliged to marry his brother's widow to raise up children to his brother's name and inheritance, when the latter died childless. The purpose was to provide a legal heir for the man's property and to perpetuate the family name. So the first born of the second marriage fulfilled this obligation.

The Sadducees cite a possible, but far-fetched case of a woman having to marry seven brothers and, even after all this, dying without bearing a child (20:28–32)! For them this situation showed the ridiculousness of the very notion of resurrection, for whose wife would she be in the afterlife (20:33)? In His reply Jesus spoke of two ages, the *children of this world* (20:35) and the *children of the resurrection* (20:36; see 1 Corinthians 15:35–58; Philippians 3:21), or as Luke called them in 16:8 *children of this world and the children of light*. The question of marriage and procreation pertains to the first stage when we are in this world. It does not apply when history has run its course and we enter the second phase which is that of the resurrection. We will be like the angels and no longer subject to death. As sons of God, divine fatherhood replaces the need for human parentage (Acts

13:34; Romans 8:14–25). Earthly conditions do not persist in the heavenly world.

Having successfully answered the problem, Jesus calls on Moses as their highest authority to refute them. In citing the passage concerning the Burning Bush, Jesus also answers their fundamentalist tendencies by telling them that there was *an implied* meaning, as well as the literal meaning in the text (20:37). The passage quoted is Exodus 3:1–6, where God revealed Himself as the God of Abraham, Isaac, and Jacob, who were long since dead at that time. Since the Living God is also the God of the living, not the God of the dead, somehow the patriarchs were still alive in God's presence, for Jesus says: *"for him all men are in fact alive"* (20:38). Resurrection, therefore, does not imply a resumption of life in the limited bodily sense. The patriarchs, though unseen – like God and the angels – were alive, now. Those Scribes who belonged to the Pharisee school, and therefore believed the doctrine of the resurrection of the dead, congratulated Jesus on His scholarly reply, but no one dared ask Him anything else, since they could not cope with His wisdom, or His insight into Scripture (20:39–40).

David's Son and Lord (20:41–21:4)

Having silenced His opponents, Jesus proceeds to question them on a thorny problem of exegesis which they could not handle, and did not dare respond to. It was a question concerning the Messiah, one that sums up the mystery of Jesus Himself. Quoting Psalm 110:1, which states that: *"The Lord declared to my Lord, take your seat at my right hand, till I have made your enemies your footstool"*, Jesus asked how could the author, King David, call the Messiah "My Lord" when the Scribes referred to him as "Son of David". How could he be son and Lord at the same time (20:41–44)? Luke uses *Kyrios* for Lord, so in what sense is David's son superior to him? The Scribes, and the people in general thought of the Messiah as a mere human being, a nationalistic political Son of David much like David himself, but this does not leave him superior to David. Jesus is obviously asking them to see more in Him than the answer to political needs.

The early Church saw the answer to the riddle in the resurrection and exaltation of Jesus to God's right hand (Acts 2:32–36). They saw that the Lord Christ was seated at the Lord God's right hand until all His enemies were vanquished. It is as Son of God that Jesus is superior to David (see 2 Samuel 7:12–16). One must also remember the mysterious title that Jesus preferred for Himself too, "Son of Man". There was much, much more to the Messiah than even the experts thought.

Having criticized the theology of the Scribes, Jesus again criticized their way of life (11:37–54). He addressed this criticism to the disciples in the hearing of the people. Clearly, He was warning those "on the way" with Him not to imitate the falsity of scribal religion, with its theoretical theology, and a behaviour full of pride, ostentation and greed, cloaked by a showy piety. Jesus attacks them for using their position as teachers to further their own prestige in both religious and secular life. As lawyers they abused their positions of trust as guardians of property, especially with that very vulnerable group – widows, for whom the Law commanded special concern. A severe sentence awaits them, Jesus said (see James 3:1).

To confound them completely, Jesus compared a poor widow putting a few worthless coins into the treasury with their ostentatious offerings (21:1–4). The poor woman gave God all that she had to live on, whereas the greedy, self important Scribes, and the self-sufficient rich, donated from their surplus funds. Jesus pointed out that what mattered was not the amount one gave, but the amount one kept for oneself! The widow's gift expressed her faith and trust in God to provide her needs (12:22–32).

The Eschatological Discourse (21:5–38)

This final discourse on the destruction of the Temple, Jerusalem, and the end of the world, was given by Jesus in the Temple in the presence of both disciples and people. It marks the climax of Jesus' public ministry, and puts the stamp "prophet" on Him once and for all, insofar as He foretells future events concerning Israel and the nations of the world. The discourse began by some people remarking to Jesus about the splendid stonework and adornment of the Temple (21:5), which was a cause of wonder even to its destroyers. Jesus replied by predicting that the time would come when *"not a single stone will be left on another; everything will be destroyed"* (21:6). Naturally the listeners wanted to know when it would happen, and what signs they should look out for (21:7).

Luke has already given apocalyptic teaching by Jesus in 12:35–48 and in 17:20–37. In chapter 12 he gave warnings about being ready at all times for the coming of the Son of Man. In chapter 17 he spoke of the danger of being misled by false prophets, for when the Son of Man comes, there will be no mistaking His arrival. Then in chapter 13:34–35 Jesus spoke of the desolation of the Temple, and in 19:42–44 about the destruction of Jerusalem. Since He had said so much, perhaps the disciples and others in His audiences felt that the coming of the Son of Man, and therefore, the final manifestation of the Kingdom, coincided with the destruction of Jerusalem?

The present discourse clearly separates them, and is also concerned with the signs of the End. Contemporary apocalyptic teaching gave many signs by which people could recognize the End approaching. Luke has already shown that Jesus rejected as such, the use of signs to calculate the nearness of the End, on the grounds that it would be sudden and unexpected. This left no excuse for careless living in the vain hope of a last minute conversion. Luke is anxious to point out that many signs *look like* signs of the End, but are not, in fact, such. Even the fall of Jerusalem, and the Lord forsaking the Temple, would not herald the End. Moreover, Jesus had given signs even though He said that the End would be sudden for all. If this is written after AD 70, when these dreadful events occurred, then Luke is trying to explain the interim period of "the times of the Gentiles" (21:24). Also trying to encourage the early Christians to endure the trials and persecutions which befell them. He wants them to know that the End is certain, but its timing is God's secret.

Jesus gave this frightening prophecy in the Temple, the heart of life and worship in Israel. The present building was the third Temple, which had not been completed in Jesus' time. Its construction began under Herod the Great, and was finally completed in AD 64, just before the Jewish war which culminated in its destruction in AD 70. The stonework was massive. Those parts not overlaid with silver or gold were pure white, and gleamed in the sun, sometimes making it impossible to look at its brightness. Josephus says that the magnificence of the Temple and its contents constantly aroused wonder among spectators and visitors alike (Josephus, *Antiquities* 15:391–402). Grateful worshippers made wonderful votive offerings that adorned it too. It was one of the wonders of the world – a shrine of immense wealth, but Jesus did not appear to have been impressed by it. He told His amazed audience that it would be a heap of stones, and His prediction was fulfilled some forty years later.

Warning Signs (21:8–19)

Everyone wanted to know when such a disaster would happen, and what would bring it about. As usual Jesus went beyond the question to deal with weightier matters. There is a clear two-level reading here, as Luke pleads with his church not to listen to false teachers. The early Church was very concerned about false teachers as we see from Acts 20:28–32; 1 Timothy 4:1–16, 6:3–10; 2 Timothy 2:14–26; Titus 1:10–16 etc. Jesus warns that many – in every generation – would come using his name and making false claims. Some would go so far as to *claim to be the Christ* (21:8), while other over-excited preachers would claim to know the timing of these events (21:8). Luke uses *kairos* for "the time", hence it is God's time in His eternal diary, not the chronological time of historical events. Even so, preachers in every generation would mistakenly claim to be able to pinpoint *the event*.

Jesus said simply. *"Refuse to join them"*, for under the stress and insecurity of great events people might want an easy "guru". God is the Lord of history, and the future lies in His hands. Human history will produce wars and rumours of wars and revolutions in every age. There will also be natural disasters, like earthquakes, plagues and famines, but none of these separately, nor all of them together (as we have experienced in the twentieth century) are signs of the End. Not even cosmic signs in the heavens (21:9–11), which Josephus claims happened before the fall of Jerusalem. Luke was probably referring to the Jewish war of AD 66–70, and the many wars and revolutions associated with the Roman Empire, with their consequent plagues and famines. There was also the eruption of Vesuvius in AD 79 which destroyed the famous Pompeii and several other cities, so there were enough signs to disturb the early Christians.

An even more disturbing fact is that Jesus said that the persecution of His followers would begin *before all this happens* (21:12). The disciples were to be more concerned about not succumbing to persecution, than wondering about the End. Persecution was to be their lot from the beginning and they must deal with it. It will begin with Jesus and His Passion, and continue throughout the life of the Church. These other signs would come and go. In the meantime they were to use the opportunity that persecution gave them to witness before religious and political leaders (21:12–13). The persecution would come because of Jesus, and they must witness to Him. This was to be a fact of their existence among Jews and Gentiles as Acts bear abundant testimony to (chapters 3, 4, 7, 14, 16, 17, 18).

Christians would have to answer to both Jewish and Gentile leaders for their faith in Christ, but there was nothing to worry about because Jesus Himself would be with them in His indwelling presence. He guaranteed them wisdom to confound their opponents (21:14–15; Acts 4:8–13, 6:10–15). They will be Jesus' official witnesses and, like the Lord in the Old Testament, He will give them speech and eloquence (see Exodus 4:11; Ezekiel 29:21; John 14:15–26). They are not to view these events as either disasters or signs of the End. These persecutions were to be a normal part of their witness for Christ, so Luke sounds a note of confidence in the final victory here.

A more difficult aspect of persecution is now put forward in that family members will betray each other under stress, or threats, and some disciples will be executed as a result. And besides all that, they will be hated by everyone on account of Jesus (21:16–17; see John 15:18–16:4). Yet God is not blind to these harsh realities, and will take care of them ultimately. They can trust the One who determines eternal destinies (12:4–12, 22–32) *"Your endurance will win you your lives"*. Luke uses the word *hupomone* for endurance, and he means the triumphant acceptance of suffering that can make it redemptive for ourselves, and for others too. Disciples will need fortitude for the coming days, yet both persecution and martyrdom will see to it that many of them will not live until the End. It is, therefore, more important to deal with living for Christ now, than in speculating about what might happen in the future. There is not much glory offered to the disciples at this stage of the Kingdom. The glory is reserved for the final stage of the Son of Man (21:29–30).

Judgement Comes to the Holy City (21:20–24)

Just as the prophets of old had correctly forecast the fall of the holy city, so here Jesus can already see her surrounded by the Roman army in the fateful siege that preceded her downfall (21:20). Jesus warned that the sight of the invading armies should be the signal to flee. The citizens should escape to the mountains far away, and the country people should stay away, because it was the *kairos*-time for vengeance, and the fulfilment of all that Scripture had predicted. In a note of sadness, Jesus thinks of the very vulnerable people, like pregnant and nursing mothers, who will not be able to flee (21:21–23), *"for great misery will descend upon the land and wrath on this people"*, who will fall by the edge of the sword, or be taken into slavery in pagan lands until the age of the pagans is fulfilled (21:24).

This was a fairly accurate description of what took

place when Jerusalem fell to the Romans in AD 70, after a long and desperate seige that reduced the people to desperate acts of survival, even cannibalism. Josephus says that an incredible one million people were slaughtered in the capture of the city, that fell, literally, stone by stone. On top of this, close on 97,000 were taken into slavery, the Temple was desecrated and burned down, and the Jewish nation obliterated. In all the carnage that took place, pregnant women had their children slain in the womb while the mother still lived, and nursing mothers had their children torn from them and slaughtered, while they were violated before being killed. The long siege began in April AD 70 and the carnage was completed by that September (see Zechariah 12:3; Revelation 11:2).

In a strange way the fate of Jesus, the man of peace, and Jerusalem the city of peace, were bound up. Both were to be handed over to the Gentiles to be mocked, scourged and crucified, yet both would rise again. The death of Jerusalem is not the end of the world, but the beginning of the Age of the Gentiles. The death of Jesus heralded the Christian Age, and both of these ages coincided. Paul in Romans 9–11 believes that the end of the age will be heralded by the conversion of Israel to Jesus as Lord.

Luke says that the destruction of Jerusalem was a day of vengeance visited on a city that had so consistently, over the centuries refused to take heed of the Word of God spoken through the prophets. The end of the city is therefore seen as something she drew upon herself (2:34, 4:28–30, 6:11, 7:31–35, 9:22, 44–45, 10:1–16, 11:29–32, 12:54–59, 13:22–35, 17:22–37, 18:31–34, 19:41–44), and should be no surprise to anyone who reads the Scriptures. The Old Testament prophets had indicated that the reason for the destruction of Jerusalem in 587 BC was exactly the same (Deuteronomy 32:35; Hosea 9:7, 11:1–7; Jeremiah

5:1–17, 7:1–8:3). Luke is probably thinking of Daniel 9:27 when the devastator put a stop to all sacrifice and oblation in the Temple until the End. When God's *kairos*-time of judgement comes there is no escape, as there was none for Jerusalem's citizens that fateful year. Except, of course, for those who heeded the prophecy of Jesus and escaped in time as early Christian history attests.

The Coming of the Son of Man (21:25–36)

The end of the Age of the Gentiles heralds the Coming of the Son of Man, and cosmic signs are given for this cosmic event, which, again, no one will be able to escape. The fearsome signs for the end of Jerusalem are nothing compared with what will precede the triumphant return of the Son of Man in glory. Here whole nations will be in agony, as it will seem the very fabric of the universe is falling apart. There will be people dying of fear as the oceans break their limits. Dreadful signs appear in the sky, and nations await a menace that threatens the very planet itself (21:25–27). Following this fear and foreboding comes the return of the Son of Man as prophesied in Daniel 7:13–14. He will come with power and glory, and since the event is cosmic in scope, everyone will see Him. As He leaves the earth on the Cloud of God's ineffable Presence (Acts 1:9–11), so He returns in the same Presence and power, as universal King and Lord (21:28). For all those who have listened to, and obeyed the Word of God, this will be a moment of liberation from all trials and distress, for now the Kingdom of God is being established in power (see Hebrews 10:32–39; Romans 8:18–27). Christians will have a rough passage through the Age of the Gentiles, but it will have a glorious outcome.

Jesus gave them a sign: just as the fig tree heralded

the approach of summer for the Israelites, so these signs announce the nearness of the Kingdom of God. The fig tree looked so bare in the winter, yet its early blossom made it the pointer for good things to come. It is not the present phase of the Kingdom of God that is under discussion (17:21) but its final manifestation. Jesus finished solemnly by assuring them that heaven and earth would pass away quicker than His Word, which would be fulfilled when the time for it came (21:32–33).

Jesus finished with an exhortation to watch and remain prepared by holy lives, full of prayerful contact with God. Because, even though signs have been given, the End will come suddenly, and it will be universal (21:34–36; 1 Thessalonians 5:2; 2 Peter 3:1 ff.). If Christians lose faith and fall into immorality and debauchery, they may suddenly find themselves caught like an animal caught in a trap (21:34; Isaiah 24:17). These would be like those servants who abused the Master's trust in 12:35–48. Those wrapped up in the "cares of life" recall the parable of the Sower in 8:11–15, where they produced no fruit. The exhortation to pray constantly echoes the teaching on prayer in 11:5–13 and 18:1–8. Just before we launch into the Passion of Jesus and all the dreadful events that accompany it, Luke gives this short summary to the disciples to be ever-ready for the Lord, ready to preach, witness, suffer, or die at any moment.

The Last Days of Jesus (21:37–38)

The Temple events concluded with a scene that recalls 19:47. Jesus spent the last days before the Passion teaching every day in the Temple, and spent the night on the Mount of Olives. This could mean that He spent His nights saturating himself in prayer, preparing for the greatest trial of his life. Or it could mean that, like so many pilgrims in Jerusalem, He slept out on the hill which was a common practice at Passover (see John 18:2; Josephus *Antiquities* 17:217).

Chapter Six

The Sun Sets: The Passion and Death of Jesus

Before entering the Passion narrative let us remember the foreshadowing event which took place in the Temple when Jesus was twelve years old (2:41–50). He went there for Passover and disappeared during the feast for three days, only to be discovered in the Presence of God, doing God's Will, and the event had to do with the fulfilment of the Scriptures. In the present narrative Jesus has just completed His ministry in the Temple as the Passover approaches. Again He will "disappear" for three days and will be discovered by His disciples in chapter 24 to be in God's Presence in Resurrection glory. Somehow they come to grips with the fact that it was God's Will and the fulfilment of the Scriptures (24:27,44). In both cases the sorrow of loss is turned into the joy of finding. Luke also informed us in 4:13 that the devil left Jesus after the temptations in the wilderness, but he would return *at the appointed time*. The appointed time has come in the Passion, and the devil shows his presence again, this time through willing agents.

For Luke, the Passion is Jesus' pathway to glory (24:26): "*He who humbles himself will be exalted*" (14:11). Jesus' journey to Jerusalem is, in reality, His pathway to God, which goes through the Temple, Calvary, the Mount of Olives, and then on the Cloud of God's ineffable Presence into glory (24:51; Acts 1:9). It is the ascent to glory that parallels His descent in the Incarnation (see John 1:14). Like the other gospel writers Luke sees Jesus

256

fully revealed as God's Son, humble servant (Acts 3:13; 8:32–33), mysterious Son of Man and crowned King en route to enthronement in glory (23:40–43) in the following narrative.

He is the righteous man who dies a martyr's death for God's cause, and is lifted up as the model for all Christian martyrs who follow His way (23:4, 14, 22, 41, 47). In Acts Luke portrays the first martyr Stephen as a photocopy of his master, dying as an innocent victim out of love for God and forgiving his murderers (23:34; Acts 7:60).

The Passion presents two opposing camps, one on the side of the forces of evil, who are knowingly or otherwise the agents of Satan in killing Jesus. The other camp consists of Jesus and those committed to God's Will and the Kingdom. The story reads very differently from either side. For one, the leaders succeed in getting rid of a dangerous nuisance, whom they can neither control nor manipulate. As far as they are concerned He is a pretender like so many others (Acts 5:34–39), making claims that are dangerous in the extremely delicate political climate of the day. They want to be rid of Him.

Christians, contemplating the mystery of the cross and human suffering, guided by the Holy Spirit, and, therefore, approaching the mystery with insight, see the great spiritual warfare between the forces of good and evil in the world. They see Jesus' personal surrender to God, and the ultimate gift of Himself for His neighbour. They see Him die as He lived, a man of prayer, concern for others, with an attitude of unconquerable benevolence towards those with malicious intent towards Himself (23:34). Those who watched saw His incredible personal freedom under pressure from torture and injustice and His personal peace amidst atrocious suffering. His love for His neighbour, is shown towards the high priest's servant in 22:50, to Peter (22:61), the women (23:27), the good thief (23:43). His love of neighbour and trust in God persist up to the very last breath. Looking at this, they realized that the Passion may *look* like failure, but in fact Jesus conquered death by His own heroic death. Those who watched it were moved even to conversion (23:42, 47–48).

Furthermore there are two stages in the narrative. First, there is "what happened back there" in those historical events, namely, what happened to Jesus. And second, there is the Christian stage where lessons are being taught concerning how to behave during trials and persecutions. Lessons have to be learned about betrayal and desertion too (22:21–23), and repentance after a fall (22:54–62). They had been taught the importance of prayer, especially about the time of testing (11:1–13). Here they find that without prayer no one survives the test (22:31–34, 39–46). When the pressure is on, only that disciple with the inner commitment to God that Jesus had, will survive the test (23:34, 46).

It goes without saying that the reader is meant to cash-in on the experience of the early Church, and learn from both the negative and positive examples given. We are meant to see also that the Christian without the cross is as much an anachronism as Christ without His. Like it or not, we follow a crucified, but glorious Saviour, yet the temptation is to follow a glorious Saviour as the Apostles did on Mount Tabor, and reject the cross, as they did immediately. Inherent in the story is the challenge to participate in the mystery of redemption with Jesus for the salvation of souls (see Acts 9:4–5). To this end, Luke tones down some of the cruel details of the Passion, preferring to use the narrative as a ringing call to Christians to take up their cross and follow Jesus (23:26, 9:23–26, 12:49, 21:17; Acts 9:16).

Passover Preparation (22:1–13)

The events of the Passion and death of Jesus take place at Passover. The Passover proper was eaten on the night of the 14th-15th Nisan (Easter time), and the feast of Unleavened Bread followed it for a week. These two feasts commemorated the deliverance of Israel from slavery in Egypt under Moses the Liberator (Exodus 12). It was on the night of Passover that the final plague hit every household in Egypt with the death of the first-born. Because of the Passover sacrifice of Moses the angel of death literally *passed over* the houses of the Israelites because the blood of the sacrificed lamb was smeared on their houses. That same night the people hastily left Egypt with no time to bake leavened bread, so their unleavened bread became the symbol of their physical and spiritual journey from slavery to freedom, also their commitment to the Lord, since leaven was mostly looked upon as a symbol of evil influence (see 1 Corinthians 5:7).

Each year Jerusalem made elaborate preparations for Passover as pilgrims from all over the world returned home to celebrate this most sacred event, which they understood as a re-enactment of those events, and it was their way of participating in them. It was not just a dead memorial or ritual but a continuation of the commitment and reception of the graces of Passover. Because of the vast numbers of pilgrims (which sometimes rose to two million) the city was overrun, and thousands camped out on the hills surrounding the city or simply slept out in the open. Among these vast throngs religious and nationalistic feelings ran high and the atmosphere was often explosive. To prevent an uprising at this time, the Roman Governor, who had his headquarters at Caesarea by the Mediterranean, took up residence in Jerusalem and drafted in troops to keep the peace. The presence of the soldiers (who were pagans) at such a sacred feast did nothing to lessen the temperature politically or otherwise! The problem that faced the chief priests and Scribes was to arrest Jesus without provoking a riot, since so many of the pre-Passover residents were manifestly on His side (22:2). The Passion narrative is complicated by the presence of crowds who do not know Jesus, but whose passions could easily be roused.

Jesus' enemies are now named as the chief priests and the Scribes with a noticeable absence of Pharisees. A new group is introduced in 22:4 called the officers of the guard. These were Temple police chosen from the ranks of the Levites to keep order in the Temple, and in all matters concerning the Sanhedrin, which operated both as the supreme religious body in Israel as well as the supreme court (22:63–65; Acts 4:1, 5:24; John 18:22–23; Mark 14:65). This is an interesting observation considering that the Pharisees were the main opponents during the public ministry. Perhaps they were content to oppose Jesus doctrinally, but stopped short at violence (see Acts 5:34–39)? Yet they were members of the Sanhedrin and closely associated with the Scribes, so maybe we are meant to see them included under the umbrella of the Scribes?

The Sanhedrin receive an unexpected opportunity in Judas' willingness to betray his master for money, a point that must have galled Luke, after all he said about the right use of money in this gospel (6:30, 38, 11:41, 12:13–34, 16:1–16, 18:18–30, 20:25)! Perhaps it was Judas' betrayal that led to the teaching on money? It was such an evil act to betray the Son of God (1:35–36), Son of David (1:33, 18:38–39), the Son of Man (17:24, 19:10), the Lord Christ (5:9, 9:21), that Luke says it could only have come from the very source of evil, namely, Satan himself, now returned to set the reign of darkness in motion (22:53). He used the unrepented weakness of Judas (see John 12:6;

13:27) which allowed him entry into his life (22:3,31). Whatever Judas' motivation for his cold-blooded decision to betray Jesus quietly was, Luke is more interested that we don't repeat the process by opening the door of our hearts to evil and its consequence of betraying the Lord in our lives, (John 14:30; 1 Corinthians 2:8).

Disciples are meant to be on Jesus' side overthrowing satan's power (10:18–19). Any opening to evil is incompatible with work for the Kingdom (11:18–22). In fact disciples are meant to set people free from Satan's vice-grip (13:10–17; Acts 26:18), not to collaborate with him which means being the opposer of the Holy Spirit who governs the life of the Christian community (Acts 5:3). The sadness of Judas' case is that he betrayed Jesus in the absence of pressure from persecution or threat of death. The problem was within himself as it was for Ananias and Sapphira later (Acts 5:3).

The powers of evil are not the only forces preparing for this fateful Passover. Jesus and His disciples prepare for it too (22:7–13), for this Passover will provide the fulfilment of all that Israel treasured in this feast, and also a transition to open up to the triumph of the Kingdom. The hour of darkness (22:53) when Jesus' enemies will appear to triumph will be brief and illusory. Jesus was firmly in control of events and commissioned Peter and John to go and prepare the Passover meal. This meant preparing the Passover lamb which was served with unleavened bread, bitter herbs and wine (Exodus 12; 22:7–9).

As in the case of His triumphal entry into Jerusalem Jesus gave a pre-arranged sign to His disciples so that they can have the Passover meal in the city – as was necessary according to custom, and yet be free of threat of arrest, hence the secrecy. The sign was that of a man carrying a pitcher of water, which was most unusual, as this job was normally done by women. The owner of the house where the man lived – or worked as a servant – obviously had reserved the guest room on the flat roof for Jesus and His disciples. The inhabitants of Jerusalem were all obliged to keep a guest room for these occasions as the Passover meal had to be eaten within the confines of the city.

In connecting these two events, of the entry into Jerusalem and its climax in the Passover meal, Luke is clearly pointing to the true Lamb of God who will be sacrificed that Passover. This divine "necessity"(22:7) had to do with the liberation of all sinners from slavery to sin, death and hell, the real bondage. It thus presents the final fulfilment of His promise in 4:18 to set the captives free. History is, therefore, being fulfilled before the blind eyes of Jerusalem, which will interpret the Passion and death of Jesus in a very different way.

Moreover, Jesus was not alone in this Passover fulfilment. He celebrates it with His new family, those who will form His beloved community later to perpetuate its meaning, and make its grace available to all nations in the Eucharistic meal which will form the central act of its worship in the post Resurrection era. Not only then, but now, Jesus is one with His disciples. *"Go and make the preparations for us to eat the passover"* (22:9). Those disciples represent all of us who are associated with Jesus in His Passion, death, resurrection and in the work for God's Kingdom. The sacrifice of the lamb followed by the death of Jesus prepares us to understand the nature of our trials and persecutions for the Kingdom.

The Last Supper (22:14–38)

However great the number of sins committed, grace was even greater (Romans 5:20). In the sombre atmosphere of plotting and betrayal "the hour" arrived when Jesus, in the company of His Apostles (22:14) share the Paschal meal, during which Jesus offers His life, and interprets the coming events for them. The Twelve are intimately associated with Jesus in His hour. As Jesus indicates in 22:15 this is clearly a definitive meal before Passovers' fulfilment in the Kingdom of God. As such it can be seen as a farewell banquet, and Jesus' words as a farewell discourse (22:15–38).

Jesus begins by solemnly declaring that He has longed for this day (12:50). Now that the hour has come He does not try to escape its realities, but they must know that He will not eat with them until all that the Passover signifies has been fulfilled. As they begin the meal that will be the centre of their lives from this moment on, Jesus looks forward to the cross, just as they will always look back (Hebrews 9:11–28; 1 Corinthians 10:16, 17).

Taking the cup – which symbolized suffering – Jesus asked them *to take it*, and all that it stood for. They were to share it among themselves, for He will not drink wine again until the Kingdom of God comes (22:17–18). Unknown to them now, they were destined to drink from the common cup of suffering with Jesus. The old Paschal meal is over. Jesus institutes a new one, which is the Messianic Banquet, which commemorates His sacrificial death, and the salvation of the New Israel. Like its antecedent, this meal looks to the future in two steps, first the Eucharistic meal, whereby He will be among them sharing His banquet (24:28–32, 42–43), and then the final outcome of the Kingdom (22:16, 17; 1 Corinthians 11:26; Romans 6:5).

At this point Jesus broke with Jewish tradition and did something completely new. He instituted the Eucharist, His dying gift to his Church: *"This is my body which will be given for you; do this as a memorial of me . . . This cup is the new covenant in my blood which will be poured out for you*" (22:19–20). This clearly points to Jesus' redemptive death, and the spiritual food He can provide in the post resurrection era. Leviticus 17:11 says that it is blood that atones for the life, so it was forbidden for Jews to eat meat with the blood in it. This was normally poured over the altar as God's portion. Jesus was clearly giving His life for us, and thus completing His total self-giving in love.

Luke's expression of the institution of the Eucharist is closest to that of Paul in 1 Corinthians 11:23–25, yet Paul called this meal the Lord's Supper. Luke called it the Breaking of Bread (24:35; Acts 20:7) a designation which emphasizes the community sharing aspect of the Eucharist. All redeemed by the same Lord would eat the same Bread and share the same Cup until the Parousia. Thus Jesus fulfilled the prophecy of Jeremiah 31:31–34 regarding the New Covenant and Psalm 23, regarding the celebration meal in the sight of our foes and the cup of joy brimming over in spite of persecutions and trials.

Jeremiah clearly gave the terms of the covenant: "*I will write it on their hearts . . . they will know me . . . they will all be taught by God . . .*".All those who accepted redemption through the blood of Jesus, the Lamb of God, could now enter God's Kingdom. This first phase of the Kingdom would begin as soon as the sacrifice was complete on Calvary and the covenant therefore sealed in His blood.

Jesus proclaimed a New Covenant in His own blood that constitutes a new people of God just as the covenant of Moses on Sinai did. That covenant was sealed by the blood sacrifice of animals (Exodus 19–24) and expressed in the Ten Commandments and conditional promises and warnings (Deuteronomy 28). This put Israel into a special relationship with God (see Romans 9:4÷5). This covenant relationship was not due to merit on Israel's part but on God's sovereign choice of them in love. The covenant was sealed only after they freely chose to accept its terms. The Old Testament is a record of God's fidelity to His promises and Israel's infidelity. The whole sacrificial system developed due to Israel's desire to restore this relationship with God, after sin had broken it. Jesus' sacrificial death is to be seen in terms of sealing the New Covenant and thus restoring relationship between God and the human race, thus rendering all animal sacrifices unnecessary (see 1 Corinthians 11:27; 2 Corinthians 3:6). This covenant made forgiveness of sin available to all nations (1:77; 24:47–48) enabling everyone to cry "Abba, Father!" (11:2).

"Do this in remembrance of me" (22:19). Just as the Passover somehow made the past present as Israel re-enacted it each year – they understood that it made the grace of that first Passover available and looked to the future to their final liberation through the Messiah (Deuteronomy 5:3; 1 Corinthians 11:24; Romans 6:5; Hebrews 10:11–18) – so the Eucharist makes the grace of Calvary available to us as we look forward in joyful hope to the final manifestation of the Kingdom of God.

Betrayal by a Friend (22:21–30)

The first shock waves go through the group as Jesus announces that the agent of evil is in their midst. It was not some sinister external power that would bring about the death of Jesus, but one of His own, a disciple whom He loved, called, guided, taught and helped (22:21). For the first, but certainly not the last time, the Apostles take a good look at each other to discern "who's who" at the Eucharistic meal. From the beginning of its history this symbol of love and self sacrifice was infiltrated by those who had power and dominance, even money in their minds, who could lead the brethren astray (see Acts

265

20:28–30; 1 John 2:18–19; 2 Corinthians 6:14–18). As 1 Peter 1:20 says, all this was foreseen in the mind of God long ago, yet this does not excuse Judas, who with the full use of his faculties must take responsibility for his actions (22:22; 17:1–2). Despite his action, God, in His power, will take account of Judas's free decision to bring about a decisive victory over Satan, evil and death, but no thanks to Judas! It will come about through Jesus' heroic love.

In case the finger would be permanently pointed at Judas, leaving all other disciples feeling smug, Luke inserts a passage that the other synoptists deal with elsewhere (Matthew 20; Mark 10). All the gospels emphasize the blindness of the Apostles right up to, and including the cross, in spite of all that Jesus had said previously in 9:46–48, 14:7–11, 18:9–17, 20:45–47 concerning humility and lowliness of heart, and that the principles on which the Kingdom would be run were the opposite of what you see in the world. Nevertheless, no sooner has a discussion arisen about the betrayal than the more pressing problem of precedence in the Kingdom came up, perhaps the very reason why John inserts the foot washing scene right here (John 13:4–15)?

It was customary that guests arriving at the Passover feast should be met at the door by a slave, or failing that a servant, or if a family couldn't afford a servant, the youngest in the group. This person did the humble service of washing the feet of the guests before they reclined at table (22:13). Since the discussion among the Apostles only concerned the greatest, there was no one to do the menial task except the One who had taken the lowest place in God's Kingdom, the One who was about to wash everyone in His precious blood, His humble service to the human race.

They could not see that Jesus was among them all

through His ministry, not just here, as one who served (22:27). Unless they could grasp that in the Kingdom the greatest person was the one who gave the greatest service (*diakonia*), then they could never understand either Jesus or the Kingdom. They would revert to the worldly position of seeking status and power, imitating the kings of Syria and Egypt who took the title "Benefactor" while tyrannizing their people! Jesus emphatically said: *"This must not happen with you"* (22:26) because it would destroy the community by inserting worldly and destructive principles into its working. These were the very attitudes He condemned in Israel's leaders. The disciples were to take Jesus as their model, not worldly men (22:27). This meant a whole life defined by self-denial, and self giving humble service to others, even to the laying down of life (22:19–20; John 15:13). Service (*diakonia*) would become the key word in describing a disciple in the early Church (Acts 6:1–6, 2:42–47, 4:23–37, 5:12–16; especially 1 Timothy 5:10).

In stark contrast to their power seeking and the service of self, which truly betrays all that He stands for, Jesus now confers authority and power in the new Kingdom upon them, to be used in the way that He has shown. To those who have continued with Him in His trials before Calvary, and in the interim period between the Ascension and the Parousia, Jesus confers the Kingdom, just as the Father conferred it on Him (22:28–29), thus passing on immense responsibility to them. This is an allusion to Daniel 7 (see also 12:32, 13:25–30, 14:15–24, 18:30). They will share the Messianic feast with Jesus (14:15 ff.) and His rule over the church, in both the interim phase and the final phase of the Kingdom. This can be seen in Acts where the Twelve rule over the new expanding community as it spreads its wings to the rest of the world. There, with the help of the Risen Lord and the Baptism of the Spirit, they understand the service Jesus spells out here, and they gave it.

This conferring of the Kingdom on twelve leaders shows that Jesus intended the founding of a New Israel on twelve stones, just as the "old" Israel had its foundation on twelve tribes. Their "judging" of the new community is to be seen in terms of Israel's judges – those charismatic leaders raised up by God to lead and guide His people. Perhaps at the end of the age when the Son of Man comes in glory, they will, according to Daniel 7:9–10 literally take their place on thrones, in that everlasting kingship (see 1 Corinthians 6:2; Revelation 2:26–28, 3:20–21, 20:4–6, 21:13–14).

The Hour of Testing (22:31–38)

Following immediately on the promise of fellowship with Jesus, and authoritative positions in the Kingdom, comes the shock of Jesus' prophecy concerning their failure to serve Him. Omitting the references in the other gospels to the fact that they *all* deserted Jesus in the Passion, Luke concentrates on Peter's fall (22:31–32) and, as in the case of Judas, goes on to explain how we all fail Jesus, and need to learn from Simon Peter the lesson of true repentance. Luke also gives the reason for their defection. It was part of Satan's ruse to bring them all down, but he only succeeded with Judas (22:31). Jesus' powerful intercession for Peter gained him the grace of recovery, and then Jesus asked him to strengthen the others (22:32). Peter is again seen as the leader of the Twelve as in 5:1–11, and Luke concentrates on him. The Passion will shake them violently, like wheat being sifted. God had permitted this because of their involvement in the redemptive mystery with Jesus, (see Job 1 where God permits Satan to test His servant with severe trials).

At this point Peter is unaware of the testing ahead, and boasts of his loyalty to his master. He was ready, he said, to go to prison, or even death for Jesus. But Jesus knew better, and prophesied that on the same day as his boast, Peter would deny three times that he ever knew Him, which is very solemn (22:34). At the beginning of this conversation Jesus addressed His beloved disciple affectionately as "Simon, Simon!" and ended by calling him Peter (the rock) for the first time. Simon, known and loved by Jesus, was still very much "the old man" (in the sense of the incompleteness of his conversion: Colossians 3:9), relying on himself, unaware of how he would behave under the pressure of trials and tribulations. The new man, Peter, will emerge after the fall of the old man, when repentance does its cleansing work. Then, relying completely on the grace of God, and strengthened by Jesus' forgiveness, acceptance and love (John 21:15–17) he will be able to lead the flock and strengthen the brethren. Unlike Judas, Simon's faith does not fail him in the coming violent test (22:32).

Just as Luke inserted a passage to show that Christians can betray Jesus just as Judas did, so here he shows the possibility of an on-going denial of Jesus in a refusal to live as he asked. In sending out the Seventy-Two in chapter 10, Jesus had challenged them to take nothing, and to rely on God for everything, even for survival (9:3, 10:4, 22:35), and they found that it worked then. Now they were facing into a time of unprecedented hostility and the call to stand by Jesus faithfully in His trials (22:28), both now in the Passion, and later when they move into the hostile world (John 15:18–16:4; Luke 9:22–17, 12:4–7, 21:18). Up to now they have been protected by Jesus from both hostility and failure, but from now on they will be on their own, and therefore, need to take

269

normal precautions, as he did about the place and time of the Last Supper, not even telling *them* until the last minute (22:36). He does not demand a heroism they cannot give. Things were easier when He was physically present. The Scriptures concerning the Suffering Servant (Isaiah 52–53) are about to be fulfilled, and it will shock and shake them, when He allows Himself to be taken and dealt with as a criminal (22:37). Again this involves a divine necessity they will not understand until afterwards (22:37; Acts 8:32–35).

Misunderstanding Jesus' instructions, they inform Him that they already have two swords hidden under their cloaks, which they were quite willing to use (22:50)! They do not see that if they remain blind to the realities of the Kingdom, and think that they can use worldly means to achieve spiritual ends, if they fail to trust God for all the needs of the mission, then they, in effect, continue to deny Him and to deny the people the reality of God's Kingdom. Later, Paul expressed it clearly in 2 Corinthians 10:4 when he said: "*Our war is not fought with weapons of flesh*". Jesus abruptly terminated the discourse with: "*That is enough!*" This rebuke to the uncomprehending Apostles is meant for all of us if our lives and attitudes deny the reality of the Kingdom to ourselves and others. Like Peter here, we could be blocking the way for Jesus in our own day.

A Son's Agony (22:39–46)

Omitting most of the details concerning the stages of the Passover meal, including the singing of the Hallel (Psalms 113–118), which forecast what Jesus was about to experience, Luke has Him emerge from the upper room and go straight to the Mount of Olives to pray. This was where He had gone to every night that week (21:37–38). It was *usual* for Him as Luke says in 22:39. Both Jesus and the disciples accepted the cup and what it meant during the supper, now it was time to begin to drink it.

Jesus went to Gethsemane (Mark 14:32), but Luke omits the name of this garden so beloved of Christians. Space within the city was so limited that well-to-do people bought gardens out on the hills. A friend allowed Jesus to use his garden as a place to pray at night. Later, Christians saw meaning in the oilpress which gave the garden its name, and the agony of Jesus who was crushed to bring forth the New Wine of the Kingdom (22:18; see Isaiah 63:3. "*I have trodden the winepress alone.*" Here, in loneliness and isolation, Jesus was subjected to the final onslaught of the evil one, and his final temptation (4:13). He knew that the secret of heroic endurance was prayer, deep sustained prayer (21:19), so while the disciples begin to fail the test to watch and pray, Jesus obeys His own teaching, and in so doing, showed us how the Our Father is prayed in agony. Both He and the disciples were moving into a time of testing, but they will be unprepared, and fail the test (22:40), both in its first phase of supporting Jesus faithfully in *his* trials (22:28) and in obeying His teaching with regard to their own. While He moves a stone's throw away in order to pray in privacy they take refuge in sleep (22:45).

All alone, Jesus shows His humanity as He kneels to pray that if it be possible He would like His Father – His Abba – to remove the cup. Luke wants his Church, and his readers, to look carefully and see that suffering and persecution are abhorrent to human nature, especially for one who is young and vibrantly alive. Even Jesus was tempted to evade the cup He had accepted at the Passover meal (22:17), and the Christians were tempted to shun the outcome of drinking from the same cup at the Eucharist. Luke will not permit an empty liturgical

271

rite with no social consequences – nor will Paul (1 Corinthians 10:16–17, 11:20–34). To accept the cup at the Eucharist is to commit oneself to drinking its contents in suffering for the Kingdom. Our words of praise and thanks can be cheap. The ones who leave their footprints in the sands of time are prepared to write their commitment in blood.

There was no desire to escape in Jesus. He could easily have escaped the clutches of His enemies, as He did at Nazareth (4:30). His agonizing prayer is a plea to God to redeem the human race by some other means, *if possible*. But in the absence of that "possible", He surrendered fully, if fearfully now, to the Will of God (22:42–43). The silence of heaven to His agonizing prayer, told Jesus there *was* no other way than the way of the cross which He had so clearly foreseen in His own predictions of it.

During his temptation in the wilderness Satan had wrongly predicted angelic help would be given on the grounds of Psalm 91 (4:10), if Jesus succumbed to the temptation. Here Jesus experiences the angelic help in accordance with that psalm, which promises help to the one who clings to God's Will (see Daniel 10:17–19). Even though Jesus' heart clearly chose God's Will, that did not take the pain away, for clinging to God's Will (see Sirach 2) is not an anaesthetic, but a reaching out for the fortitude that enables one to endure faithfully. Luke alone describes the sweating of Blood, perhaps to warn us that the Baptism of Blood begins now (12:50). Perhaps, too, he wants us to remember this unseen divine help as we proceed.

The disciples fail Jesus partly because of their sheer blindness to the deeper meaning of the events, and partly through lack of prayer and preparation. Perhaps mostly because they wanted a glorious Messiah as seen on Mount Tabor. Even the first sight of the Suffering Servant was too much for them. For the second time, Jesus in 22:46

asked them why they slept when they should be praying not to be put to the test themselves. For Jesus there was to be no more sleep. He would keep His vigil faithfully until death closed His eyes. Yet when He conquered death he would call everyone from their slumber to live and work in God's Kingdom (see Matthew 27:51–52; 1 Peter 3:18–19).

There is a solemn warning here to Church leaders not to sleep – in the metaphorical sense – during their long "night" as they await the glorious coming of their victorious Messiah. Like Jesus, their master, and Lord, they must arm themselves with a life of prayer and clinging to God's Will, no matter what the cost. It would be tragic if the glorious Son of Man had to ask His Church leaders on that great and terrible day why they had slept on the job.

Luke tones down the failure of the disciples here. Unlike the other synoptics he does not distinguish the three special disciples (who had seen Jesus on Mount Tabor and witnessed the raising of Jairus' daughter), from the others (Matthew 26:37; Mark 14:33). He vaguely refers to them all as disciples (22:40) rather than Apostles, thus taking the heat off their personal failure, and enabling him to widen the context to include later Church situations. Luke appears to be anxious that disciples in other generations do not perpetuate the sufferings of Jesus by their errors. There are lessons to be learnt here in the Passion narrative.

The Binding of the Son of Man (22:44–53)

Once Jesus fully surrendered His agonized heart to the Father's Will with all that it entailed, He got His peace back. For the rest of the Passion He shows remarkable serenity, and an inner freedom and peace of soul. So much so, in fact, that both Luke and John portray Him as very much in control of events, which turn out to be very different to what one would expect. Jesus is not presented as a hapless victim of politi̇̄al or religious violence, and one must continually read the deeper meaning of the events to even follow what the evangelist is saying.

Just as Jesus was trying to arouse His sleeping disciples to *"Get up and pray not to be put to the test"* (22:46), the test came upon them. Judas, one of the Twelve, appears, with a high profile arresting group from the Temple, consisting of chief priests, elders and captains of the Temple guard (22:52) – a dramatic fulfilment of the prediction of 9:22. Luke omits all reference to a crowd or rabble accompanying them (see Matthew 26:47; Mark 14:43) as he presents the Passion of Jesus as a problem stemming from the leadership, not the people.

Judas has already lost faith and entered into temptation. He approached Jesus as a beloved disciple should, to kiss his master. This involved putting his hand on the master's shoulder and kissing the cheek. But Jesus held him off asking him to reflect on his action, for this would open the way to repentance for this prodigal son (15:17–20). Why did he twist the sign of love and respect into one of betrayal? Did he realize the betrayed one was the mysterious Son of Man? Was that what he wanted by his action, or was it an unreflected response? Was he aware of the power that moved him? Only Satan, the one who opposed all that God stood for, would want to prevent love, respect, and fidelity among people.

The early Christians used the holy kiss at their assemblies (1 Corinthians 16:20). Under pressure of persecution they were not to pervert this sign of love into betrayal to save their own lives for this world. They, too, would not fully grasp how terrible would be the crime to implicate oneself in the destruction of the Mystical Body of Christ in the world. Yet they need to cope with the fact that there will be cockle among the wheat always (see Matthew 13:24–30, people among them who are not really of their group, who can act as spies and anti-christs (22:24–27; see 1 John 2:18–19).

The rest of the disciples enter into temptation now, which would not have happened had they kept vigil in prayer as they were instructed to do (22:40, 46). They think this is the time to defend Jesus with the sword. In a clumsy attempt, one of them cut off the right ear of the high priest's servant (22:51–52). Since they do not yet grasp the nature of the spiritual warfare that God's Kingdom will bring, Jesus cuts them off by ordering them to stop, as it could provoke a riot. Then, in His compassion Jesus healed the poor servant. Luke never fails to show Jesus' concern for others, and here demonstrates His lack of fear concerning His own fate. He is more concerned about the fate of His failing disciples, who needed the sword of obedience to Jesus' Word and fortitude, to face what was coming. They must not respond to persecution with armed resistance. That was not His way. Their suffering for God's Kingdom – like His own – was more useful for the accomplishment of God's purposes.

Turning to the arresting party Jesus rebuked them for treating Him like a terrorist with their armed force. They have approached Him as if He were a political man of violence, even though He is the Prince of Peace (2:14, 19:38, 42). He said that they could have arrested Him any day in the Temple, but in fact they could not, for that arrest would have to be lawful and out in the open (19:47–48; 21:37–38; 22:52–53). They are arresting Him in secret because their deed is evil and they are the agents of Satan. Jesus solemnly says: *"But this is your hour; this is the reign of darkness"* (22:53). For a brief moment in history Satan is permitted to test the Beloved Son and

Servant of God, and, as was said earlier, woe betide those who, like Judas, act as Satan's active agents in this drama (22:22).

Jesus surrendered to them, for unknown to them, this is not just the hour of darkness, it is also Jesus' hour, when He will glorify the Father (John 17), and show His heroic love for His neighbour by laying down His life for them (John 10:18). In reality this is the next stage on Jesus' journey to God and glory (1:78–79; John 12:31–32; 14:30–31; Colossians 1:13 etc).

As soon as Jesus surrendered to His enemies they seized Him and took Him away to the high priest's house (22:54). He who had come to set the captives free (4:18) was now a prisoner Himself and would never be freed by His captors. From this moment onwards, a complete reversal of Jesus' own actions is seen in the behaviour of those who killed Him. His entire ministry can be put under the heading of unbinding, as we said in the section on the Lord's Power in 11:14–36. As such He was the agent of Light and the solution to the crippling problems of people's lives.

As the agents of darkness seize Him they behave according to the principles of the world, and of the powers of darkness. They bind Jesus with cords to make a physical prisoner of Him first. Then they attempt to make an emotional prisoner of Him by injustice, rejection, malice and torture. Finally, they bind Him physically to the cross and seal him in a tomb, even as Matthew says putting guards upon it. Darkness closes in on Him with its suffocating effects and we must watch the sun setting.

It looks like victory for the agents of darkness on Friday, but when the Sun rises three days later, the world gasps as Jesus breaks the cords of death, breaks the seal of the tomb to emerge into eternal light and glorious freedom as the first-born from the dead. His freedom now includes freedom from all material restrictions and the binding of time and space (24:36). It is the glorious freedom of the sons of God (Romans 8) that changed the gloomy hour of darkness into one of permanent glory. It transformed the almost blind disciples into fearless witnesses for Jesus, who commissioned them to go out and unbind the world and then follow Him in laying down their lives for their brethren. This is the key to unlocking the universe which is passed on from generation to generation until the Son of Man comes on the clouds of heaven.

The Trial of Peter (22:54–62)

This dramatic story begins with the words: *Peter followed at a distance*. In 5:11 Peter had left all to follow Jesus and knew that this entailed picking up the cross and following on a daily basis (9:23). He also knew that if he tried to save His life he would only lose his real life (9:23–24). He should remember too, that if he is ashamed of Jesus and his teaching before others, that the Son of Man will be ashamed of him in the Presence of God and His angels (9:26). This trial is serious. Peter should have prayed not to enter into temptation. Now we hear that ominous warning that he is following, but at a distance. There is quite a distance between Jesus and Peter right now. Peter has no idea that he will be tried first . . . and found wanting as a disciple. Not only will he not defend his master to the point of going to prison or death for Him (22:33), but he will experience Jesus as a true prophet when His prediction concerning him comes true. When he met Jesus first, Peter was aware of his sinfulness (5:8), now he must confront it and his complete inability to serve the Lord without grace and a deep prayer-life (see John 15:4–5).

Peter's trial took place in the middle of the high priest's

courtyard where the agents of darkness had lit a fire and
Peter sat down among them (22:56). He has made the
mistake of associating with those who try to destroy Jesus.
He is in the wrong company (Psalm 1:1). Thus distanced
from the Lord – and the community – he cannot stand
on the day of trial. He denies that he ever knew Jesus,
and that three times: *"I do not know him"* (22:56–60).
Those around clearly recognize Peter as an associate of
Jesus, but in these circumstances, Peter does not see that
as an advantage. He is ashamed of Jesus, and denies his
discipleship. This is in stark contrast to Jesus during his
trial where he steadfastly proclaims who He is and why
He came, and remains faithful to His divine sonship and
His mission to the end (22:66–71).

It is not difficult to hear Luke exhorting his church
here. He is not worried about Peter "back there" in history.
With Jesus' help (22:61) and intercession (22:31–32) he
repented. But what about Christians today? Have we
learned from history the clear lesson of Peter? Are we
consorting with worldly people, or even with elements in
society that oppose the gospel? Peter sat at the wrong
fire. Jesus came to cast fire upon the earth (12:49), and
this cleansing fire of God's love entailed the suffering of
the Passion. Christians, too, are given that fire (3:16),
and the help of the Holy Spirit in their spiritual rebirth
(Acts 2:3). When confronted by the mystery of suffering
Christians, like Peter, are tempted to deny Jesus and be
ashamed of their association with Him. They must choose
first, what kingdom they want to live in, and second,
what fire will enkindle their lives. Like Judas and Peter,
we too, have to live out the consequences of our choice.

Jesus is with us in our trials, just as He is present to
Peter now. Even though Peter turns away from Jesus,
Jesus turns towards Peter, to hold him by his love,
acceptance of His weakness, and forgiveness of his sin,

(22:61). In fact Jesus is so concerned about Peter, that one almost forgets that Jesus, too, is on trial! It is as if His own sufferings were nothing. His present anguish is to see this disciple through to repentance: *The Lord turned and looked straight at Peter, and Peter remembered.* (22:61). He had been warned. He needed to remember, or to keep in mind, the teaching of Jesus if he is to remain faithful. The signal promised by Jesus to jolt Peter's memory is given now, and Peter realized that he had received a truely prophetic word from God through Jesus. Up to this moment he could not hold his testimony even before the gaze of a servant girl, but now, under the loving gaze of his master, he repented *And he went outside and wept bitterly* (22:62). Jesus had triumphed, and Satan had lost His prey (22:31–32). Peter's faith had not failed. He would recover. The shepherd had snatched his sheep from the lion's mouth.

Jesus Tried by the Great Sanhedrin (22:63–71)

Peter was not around to witness the mockery and maltreatment of his master by the Temple guards, men who were employed to protect God's Holy House. They were not aware that it was God's Son (22:70), and God's Messiah (22:67) whom they blindfolded, mockingly asking Him to play the prophet even though His prophecy to Peter has just been fulfilled, and all His prophecies against the Temple and Jerusalem were fulfilled even as Luke wrote his gospel. Jesus is indeed a prophet, but not according to the simplistic and shallow notion of His mockers. Of course, if Jesus is a prophet, then they are the slayers of the prophets (13:34). In their blindness they do not realize that they are transforming the mysterious Son of Man into a man of sorrows, one familiar with grief (Isaiah 53). Jesus has already been through the trauma of the agony and the desertion of the disciples, which Luke gently glosses over. It is indeed a dark night (John 13:20). Whether this mockery went on all night, or whether Jesus was given respite in the small hours of Friday morning we are not told.

Luke merely relates that the Sanhedrin convened (or re-convened if you follow the other synoptics) at daybreak as it was illegal for them to do so during the night (22:66). Jesus was brought in as a prisoner to stand trial for His life before the Jewish high priest and the council who had already decided His case in advance (John 11:45–54). The men seated about Jesus were His principal opponents in 20:1–21:4, where His wisdom had confounded them. The Sanhedrin normally sat in a semi-circle where every member could be seen, with the students and disciples of the rabbis at the back. The prisoner stood in the centre. All the rules of the trial tended towards mercy. Witnesses had to concur on their statements, and Deuteronomy 17:6–7 laid it down that two or three witnesses were required to carry the death sentence. The trial of Jesus is presented as a mockery of true justice which treats a man as innocent until proven guilty.

The question at issue for the Council is whether Jesus is the Christ (22:67) but Jesus did not reply, and for the same reasons dealt with in chapter 20. They will use His words against Him – which was against the Jewish Law. So He replied that it wouldn't make any difference what He said since they would not believe Him anyway. Nor would they reply to His questions as we saw in 20:7, 26, 40, where they refused to be open and honest with Him. If Jesus' reply was "yes", then they would send Him to Pilate as a Messianic pretender – which they did anyway (23:38). In 9:20–22 Luke had already put the titles of Messiah and Son of Man together in relation to the Passion. Here Jesus announces prophetically that *from now on*, from the time of his hour, *"the Son of Man will be seated at the right hand of the Power of God"* (22:69).

Jesus looked beyond the narrowness of a political Messiah to the ascension of the triumphant Son of Man in the Resurrection. He is indeed their Messiah, but His concern is not for political liberation but for the ultimate liberation of the human race through the action that they participate in so blindly, namely, His Passover. For the Sanhedrin this claim to sit at God's right hand is tantamount to a claim to divine sonship, so they question Him concerning this, for them, explosive issue. Christians know of Jesus' divine sonship, but for this audience at His trial it is blasphemy, and worthy of the death penalty. At last they've got Him, even though He answered mildly: *"It is you who say I am"*. He cannot deny it, but they are the ones who brought up the subject.

Contrary to their own law they dispense with witnesses, and condemn Jesus out of His owm mouth. The whole assembly rose and brought Him to Pilate. There was no further discussion. It is at their hands that the Son of Man will ascend to whence He came from. In His trial, Stephen, the first Christian martyr (Acts 6:8–7:60) stood before the same Sanhedrin for the same reasons, and saw in vision during his trial that Jesus was standing at the right hand of God in glory. As they reacted violently to Jesus' prophecy in 22:69, so they reacted to its fulfilment, by killing Stephen. They still refused to hear the Word of God through His prophets.

Jesus Tried by Civil Law (23:1–25)

There is one name forever linked with the death of Jesus by historians, evangelists and believers alike. That is

Pontius Pilate, the Roman Procurator of Judaea from circa AD 26–35. He has gone down in history as the man who examined the Jewish claims to put Jesus to death and found Him not guilty. After three separate declarations of innocence he still handed Him over to be executed by the horribly cruel process of crucifixion. Historians of the time relate many inhuman acts whereby Pilate tried to break the Jews. One of them is alluded to in 13:1. This cruel leader, who could be manipulated by a crowd to act contrary to the truth, was the representative of the highest civil authority in Israel, and in the Roman Empire. The highest religious body in Israel had condemned Jesus. Now he must bear the scrutiny of the Gentiles only to find no justice there either. Taken together, these groups represent "church" and "state", or authority in the world as we know it. The rejection and condemnation of Jesus – albeit without cause (Psalm 69:4) – was, and remains, universal, but for a remnant of faithful followers, some of whom we will meet at the cross and afterwards.

The Romans did not allow the Sanhedrin to carry out the death penalty. Capital crimes had to be scrutinized in the civil court and the charges ratified. The Roman authority usually did not initiate the proceedings, but pronounced on the charges. It was obvious to the Sanhedrin that a Roman court would not handle a charge of blasphemy (see Matthew 26:66; Mark 14:64). Blasphemy was a religious problem, and the civil court dealt only with civil matters.

To this end, the Sanhedrin changed the charges to political ones, accusing Jesus of inciting the people to revolt – a matter the Romans would have suppressed without their help. He was also accused of opposing payment of taxes to Caesar, a clear contradiction of 20:20–26, and to being a royal claimant "Christ the King", therefore, a subversive. Their accusations actually reflect what they would have liked their Messiah-King to be like, since the Messianic hopes were political, and included overthrowing the Romans (23:2). Pilate ignored the Christ question, for the Messianic claim was irrelevant to him, but he had to deal with the question of kingship. Mark 15:10 says that Pilate saw through the charges, and realized that it was out of jealousy that they had handed Jesus over.

Pilate was an experienced soldier, whose jails were full of subversives (23:19), so even a cursory examination of Jesus convinced him that whatever this man was up to, it wasn't political – which was the point at issue. This, even after Jesus did not deny His kingship in His enigmatic answer: *"It is you who say it"* (23:3). John 18:36–37 says that Jesus explained to Pilate that His kingship was not of this world. Earthly power was not how God's Kingdom would spread, as we learned on the journey to Jerusalem. Since Jesus made no specific claim Pilate declared Him innocent, but that only made the Jewish leaders even more determined. They pressed the case of Jesus' popularity with the crowds everywhere, saying that *"He is inflaming the people with his teaching ..."*. even in Galilee, where it all began. They acknowledge that the Word of God has spread all over the land. The seed has been sown, but now, to make it fertile, it has to be drenched with the tears of Jesus' martyrdom.

Mention of Galilee provided Pilate with a loophole to escape the trap set for him, as he began to see that this was a power struggle between himself and the Sanhedrin, who had it in for him for a long time. They were going to force his hand to do their will this time. Herod Antipas was the tetrarch of Galilee, and he was in Jerusalem for the feast. As a Galilean Jesus came under his jurisdiction even though he was a lesser authority than Pilate. Perhaps

Pilate sought a Jewish civil opinion on the matter? Luke had mentioned earlier that Christians would be dragged before synagogues, kings and governors (21:12; 12:11–12). Here he presents Jesus being tried by all these authorities. Paul experienced the same when he was tried by the Roman Governor Festus, at Caesarea (Acts 25:6–12; 26:24–32), who insisted on calling King Agrippa in on the case (Acts 25:13–26, 26:23, 26–32). Like his Master, Paul too, had been previously tried by the Sanhedrin (Acts 22:30–23:10). The Romans obviously had difficulty understanding Jewish issues, but seemed sure of the innocence of the prisoner.

Herod was delighted to see Jesus, but this sentiment was not reciprocated as Jesus saw through him (9:9, 23:8). He only wanted Jesus "to perform" in front of him like a magician, but this idle sign constituted no temptation for one who resisted stronger approaches of the Enemy (4:1–13). Jesus' interest lay in the casting out of devils, not in collaborating with evil – perhaps a warning for Christians? He had nothing to say to Herod, which was Herod's condemnation. This petty king was not permitted by the Lord to interrupt or even influence the journey He undertook to God (13:31–33), so Jesus made no reply to his cross examination, even though the chief priests were violently pressing their charges (23:10). This interrogation added nothing to the case, beyond providing a second witness to Jesus' innocence (23:15; Deuteronomy 19:15). This means that, according to Jewish law, Jesus cannot be condemned. It is read differently, however, by Luke's church in Acts 4:25–28 as the fulfilment of Psalm 2:1–2, according to which kings and rulers plotted together against the Lord and His Anointed One.

Herod failed to move Jesus to speech or action in the interrogation. Now he descends to making fun of Him, treating Him with utter contempt (23:11). For

Herod, Jesus' royal claims were so ludicrous that he dressed Him in his own royal robe, and thus attired sent Him back to Pilate, who read this message correctly, that Jesus was innocent, no matter what the chief priests said. This incident, and perhaps this sign, cemented the relationship between these two enemies, who were reconciled over this matter. Perhaps Herod was pleased that Pilate should consult him, thus recognizing his authority (23:12)?

Herod, whose petty kingdom was definitely "of this world" could not have known the significance of sending the king of the Jews back to the Gentile court dressed in his royal robes. The kingship of Jesus is acknowledged, albeit in mockery, but Jesus was willing to wear the robe of mockery so that one day His disciples could wear the robe of glory, and that sinners could wear the robe of righteousness (15:22). This humble King of the Jews works away quietly for His divine purpose without interference, for His silence and personal freedom makes these treasures safe. It is important to note that unjust accusations combined with violence and mockery don't shake Jesus' personal control, or His freedom. Unlike His captors He is in control, and demonstrates by His words and actions that He is the Son of God. Christians are asked to look to Jesus as their model, then they too, will be able to remain silent under the lash and bear witness to who they are.

Neither Herod nor Pilate found Jesus guilty, is the verdict given on the case (23:13–17). The two witnesses agree. Nevertheless, the Jewish leaders press on more determined than ever to kill Him. The situation was becoming crazy, and dangerous for all participants, as John's account brings out very clearly (John 18:28–19:16). Here were the Jewish authorities demanding the death of Jesus on the grounds of attempting to overthrow the political authority, yet they do not accept the verdict of that authority, and proceed to force Pilate's hand.

What is more, they use the local custom of releasing a prisoner at Passover to pacify the people, in order to get Barabbas – a notorious criminal and subversive – freed. They demand Barabbas in exchange for Jesus who will take Barabbas's punishment (23:18–19). This spells trouble for Pilate, who could then be reported to Rome for releasing a known political criminal. It was time for him to assert his authority among Jesus' enemies, who, themselves, with all their shouting, are fomenting a riot (23:23). According to Jewish law one had to be innocent of the crime before one could cast the stone at anyone else (John 8:7), and they are now doing the very things they accuse Jesus of. Jesus' silence and personal freedom stands out in all the din. He is the sign causing the rise and fall of many in Israel, exposing their secret thoughts (2:34).

The Barabbas incident is a tiny gem among many in the Passion narrative. The name Barabbas means "son of the father". The two men who stand before the people have the same name. Both are called the son of their respective fathers. Israel must choose between the sinful one and the sinless Son of God. They chose the sinner, who committed the political crimes for which the innocent Son of God will die, a fact not lost on the early Church, as the stipulation for the Passover lamb in Exodus 12 was a pure lamb without spot or stain. Ironically the leaders chose correctly, if they knew Jesus was the Passover Lamb. The innocent one must die in place of the guilty one. Throughout this narrative of the trial, there is a noticable absence of the people (the *laos*, the laity, although Matthew 27:20 and Mark 15:20 include them). Luke presents these events as taking place only among the authorities, and presents them as a tour de force by the

Jewish leaders, who manage to undermine Pilate's authority in the whole affair.

Before the Barabbas incident Pilate had been willing just to flog Jesus and let him go. Obviously He was the cause of all this commotion among the chief priests, and perhaps some blood would satisfy them. Luke does not say whether Jesus was, in fact, scourged, but goes on to conclude the trial with Pilate giving in to their demands (23:24–25). While he allowed a known and wanted insurrectionist to go free, he handed over the Messiah-King, the Christ, Son of Man and Son of God (22:63–67) to be crucified. In fact Luke gives the impression in 23:25 that Pilate handed Jesus over to the Jews to crucify Him, but the other gospels state clearly that it was the Roman soldiers who did it. The Jewish penalty for blasphemy was stoning (see Acts 7:55–8:19), the Roman punishment for insurrection was crucifixion.

Luke is adamant though, that we hear what he has to say: *Pilate then gave his verdict: their demand was to be granted ... and handed Jesus over to them to deal with as they pleased* (23:25). Jerusalem kills the prophet as Jesus had predicted (13:34), and she will have to bear the consequences (19:41–44). Her day of salvation was over. The next step for Jesus was to open God's Kingdom to the Gentiles. Before we leave this scene, remember that it is only a short time ago that Jesus prayed "Abba, if you will ... so be it". Now we hear that it was definitely the will of the Sanhedrin that He drink the cup, and this at the cost of overriding political authority.

The Way of the Cross (23:26–46)

The execution followed hot on the heels of the sentence. Luke, who wants to keep to the Christian interpretation of the events, plays down the role of the Roman soldiers, who are not mentioned until 23:36. They were, after all, merely carrying out orders from legitimate authority. The miscarriage of justice cannot be laid at their door. To this end, Luke, omits the scourging, mocking and crowning with thorns by them mentioned by Matthew 27:27–31 and Mark 15:16–20. It was customary for the condemned man to carry the cross beam, by the longest possible route, to the place of execution. Before him marched the soldier carrying a placard with the crime inscribed on it. The whole procession was meant to be a warning to the people not to follow the condemned man's footsteps.

As the procession begins, Luke focuses on the participants who are to teach lessons and give example to all future disciples called to walk in the footsteps of Jesus. The first of these is Simon of Cyrene (23:26), who came from North Africa, probably fulfilling a lifetime's ambition to come to Jerusalem to celebrate Passover. The last thing he needed was involvement in an execution, thereby incurring ritual defilement. However, Jesus proved too weak to carry His cross, from His previous tortures omitted by Luke, and it would not do for Him to die on the way. Simon, therefore, was enlisted by the soldiers to carry the cross: they *made him shoulder the cross and carry it behind Jesus* (23:26). Enlisting meant a tap on the shoulder with a Roman lance, which one could not refuse.

The Lord had seen into Simon's heart, and he is called, like all disciples, to take up his cross and follow Jesus, and not be ashamed of Him in the presence of others (9:23–26). Mark 15:21 mentions Simon's two sons Alexander and Rufus who were well known to the Roman Church. Both they and their mother were prominent members deserving mention in Paul's letter to the Romans 16:13, (see also Acts 6:9, 11:20, 13:1). This means that although Simon reluctantly took the cross initially, he had a change of heart. Perhaps his eyes were opened on Calvary and he was given insight into the real Passover and the fulfilment of the rite he had come so far to celebrate. If so, then Jesus en route to His death won yet another triumph as He turned Simon's mourning into dancing (Psalm 30). Simon represents those who will come from north and south to take their places at the feast in God's Kingdom (13:29).

Luke now mentions the crowds of people who join the mournful procession. The Talmud records that middle-class and noble women were accustomed to mourn and lament a criminal on his way to death. This was seen as a good and religious act. They often gave the criminal drugged drinks to soothe his pain. To die unmourned was a terrible fate, and to die unmourned and childless was the worst fate of all. Unless the women came forward this was Jesus' fate. Perhaps without knowing it, they fulfil Zechariah 12:10, which said that the citizens of Jerusalem *will mourn for the one whom they have pierced as though for an only Son, and weep for him as people weep for a first-born child.* This mourning was expected to be given to the dead Messiah.

Jesus responded to their compassionate tears by telling them that He was OK. His death was not what it seemed. They could not perceive its deeper reality, but future believers who would penetrate its mystery, would find in it a means of giving thanks and praise to God (1 Corinthians 15:54–47). Shedding tears over His Passion was not the response He asked. It was a preparation for their own passion which would surely come. His prophecy concerning the fall of Jerusalem would come in the life-time of many of them (21:20–23, 19:41–45), for Jerusalem was about to reap the fruits of her rejection of the Messiah and God's plan of salvation. It was Jerusalem that should be wept over (19:41), for if her leaders deal with an innocent man as they dealt with Jesus, what can her guilty citizens expect? He was the green wood, they were the dry (23:31).

Jerusalem's leaders may not yet realize that they are dry wood, fit for the fire, but their rejection of the day of salvation left them outside of grace. If they continue to misuse justice as they have done now, coupled with their rejection of the Word of God, they will not be ready when the fire of destruction hits them in AD 70. Then things will be so terrible that Hosea's prediction will come true, and they will call on the mountains to cover them (Hosea 10:8). In those dreadful judgement days it is not the childless people who will suffer most, but those who are parents (23:29, 21:23). Everything will be turned upside down, even the disgrace of barrenness (1:25; see Ezekiel 3:1–4).

Crucifixion (23:33–43)

Before the unseeing eyes of everyone the Scriptures are quietly being fulfilled as Jesus is crucified between two criminals (23:32; Isaiah 53:12). Luke gives no details of the dreadful cruelty of crucifixion, which was a familiar scene in Israel at that time. Yet Jews, Greeks and Romans agreed upon one thing: it was the most degrading way to die, in which pain was maximized, yet inflicted in such a way that it brought about a slow agonizing death (1 Corinthians 1:18) Luke simply states that they crucified Him. The details would be only too clear to his church, and too upsetting to many Christians who were destined to suffer a similar fate at the hands of the Roman Empire in its desire to destroy Christianity. They were trying to come to grips with such an event, and how it could have been part of God's plan (Acts 2:23, 4:28).

They come to understand as they watch Him die, for

the way we die is the greatest statement on our lives. Jesus died as He lived, in prayer, forgiving his enemies, loving and serving His neighbour and in full surrender to God's Will (23:34, 39–43, 46). In retrospect they saw that Psalm 22 had been fulfilled. This psalm speaks of an innocent sufferer dying surrounded by his enemies, but instead of anger, he turned to God in trust (vv. 1–5) as he tried to deal with the mockery of his enemies who sneer at his trust in God (vv. 6–8). Their understanding was that God would save the righteous man from such a punishment. If he did not, then the man was guilty (vv. 6–8). The sufferer then describes how he feels about his enemies (vv. 12–13, 15–16) asking God to pity him in his plight (vv. 9–11, 17–18). Then with a heart-rending cry he pierces the heavens and God replies (vv. 19–20). Now that God has answered the cry of the poor man in his poverty (vv. 24) all Israel should praise God and look forward to the fulfilment of all God's promises to them (vv. 25–31). It ends with "all this God has done" which is the *"consumatum est"* of the Old Testament.

Following Jesus' own post-Resurrection instructions (24:27, 44) it is not difficult to see why the early Christians saw this psalm fulfilled in Jesus, including as it did details like "they cast lots for his clothes" as his clothing was shared out among the four soldiers responsible for carrying out the crucifixion (23:34; Psalm 22:18) and the mockery which followed it. Even the psalm, let alone Jesus' own teaching, reminded them that the crucifixion was a passage to glory, not to oblivion.

Luke is alone among the evangelists to stress Jesus' forgiveness of his enemies, which was an act of total heroism given the circumstances. He says that Jesus *kept* saying: *"Father, forgive them; they do not know*

what they are doing" (23:34). To forgive from the
heart, with real love, is wonderful (7:48, 5:20), but to
make excuses for one's murderers in the very act of
murder as they mocked and jeered – that is different.
That is unconquerable benevolence, *agape*-love, divine.
With such heroic forgiveness death, in the sense of
darkness and evil, is already overcome, as Paul understood when he wrote to the Romans to resist evil and
overcome it with good (Romans 12:21). In 1 Corinthians
15:56–57, Paul says that the sting of death was sin,
but we can thank God that this sting was removed by
the death of Jesus.

Jesus remained Himself to the very end. Though His
body was brutalized by torture, He remained free inte-
riorly, and chose to give one last chance to Israel to
repent. Perhaps their hardness of heart would be softened
by His broken-hearted forgiveness? It seems so from
Acts 2:37–41, 47, and especially 6:7 where we are told
that a large number of priests made their submission to
the faith. In trying to reach them, Peter, in Acts 3:17,
used this forgiveness of Jesus: *"Now I know, brothers,
that neither you nor your leaders had any idea what
you were really doing ..."* (see 1 Corinthians 2:8; 1
Timothy 1:13–14)

The people were witnesses to all that happened. They
stayed there watching (23:35), and as Jesus had shown
them how to live, He was now showing them how to
die. The people are silent spectators, but the leaders
continue to jeer Him, even as a defeated foe. In some
ways they know Him better than His disciples, even
though He found an excuse for them, for they threw
His own teaching at Him, as the sufferer in psalm 22
experienced also. A man who saved others should be
able to save himself! Had He lost that power they had
envied so much when He saved the poor, the blind,

the lepers and demoniacs? Had He not eluded them before at Nazareth (4:30)? Why is he apparently without power now?

Jesus was right. They did not understand that if He came down from the cross nothing would change, and none of them would be saved. He would still be confined to the flesh, limited by time, space and material things. By His own teaching in 9:23–25 it was by losing His life that He would save His real life, but by giving in to their temptation to avoid the cross and its shame, not only He, but all humans would lose salvation (23:35–38). For those with eyes to see the Lamb of God was laying down His life to take away the sin of the world (John 1:29). No! Jesus must stay on the cross until He dies and Christians must not seek to shed their cross either. The stakes are too high. Meanwhile the uncomprehending world of closed-minded religious people, and unbelievers, look on mocking and jeering and must be forgiven by the rest of us.

The soldiers join in the mockery and offer the king of the Jews a drink of vinegar or sour wine, perhaps out of compassion, for the suffering of crucifixion was very distressing even to onlookers. These Roman soldiers called Jesus the king of the Jews, whereas the Jews would have called him the King of Israel, so another title is given to Jesus here at the last moment (see Mark 15:32; Matthew 27:48). The drink was seen as a pain-killer, but unfortunately it prolonged the fight for life. It seems Luke may see this as a mocking gesture in the light of Psalm 69:21 which reads: "*when I was thirsty, they gave me vinegar to drink*", a hostile action therefore.

Unknown to them all, Jesus is universal king (Revelation 19:12), one who deserves the homage of Jew and Gentile, not their mockery. Matthew 27:36 says that Jesus refused the drink. He would not shirk the cup His Father offered Him (John 18:11; 22:17, 43), and, besides, He would not drink the fruit of the vine until God's Kingdom comes (22:18). The inscription over the cross proclaimed the truth: *"This is the King of the Jews"* (23:38). Pilate covered himself legally here, for Roman law would not countenance such a death for an innocent man. Jesus is dying as a king, and possible threat to Caesar, His kingship is misunderstood by all. Christians see that the king has his head lower than all his subjects, for he does the most menial task of washing the stains of sin and iniquity from us all. He is the true suffering servant of God (22:24–27; Isaiah 52–53).

The Two Criminals (23:39–43)

The green wood and the dry wood are present on Calvary (23:31), as Jesus hangs equally between two sinners, who are dying for their sins. Here is one of Luke's unique contributions to the Passion narrative, where he asks his readers and community alike, to place themselves here at the cross, and choose which way they should go, for choice there is. There in the centre is the Lamb of God, the Davidic Messiah-King, Son of God and Son of Man, dying to save us all, paying a frightful price to open the gates of Paradise to forgiven sinners. He hangs equally between a sinner who accepts and one who rejects, such is the mystery of the freedom of human choice. Both these men find themselves in the same circumstances, with the same opportunity for grace, but with different results. Yet Jesus made no distinction between them. He did not reject the one who reviled Him. No. He would be covered under the umbrella of Jesus' heroic forgiveness, but Jesus responded incredibly to the good will of the so-called Good Thief, whose only good deed was to turn to Jesus in the nick of time. A very good example of salvation through faith and without works!

This good thief is also Luke's third witness to the innocence of Jesus. Absolutely nothing in Jesus' behaviour or words indicated a criminal. Even this man in his own extremity could see that. He rebuked his fellow thief: *"Have you no fear of God at all?"* he said. *"You got the same sentence as he did, but in our case we deserved it . . . But this man has done nothing wrong"* (23:40–41). Even now Jesus is proclaimed innocent by someone who would recognize one of his own.

Instead, he turned to Jesus as his only hope, whereas the other criminal was limited to nationalistic ideas of salvation or liberation when he said that if Jesus really were the Messiah He should save Himself, and them as well. Since his idea included a Messiah who would lead them in political revolution, he only pours scorn on Jesus' apparent impotence. Again we see that it is his own mind-set that prevents him from entering God's Kingdom.

The good thief accepts Jesus' notion of kingship, even though he probably did not understand it, yet he put his trust in Jesus Himself. Jesus seemed sure of whatever He was doing, and so he asked to be associated with it. Since both of them were dying, his request to remember him when Jesus came into His kingly reality refers to afterwards. Jesus' response was speedy and way beyond what was asked. He promised, with the word of the Messiah, that the day of his shameful execution would see him into Paradise. Like Jesus, he would ascend from the cross into glory, the ideal of every follower of Jesus, who knows that their salvation is all of grace, and due to the salvation won for us by so great a redeemer as Jesus.

Luke here portrays Jesus forgiving sinners and accepting

outcasts into the Kingdom right up to the very end. For him, a repentant sinner was a great joy (chapter 15). Here was a prodigal son about to be embraced by the Father in His eternal Home (13:30, 14:2–24). This must have been the only consolation offered by the Father to His dying Son. He could still find the lost sheep, and bring in the strays off the streets into the eternal banquet. His love had conquered yet again.

The word Paradise comes from the old Persian language, and refers to an extensive park, filled with every possible luxury, enclosed by a wall attached to a king's palace. It was used as a synonym for heaven, or the dwelling place of the just after death. It doesn't make for tidy theology to have the second Adam re-open Paradise with a good-for-nothing thief in his company. It would have been more "fitting" to have Adam, Abraham or one of the saints. But that would not be the good news! The good news proclaims Paradise opened for all repentant sinners who turn to accept Jesus as their Saviour and Lord. It should then be a noisy place, where very grateful people wonder how they ever passed the "test" (see 14:15–24 for the sinners' banquet). By contrast, one of hell's frustrations will be the inability to work out why so many "good" people didn't make it (13:23–30). This man certainly is a good example of the last in this world becoming the first in the next!

The Death of Jesus (23:44–49)

The day of Jesus' death is divided up by the gospels into certain "hours", even though the entire event was His hour, His *kairos*-time. He was crucified at the third hour (Mark 15:25), approximately 9 am, three hours after sunrise. This is the Hour of Suffering. The sixth hour was about midday, when darkness came over the earth until the ninth hour: this is the Hour of Darkness. The ninth hour was mid-afternoon (usually thought to be 3pm) when Jesus died. This was the Hour of Victory.

Luke states clearly that the sun eclipsed in such a way that it refused to give its light for three hours (23:44; Joel 2:31). Here the very universe seems to want to teach blind humans that, the powers of evil wanted to extinguish the Light of the World, and apparently succeeded. Humans had rejected the Light, and now even the earth's light refuses to shine. All is reduced to darkness, the physical darkness a pointer to the more ominous spiritual darkness everywhere. The friends of Jesus who stand at a distance, see the darkness as God's judgement on a sinful world, as the plague of darkness was, which God sent to Egypt at the time of Moses (Exodus 10:21–29). That plague was meant to bring them to repentance. No one is allowed to be indifferent to the mystery of the cross.

What is more, the veil of the Temple was torn right down the middle at the moment that Jesus died. As the ninth hour was the time when the people gathered for evening prayer and sacrifice (Acts 3:1; Exodus 29:38–42), this was a dramatic sign from God that the sacrificial cult of the Temple was finished, and the exclusiveness of the Jewish people removed. The veil in question was that which covered the entrance to the Holy of Holies, the innermost room of the Temple, the place which housed the very Presence of God Himself. It was held to be so sacred, that only the high priest could enter it once a year on Yom Kippur, the day of atonement, when he asked forgiveness for the sins of the nation (Exodus 26:31 ff.; Leviticus 16). This veil effectively closed off the Presence of God from everyone, both priests and people, and the Gentiles most of all. If this veil were torn in two without human intervention, then God was giving an unmistakable message to Israel, that their exclusive access to God was now removed (Ephesians 2:14; Galatians 3:28), and that Jesus, out on that lonely hill on Calvary, had carved a new and living way for all nations to find access to the living God (Hebrews 9, 10:19–22).

The life and death of Jesus had torn the heavens open to give access to everyone (Isaiah 64:1) to walk the sacred way of the redeemed. Now the barren wastes of the hearts of all nations could rejoice, for the Lord has come to save them (Isaiah 35:1–10). The more ominous side of the message for the Sanhedrin was that the destruction or the dismantling of the Temple had already begun (19:41–44, 21:20–24, 23:27–30). It could now be compared to a climbing plant whose roots have been cut off, which does not die immediately, but the process of decay begins all the same. All the sacrifices of Israel have now been replaced by the one and only sacrifice of Jesus, the Beloved Son.

All the gospels record Jesus' loud cry before His death, an extraordinary circumstance given the extreme agony and loss of body fluids. This death is not what it seems on the outside. Jesus had chosen to drink the cup to the dregs, and now it is done. John records that Jesus died saying: "It is finished" (John 19:30) which has him very much in control, and knowing at what moment all was given. It is a cry of triumph as indicated by the tearing of the veil of the Temple.

Luke demonstrates Jesus' final surrender of His life into the Father's hands. His loving and obedient relationship with his Abba had been the very centre of his life. Now as the evening prayers are recited in the Temple they included Psalm 31 from which Luke quotes v. 5: *"Father, into your hands I commit my spirit"*. This would seem to imply that a true son of Israel was still obedient and in solidarity with all true members of Israel in their submission to God's Will. He finished His life as He began it – about His Father's affairs (2:49). The Beloved Son now surrenders into the Everlasting Arms of His Heavenly Father with grace and trust, like a child (23:46). He died as He lived, the greatest example of His own teaching. Jesus departs to take His place at the right hand of God (22:69), not, as His enemies thought, His place among the accursed (Deuteronomy 21:23). Next time they meet Him, He will be both Lord and Christ, a power to be reckoned with, as He marches triumphantly from nation to nation in and through His followers (Acts 4:33, 2:33, 36, 7:59).

The Roman centurion (captain of one hundred men) responsible for the execution stood up, deeply moved by what had occurred, and became the fourth witness to the innocence of Jesus. He knew from experience that crucifixion could reduce a decent man to the animal level, and that many of the crucified struggled for days on end, dying stark raving mad, a truly pitiful sight. But Jesus was serene, noble, peaceful, in control, a true son of God. This pagan praised God and said: *"This was a great and good man"* (23:48). Under the test of crucifixion this was no small response to wring from the chief executioner (Acts 3:14).

The people, too, had seen everything. Luke says they were there for the spectacle, uninvolved in the issues, yet they too reacted to what they saw. They went home beating their breasts, realizing certainly, that something awful had taken place, but hopefully, repentant too. Neither the Passion of Jesus nor that of his followers is to be seen as a spectacle. We are all involved in its mystery and must make decisions as a result. Perhaps this beating of breasts prepared for the mass conversions which came so soon after the event (Acts 2:41, 47, 4:4, 6:1)? This would mean that the dying Jesus achieved by

His heroic love and sacrifice, what His heroic words and deeds could not accomplish in His lifetime. The blood of the martyr was needed to make inroads into stony hearts.

For the first time Luke mentions Jesus' friends. They have been conspicuously absent up to now in the Passion. Nevertheless they are there, all of them, including the faithful women who had journeyed with Him from Galilee (8:2–3, 23:49). They had kept apart from His enemies. Instead, they stayed at a distance unable to influence events, but standing in solidarity with their beloved Master. This was not just Jesus' death, for in Him they died too, died to their own ideas of the Messiah and Saviour. Only His rising to New Life could lift them out of the mourning robes that enwrapped them all: *"Our own hope had been . . ."* (24:21). In spite of their pain they are the witnesses to His death and burial, and the women are the very privileged ones to discover the next stage of His triumphal march to God and glory . . . and to the ends of the earth. "Christ has died" they say now. "Christ has risen" they will say in three days time. "Christ will come again" they will preach to the whole world.

The Burial of Jesus (23:50–56)

As soon as Jesus died the whole atmosphere changed. The sun gave its fading light again as evening dawned and the Sabbath lights were about to be lit, for the holy day began in the evening at about 6pm. The verdict of the supreme religious body in Israel was: guilty. Now everyone awaited God's verdict which will be given in the resurrection. In the meantime various individuals and groups came to their own conclusions, and acted accordingly. King Herod and Caesar's representative both declared

Jesus innocent. This was followed by the testimony of the centurion who executed Him. Simon of Cyrene and the Good Thief join Jesus, and the women of Jerusalem, some of whose husbands or sons may have been members of the Council, mourned for Him. And the spectators went home to repent.

Now, at the last moment, a star witness appears, when the deed is done. Joseph of Arimathea was a member of that Council that had apparently, unanimously decided to kill Jesus. He must have been absent from the meeting, for his behaviour now in burying Jesus, could not be equated with a cowardly silence when he could have stalled, if not prevented the death sentence from being carried out. He was a respected member of the Council according to Mark 15:43, a rich man and a disciple of Jesus according to Matthew 27:57, but a secret disciple according to John 19:38, who also mentions Nicodemus, another secret disciple of Jesus in the Council. This man had influence with Pilate – enough to disturb Pilate badly by demanding an honourable burial for a "criminal" (23:52). If he had been present at the trial could he not have influenced it too?

Luke is at pains to tell us that Joseph was different to the other members of the Sanhedrin that he presented in such a negative light. He was an upright man, who did not consent to the Council's decision or subsequent actions in killing Jesus (23:51). In fact he was one of the true Israel, the remnant, like Zechariah, Elizabeth, Simeon, Anna and the other good people who lived in hope of seeing the Kingdom of God. It seems he could do nothing to prevent the death, but he could add the witness of his actions to the innocence of Jesus, and so a fifth witness appears, after the event. All his actions prove that to him, as an official member of the Sanhedrin, Jesus was a good and innocent man, who should and would be given an honourable burial, so he went to Pilate to request the body of Jesus (23:52).

The Roman custom was to leave the bodies of the crucified on their crosses to rot and be eaten by wild animals and birds of prey, a sign of an already accursed death. The Jews, however, insisted on burial, albeit in a mass grave (Deuteronomy 21:23), in order to remove the curse from the land. It must have disturbed Pilate – in a day of great disturbance – to find such a high ranking Jewish official wanting to honour Jesus in His death. Or perhaps it was just another instance of the inscrutable Jews? Joseph removed the body of Jesus and wrapped it in a shroud, and then, contrary to all expectation, laid it in a new tomb hewn out of rock (23:53). Jesus was buried like a king, not a pauper, as a man of God, not a criminal. Just as Jesus had entered Jerusalem on a donkey no one had ridden, so here He is laid in a tomb that has never been soiled by death. What He initiated in His entry into Jerusalem was a totally new and unique event that was to explode into new life and glory. And Joseph was rewarded by his own tomb becoming the symbol of everlasting hope and joy for every living creature, for a totally new event took place there where death was overcome.

Luke said that all this took place on Preparation Day, for no work was permitted on the Sabbath, the sacred day of rest, particularly sacred that year because it coincided with the Passover. In a real sense we are told that everything that had occurred in the ministry and in the journey to Jerusalem was only a preparation for that great day of the Lord that was about to dawn. The Galilean women remained faithful to the end and were the witnesses to Jesus' death and burial. Since the Sabbath lights were being lit, they could do nothing to wash or anoint the body. They planned to do that after the great Sabbath.

Therefore they went to their lodgings to rest as the Law required (23:56), perhaps not realizing that the Son of Man has entered into His rest after the labours of His redeeming work (Hebrews 3:1–4:11). When His rest is over, Jesus will rise to inaugurate the New Era of the Kingdom of God. But already in the events of His burial we are shown that the final verdict was: innocent.

Chapter Seven
The Sun Rises with Healing in its Rays

As we move into Luke's final chapter we open out to a completely new world where Isaiah 60:19–20 is fulfilled: *"Yahweh will be your everlasting light, your God will be your splendour. Your sun will set no more nor your moon wane ... your days of mourning will be ended."* The terrible hour of darkness culminated in a glorious dawn, the first day of the Messianic Era. Just as everything closed-in on Calvary with the suffocating pall of death, so now God opens the tomb to release the first-born from the dead into the new life of resurrection. This opening of the tomb occasioned the opening of people's homes (24:29), and hearts (24:32) to the Risen Lord. As the heavens open to receive Jesus (24:51), He also journeys with His disciples on their new mission to all the world (24:13–15) opening the Scriptures to them (24:25–27), opening their eyes, their interior vision (24:31), and opening their minds to understand the mystery of Christ from the Scriptures (24:45).

Like the other evangelists Luke states the fact of the empty tomb, and then moves on to the vital question as to how the disciples came to be convinced that Jesus was Risen, and what the implications of this were for us all. He is also concerned to answer the question: "How do we meet the Risen Lord today?" He answers these questions in a journey narrative so typical of him which has the double perspective of "what happened back there" and what is happening now among those who form the church.

Luke's thesis is that both experience the Risen Lord in essentially the same manner.

The Empty Tomb (24:1–12)

The Galilean women who had travelled to Jerusalem with Jesus, and who witnessed His death and burial there, went away to prepare spices and ointments to anoint the body of Jesus (23:55–56). As soon as the Sabbath was over, they intended to finish the funeral rites for Him. They set out for the tomb at dawn on the first working day of the Jewish week, but the new Christian Sabbath, Sunday (Acts 20:7; 1 Corinthians 16:2). This day would forever remain the day when Christians celebrate the resurrection of Jesus, the Lord. At this point, of course, they are unaware of this new dawn. Up to this moment they were loyal Jewish women, obeying the Law of Moses, but from this moment they will obey the Law of Christ.

It appears that they either thought that between them they had enough strength to roll away the stone that closed the entrance to the tomb (which was usually fitted into a groove in the ground), or they gave it no consideration at all. A tomb such as the one Jesus had been buried in would have an antechamber and an inner chamber where the body was laid on a stone slab. It would have been big enough for all of them to go in and also to receive the heavenly visitors.

On arrival they found that the tomb was open. The stone had been rolled away by an unknown agent and *they could not find the body of the Lord Jesus* (24:23). The body of Jesus was never referred to as a corpse, a dead thing, and Jesus Himself is given his Risen titles "The Lord, Jesus". The implication being that if Jesus is Lord, His body will not be found in a place of death (24:3). As they contemplate this mystery they are favoured with two heavenly visitors: *two men in brilliant clothes suddenly appeared at their side*. They came unannounced, but proceeded to interpret the meaning of what has occurred (24:23). It is obvious that the women would not have concluded that Jesus had risen. They were merely astonished and perplexed, and terrified by this supernatural occurrence (24:4–5).

The two men, without explaining either their origins or identity, proceed to reveal the Resurrection to the women. They were not now, or ever again, to seek Jesus among the dead: *"Why look among the dead for someone who is alive? He is not here; he has risen"* (24:6). The tomb is empty because Jesus is the Living One (Revelation 1:17). This is the vital piece of information to take away. The more obvious conclusion would be that grave robbers got there before them (Matthew 18:13; John 20:15), a theory that has haunted many. The women were then reminded of the predictions Jesus made concerning His Passion and Resurrection, which up to this moment none of them appear to have remembered (24:6–7). If they are to understand the mystery of the Resurrection they must remember the teaching of the Son of Man: *And they remembered his words* (24:8).

These two men – angels in 24:23 – parallel the two heavenly visitors on Mount Tabor (9:33), and the Ascension (Acts 1:10; John 20:12). This may allude to the need for two or three witnesses in Deuteronomy to ratify an important matter. The two heavenly visitors on Mount Tabor were Moses and Elijah foretelling Jesus' *exodos*. The two angels at the Ascension foretell the Parousia, and the two here tell the women to look among the living – all those who live in the spirit – for Jesus. Therefore they will find him in the community of believers. Luke's story goes on to relate how two men, obviously belonging to the Seventy-Two, found Jesus in the community and at the Eucharist.

A flashback to the Passover will remind us that Jesus had sent two disciples to prepare for the entry into Jerusalem. When they followed His instructions they found that everything was just as He told them (19:32). Likewise at the preparations for the Last Supper: they set off and found everything as He had told them (22:13). If the disciples and the women had listened to Jesus' predictions of the Passion and resurrection, they were now also finding everything just as He had said. He is Risen, so the tomb is empty (9:22, 44, 12:50, 17:25, 18:31).

From this time onwards it will be the disciples going out two by two who will announce and interpret the Resurrection to the rest of the world (Acts 3:18, 26, 26:22–23). They will be God's messengers (angels, though unwinged!) to open up the dead world to God's Kingdom, and to call the nations from the tomb of unbelief to the glorious Day of Salvation and Joy. Everyone who discovers the true meaning of the empty tomb must become a proclaimer of the glorious fact of the Resurrection.

The women, led by Mary of Magdala, Joanna, and Mary, the mother of James, went to report to the Apostles and to *all the others*, namely the Seventy-Two and other disciples (24:9). The women's testimony was not received, but treated as pure nonsense. This is a prophetic forecast of the future for the message of the Resurrection is still treated as pure nonsense by many, who will accept no one's testimony. John relates that Thomas, one of the Twelve, refused to accept it even from the apostolic witness (John 20:24–29), but Jesus did not congratulate them on their scepticism (John 20:29). When it comes to the Resurrection, the basic need for signs to confirm faith became urgent. There was also and still is, a craving for scientific evidence to "prove" it. The men waited until they saw Jesus for themselves, and shared a meal with Him, before they were convinced (24:36–43). The women's faith was simpler and more direct, and amply rewarded according to Matthew 28:9–10, where the Risen Lord came to meet them as they were on their way to bear testimony to the Church (John 20:11–18).

To his credit, Peter at least, went to the tomb to confirm the evidence. The tomb was empty except for the grave-cloths which were no longer needed by the departing Risen Lord. Peter did not take the quantum leap to faith in the Resurrection from the evidence. He just went home amazed (24:12). John said that two of them went, and that the beloved disciple did take that leap in faith, required for understanding the Scriptures (John 20:8–10), but then John had given a detailed explanation of the raising of Lazarus, who merely came back to this life with all its limitations, so he was still bound in his grave-cloths. Jesus, however, had entered into a completely new dimension of being, where He needed none of the trappings of earth. He was gloriously free of all limitation or definition of time or space. His abandoning of the grave-cloths was a vital piece of evidence, which grave-robbers would not have left behind. They would have needed extra wrappings to cover up the foul deed of stealing a corpse.

Journey to Emmaus (24:13–35)

Luke's main recognition story is told on a journey from Jerusalem to Emmaus, a village some seven miles from the city, but to this day its exact whereabouts is disputed. Here Luke's skill as a story-teller reaches new heights as he weaves many of his favourite themes into this wonderful event, whereby two ordinary disciples discovered the reality of the Resurrection. Their discovery was not at the tomb for the angelic visitors there had focused the attention of the early Church away from the tomb (24:5). The abode of the dead could not hold the Living One (Revelation 1:17–18; Psalm 16). But how are they to discover Him? And where? How will they recognize Him since no one has ever seen someone back from the dead? Will He be the same or radically different? What would they look for? How would they relate to Him? And how would His Risen Presence affect the community and relationships within the group? Who was in charge now and how would they know?

While answering all these questions Luke weaves his familiar themes of the journey with Jesus: the fulfilment of the Old Testament Scriptures, God's plan of salvation, the Messianic Banquet, Jesus' concern with the "little people", the unimportant ones, and Jesus the one who knows the way to their goal. All this is woven wonderfully into this story.

It was the same day that two disciples, obviously not Apostles since one of them was called Cleopas, decided they could take no more and left Jerusalem for Emmaus. First of all, Luke relates all the Resurrection appearances the same day, Easter Day, perhaps because it was the New Day, the New Era of grace and glory. Regarding the identity of these men, Eusebius (HE 3.11, 32, 4.22) cited Hegesippus, circa AD 180, identifying Cleopas as the brother of Joseph, the foster-father of Jesus. This Hegesippus was a Palestinian Christian who wrote down his memoirs . . . "After the martyrdom of James the just (nephew of Joseph and Cleopas) on the same charge as the Lord, his uncle's child Simeon, the son of Cleopas, is next made bishop. He was put forward by everyone, he being yet another cousin of the Lord". This Simeon succeeded James as leader of the church in Jerusalem and led the Christians back there after the disaster of AD 70. This would make Cleopas Jesus' uncle (John 19:25), thus adding a homely touch to a story that moves the heart-strings anyway.

In reading Luke's gospel it is clear that Jerusalem is the centre of everything. It is the place where the mystery of redemption comes about, and the place where God lives. The journey of life is centred upon Jerusalem, and all that must be accomplished there, for it a symbol of life's goal. To go – in this gospel – from Jerusalem to anywhere, is automatically to go in the wrong direction in life. The Good Samaritan has already shown the way to erring disciples. They may be hurt by life's events and disasters, but a fellow-traveller sent by God will join them, heal their heartaches, and put them back on the road to Jerusalem and God's Will for them (10:29–37).

When they learn their lesson, God will use them as missionary strangers to travel the roads of the world ministering to people on their life's journey, and setting them on the road to the New Jerusalem (Revelation 21–22). This is illustrated in Acts 8:26–40 with regard to Philip. For a later age there is the lovely story about the Curé of Ars who stopped a boy on a country road to ask directions to his new parish. He said to the boy: "If you show me the way to Ars I will show you the way to Heaven". It is still the stranger on life's journey. Luke has managed to encapsulate the missionary ideal in one stroke of his pen, and to fire us with his enthusiasm in the same breath. Life is all about this spiritual journey, and it is a matter of extreme, and eternal, importance where the destiny of that journey lies.

The two men are dejected and so wrapped up in their misery that they are not aware of the stranger's presence until he interrupts them in order to get their attention (24:15–16). Is it possible that the Lord is at our side, and because we are absorbed in the cares of life (8:14) we do not perceive it? Luke's first point is that we find the Risen Lord on our journey but we must recognize Him. Lack of faith and prayer keeps us blind to Jesus' presence and leaves us in an apparently abandoned state. We must do something to break through to His presence.

Since salvation comes to us on God's initiative, Jesus begins the dialogue that enables these men to get in touch with the real source of their pain and to look for the true solution. Jesus wants to know what they are talking about (24:17). This pulled them up short, and Cleopas wondered how this stranger could be the only person in Jerusalem who didn't know the happenings of these past three days (24:18)! Superb irony here on Luke's part, for Jesus is about to show them that He is the only person who really did know what happened, and they don't seem to have grasped it at all. This is parallel to Mary of Magdala's request in John 20 where she asked Jesus if He took the body, and would He tell her where he had put it so she could find it.

Jesus feigned ignorance to get the story, and its interpretation, out of them. They answered that it all about Jesus of Nazareth, and one knows immediately that we are listening to the early Church's catechesis. At this moment they do not realize that they are on a practice session for their mission to all the world, where Jesus will be with them in His invisible presence giving them the words to say. He is now told that Jesus *"proved he was a great prophet by the things he said and did in the sight of God and of the whole people"* (24:19). So the accredited signs of a prophet were given and recognized by these men, so where is the problem since all the other prophets are dead? Now He has been killed by the chief priests and elders who handed Him over (official expression for "betrayed") to be crucified ... but other prophets were persecuted and killed, weren't they (11:47–51, 13:34, 20:9–19)?

What is their problem? *"Our own hope had been that he would be the one to set Israel free"* (24:21). The problem lay in their own perception of Jesus, and now that things had worked out differently, they have lost faith and hope. In spite of the clear prediction of the Passion and Resurrection, they had persisted in a political notion of Messiah.

They had not "heard" His teaching concerning the suffering Son of Man and Servant of God. Jesus had not succeeded in breaking through their mind-set so that they could see what God was doing under their very noses. *"Father, forgive them; they do not know what they are doing"* must cover His close friends and relatives too. How sad to be so close to Jesus, and to miss seeing what you are looking at. This blindness explains their inability to recognize Jesus on the way, since they are "back there" in the Old Testament political notion of Messiah, and have not yet come up to date with the truth revealed by Jesus. How could they possibly cope with the mystery of the Resurrection when they have not even faced the reality of the Suffering Servant of God in their midst? Only those who penetrate the scandal of the cross can possibly emerge into the glory of the Resurrection, and realize, yet again, that God's ways are not our ways. In fact, His ways are as different from ours as the heavens are from the earth (Isaiah 55:8–10).

Only when we go into the tomb with Jesus carrying our own cross, like Simon of Cyrene, can we hope to grasp the wonder of light, life, hope and glory. What is wrong with these two is that they are "back there" at the scandal of the cross, and Jesus is here in light and glory, ready to initiate His mission to all the world. They are so far removed from where Jesus is, that He must now take them on a journey from the darkness of unbelief and incomprehension of God's ways to the light of faith. They must shift from Friday darkness to Sunday glory in their hearts. They must rise from the dead and live the New Life hidden with Christ in God (Colossians 3:1–3).

In their present state not even the facts of the Resurrection will get through to them, as they now relate. Even though it is the third day, and the women have found the tomb empty; even though the women have had a vision of angels revealing the fact of the Resurrection; even though some of their friends, namely Peter and John, had gone to the tomb to verify the facts; even though they found everything just as the women had said ... they still would not believe (24:21–24)! The crux of the matter comes now: *but of him they saw nothing*. Only now can these men verbalize their broken-hearted loss. Jesus was everything to them, in spite of all their wrong notions. They could not accept theories about a Resurrection. They wanted Jesus Himself! At long last it is out. Jesus is the very centre of their lives and they cannot live without Him.

How poignant for the reader – who has more information than the participants – who cannot shout to these men as children do at actors in a pantomime "he's there, beside you! Turn around and look at him. He was with you all along the road, participating in your sorrow and waiting for His moment to give you the joy and peace that will last forever" (John 14:27; 15:11). With these or similar words, Luke in his genius has made the readers preach a really good sermon to themselves, for this is the message for each one of us. He is there all the time with you, on every step of the way from the beginning to the end of life's journey, but we must give Him entrance through faith and prayer.

Luke has answered the first question. You find the Risen Lord on your journey through life. Now he proceeds to take us on a second journey through the Scriptures, for ignorance of the Scriptures is ignorance of the Christ, whom those Scriptures speak about. Those on the spiritual journey must be fed with the right food, and this is pointed out now, the Word of God (24:25–27) and the Eucharist (24:28–31). These bring us back to Jerusalem and the Church community (24:44–53).

Jesus scolded the men for their slowness in accepting the testimony of Scripture, for He had already taught them that if they did not listen to Moses and the prophets, that neither would they listen to someone back from the dead (16:31). So He brought them back to examine the books of Moses (Pentateuch), and all the prophets, while *he explained to them the passages in the scriptures that were about himself* (24:25–27). Since they had accepted Jesus was a prophet and the Davidic Messiah, what they needed to look at were those texts pertaining to the Suffering Servant, which could be found in the four servant songs of Isaiah: 42:1–9, 49:1–6, 50:4–11, 52:13–53:12. (See also Jeremiah 31:31–34; Zechariah 6:12–13, 9:9–10, 11:13, 12:9–13, 13:7, 14:1–21, Malachi 3–4; Psalms 16, 22, 30, 41:9; 55:12–14; etc.)

Jesus had chosen a reading from the prophets to explain His ministry at the beginning (4:18). Now that the Paschal Mystery is complete He refers to all of the Old Testament Scriptures. They must look for Him under the titles of prophet, priest, king, Son of Man, Son of David, Son of God, the wisdom greater than Solomon, etc. Once they have put the pieces of the jigsaw together from their own searching of the Scriptures, they will be able to teach it to others (Acts 3:18, 22–26, 4:25–31, 17:2–4, 26:22–23, 28:23).

The journey through the Scriptures leads to Jesus as the Messiah, the one who feeds us with the Eucharist, which symbolizes the New Covenant in His own blood. Through the mystery of the Eucharist He leads us into intimacy with Himself, for He wants us to draw life from Him as He drew life from the Father (John 6:57). The third journey is into table fellowship with Jesus and with each other – the mystery of His presence today, for He has given us two tables: the table of the Word and the table of the Eucharist. It is in feeding from the table of the Word that we are made ready for the recognition of Jesus' risen but unseen presence at the sacred meal, and in the sacred meal.

As they drew near to the village the stranger appeared as if he would go on, but the disciples pressed him to accept their hospitality for the night (24:28–29). Their excuse was that night was fast approaching – which was in a manner beyond their comprehension – the long night of Jesus' physical absence, when they would have to take up their cross and follow to persecution and death in His name. They needed the solace and strengthening grace of the Eucharist where they could draw life and grace from Him. Jesus went in with them, but instead of acting like a guest He was the host at table: *He took bread, and said the blessing; then he broke it and handed it to them*. Only Jesus Himself could open their eyes to the glorious truth of His spiritual presence among them.

The words used by Luke here recall both the miracle of the loaves (9:12–17) and the Last Supper (22:14–27). As soon as they recognized Him He vanished from *their* sight, but He was still there. They had recognized Him, they realize now, in the spiritual journey itself, in the study of the Scriptues, and here in the Eucharist (24:31–32). From now on "recognizing the Body of the Lord" will not refer to apparitions or visions of the Risen Jesus, but to His Eucharistic presence among the community for all time (1 Corinthians 11:28–30). Once Jesus' invisible presence has been discerned there is no further need of visual aids in this search, for we walk by faith, not by sight (2 Corinthians 5:7).

The next stage of this spiritual journey is mutual up-building, where the disciples acknowledge to each other and testify to what the Lord had done for them up to this point (24:32). They acknowledge that insight and understanding came first from Scripture study. This was where the hearts softened to God's grace and opened up to God's possibilities. Here was where the soil of their souls was made ready for the gift of Jesus' love in the Eucharist and the realization that nothing – no, not even the Resurrection of Jesus – was impossible with God (1:37, 8:4–10). Only then could they penetrate the fact that what occurred on Calvary was not the failure of their Messianic hopes but the fulfilment of them, as God pulled down the Prince of Darknesss from his throne and raised up the humble and lowly servant, Jesus (1:52). All that was lacking on Calvary and afterwards, was that their eyes were not opened as they are now.

This new-found faith in Jesus' Risen glory profoundly transformed these men. They have not only risen from the death of their old understanding of Jesus, but they rise up physically and go to proclaim this good news to the Eleven, who at that moment were already assembled as the infant church needing the breath of the Spirit (John 20:23) to make them alive in Resurrection faith. With no regard to the dangers of the journey or the fact that for the rest of the world it was night, the two disciples hurry back to Jerusalem and all that God's call held for them there (24:33–34). To their surprise they found the church not only assembled, but risen from the dead too! To a man they stood behind Peter's testimony that Jesus was risen. When they left that morning Peter was as puzzled as they were (14:12). When they returned with their new-found faith Peter has seen the Risen Lord and the other Apostles accept his testimony.

The great sadness is that Luke gave no details of what

occurred between the Great Shepherd and the shepherd, but whatever it was, the Apostolic witness fully backed Peter who now fulfilled Jesus' injunction to strengthen the others once he had recovered himself (22:32). This is the first picture of the post-Resurrection Church, with Peter the clear leader and the other Apostles fully behind him, and this "in the presence of all their companions", which must include the Seventy-Two and the women (24:34–35). Only after the Church gave its official testimony to the Resurrection, were these two laymen permitted to add their voice to the chorus of praise rising up to God (24:35).

Jesus Comes to His Own (24:36–53)

As the assembly still talked about these new experiences of Jesus, suddenly, without warning, and obviously without sound, Jesus startled them by appearing among them (24:36). His new-found ability to appear and disappear at will, and His freedom from all material restraint, must have been disturbing to say the least! Luke unabashedly says that Jesus' greetings of peace fell on deaf ears, for they were *in a state of alarm and fright* (24:37). Humans as a whole, do not care for the supernatural world breaking in on their everyday life; it is too uncomfortable and too challenging.

Luke wants to answer some more questions regarding the Resurrection. In the Emmaus story he emphasized the spiritual presence of Jesus in the Church, but that could lead to the docetist heresy, whereby people could deny the bodily Resurrection of Jesus. Luke wants to answer these questions: Was it *really* Jesus? How did they know? What kind of a body did He have? Perhaps it was just a ghost giving the impression of substance, deceiving their troubled hearts?

317

Jesus stood in the midst of His assembled Church who were very agitated, wondering what to think (24:37–38). He then began to reveal Himself to them and to remove their doubts (24:39). It really was Jesus standing there. He invited them to examine His body which still bore the marks of crucifixion (John 20:25–27). Upon examination they discovered that it really was a "flesh and bones" body, not a shimmering mirage such as a ghost presents. The stranger whom the two disciples met on the Emmaus road was a real flesh-and-body person too, one who could share a meal with them, which Jesus invites them to do now with the whole assembly. Clearly it was not enough for one or two to have seen the Lord, *the whole Church* must come to this new faith in the Risen Lord. Jesus ate the grilled fish presented to Him, as they looked on trying to comprehend (24:42–43). The Church in later times will relate that this assembly ate and drank in His presence after He rose from the dead (Acts 10:4), as Moses and the Seventy elders did on Sinai (Exodus 24:10–11).

Jesus assured them regarding His identity: *"it is I indeed"*, here reserving the divine name *"I AM"* for Himself. They stood there dumbfounded, their sorrow turning into a joy so great that they could not cope with it yet. If what stood before their eyes was true, then Jesus was *greater* than they had ever comprehended, and the implications for the salvation of the world very great (24:40–41). At this point the whole assembly recognized Jesus, and Psalm 30: 11–12 was fulfilled for them, for Jesus had turned their mourning into dancing. He had taken off their sackcloth and wrapped them in gladness. Their hearts will be silent no longer, and they will go to all the world praising and gloryifying God for all He had done for us.

Just as the two on the Emmaus road were instructed

by Jesus in the Scriptures, so here He does the same for the whole assembly (24:44). He opened their minds *to understand* the scriptures (their problem up to now), having revealed that the whole Old Testament spoke about Him. They were to look for Him in the Books of Moses, the prophets and the Psalms – the three divisions of the Old Testament Scriptures. Very particularly they must come to understand the Paschal mystery, so that they can go to the world to preach repentance for the forgiveness of sin (Acts 10:42–43). Their mission was to begin in Jerusalem, but to branch out to all nations (24:47–48). They were now constituted His official witnesses, whose testimony the Church will rely on for all time. Thus Luke shows that Jesus is the originator of the Apostolic teaching and the kerygma of the early Church.

They are being sent out in power, not in weakness or fear. So they must stay in Jerusalem for the Promise of the Father, which is the Pentecostal outpouring of the Holy Spirit on all of them (Joel 3:1–3), that Fire that Jesus had longed to cast upon the earth (12:49). This Fire will cleanse, heal, strengthen, anoint, and empower them, giving them the Gifts of the Spirit, and transforming them into fearless witnesses (3:16, 24:48). They will be literally "clothed with power from on high" (Acts 1:8, 2:1–4). Now that Jesus has triumphed, everything He promised would be experienced by His wondering disciples.

The final stage of the journey takes place now as Jesus took them out as far as the outskirts of Bethany, on the slopes of the Mount of Olives (Acts 1:12), the place where the entrance into Jerusalem began (19:29), and where for a brief moment they had hailed Him as "the one who comes in the name of the Lord". Now He is about to enter the Heavenly Jerusalem, the City of God (2:49, 23:46; Revelation 21–22). Before His departure for the last time before the Parousia, He blessed them as the

319

High Priest of Christianity, as He ascended into the Holy of Holies forever. He stands in absolute contrast to Zechariah at the beginning of the gospel, who could not give the blessing of the Aaronic priesthood because of his dumbness and unbelief (1:22). As Jesus withdrew from them into the Father's Presence, they realized that the promises to Abraham that all the families of the earth would be blessed (Genesis 12:2–3; Acts 3:25) are to be fulfilled in Jesus from His place at God's right hand.

The assembly of believers are now the heirs of the promises made to Abraham (1:72–73) and they worshipped Jesus before making their way back to Jerusalem (as the Emmaus two had done) full of joy and ready to obey all that the Lord wanted from them. They went to the Temple, and continuously praised God there (John 14:28). Luke's gospel begins and ends in the Temple with the remnant of believers in prayer, and waiting for the Kingdom of God to reveal itself. It opens with the devout believers praying for the longed-for Messiah, and closes with devout believers praising God for answered prayer and redemption accomplished.